2011 Supplement

Constitutional Law

2011 Supplement

Constitutional Law

Sixth Edition

Geoffrey R. Stone
Harry Kalven, Jr., Distinguished Service Professor of Law
University of Chicago Law School

Louis Michael Seidman
Carmack Waterhouse Professor of Constitutional Law
Georgetown University Law Center

Cass R. Sunstein
Felix Frankfurter Professor of Law
Harvard Law School

Mark V. Tushnet
William Nelson Cromwell Professor of Law
Harvard Law School

Pamela S. Karlan
Kenneth & Harle Montgomery Professor of Public Interest Law
Stanford Law School

Wolters Kluwer
Law & Business

Published by Wolters Kluwer Law & Business in New York.

Wolters Kluwer Law & Business serves customers worldwide with CCH, Aspen Publishers, and Kluwer Law International products. (www.wolterskluwerlb. com)

To contact Customer Service, e-mail customer.service@wolterskluwer.com, call 1-800-234-1660, fax 1-800-901-9075, or mail correspondence to:

Wolters Kluwer Law & Business
Attn: Order Department
PO Box 990
Frederick, MD 21705

Printed in the United States of America.

1 2 3 4 5 6 7 8 9 0

ISBN 978-0-7355-0737-1

Library of Congress Cataloging-in-Publication Data

Constitutional law / Geoffrey R. Stone ... [et al.] — 6th ed.
      p.   cm.
   Includes index.
   ISBN 978-0-7355-7719-0 (case bound)
         978-0-7355-0737-1 (supplement)
   1. Constitutional law — United States. I. Stone, Geoffrey R.

KF4549.C647 2205
342.73 — dc22   2005000567

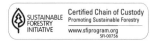

About Wolters Kluwer Law & Business

Wolters Kluwer Law & Business is a leading global provider of intelligent information and digital solutions for legal and business professionals in key specialty areas, and respected educational resources for professors and law students. Wolters Kluwer Law & Business connects legal and business professionals as well as those in the education market with timely, specialized authoritative content and information-enabled solutions to support success through productivity, accuracy and mobility.

Serving customers worldwide, Wolters Kluwer Law & Business products include those under the Aspen Publishers, CCH, Kluwer Law International, Loislaw, Best Case, ftwilliam.com and MediRegs family of products.

CCH products have been a trusted resource since 1913, and are highly regarded resources for legal, securities, antitrust and trade regulation, government contracting, banking, pension, payroll, employment and labor, and healthcare reimbursement and compliance professionals.

Aspen Publishersproducts provide essential information to attorneys, business professionals and law students. Written by preeminent authorities, the product line offers analytical and practical information in a range of specialty practice areas from securities law and intellectual property to mergers and acquisitions and pension/benefits. Aspen's trusted legal education resources provide professors and students with high-quality, up-to-date and effective resources for successful instruction and study in all areas of the law.

Kluwer Law International products provide the global business community with reliable international legal information in English. Legal practitioners, corporate counsel and business executives around the world rely on Kluwer Law journals, looseleafs, books, and electronic products for comprehensive information in many areas of international legal practice.

Loislaw is a comprehensive online legal research product providing legal content to law firm practitioners of various specializations. Loislaw provides attorneys with the ability to quickly and efficiently find the necessary legal information they need, when and where they need it, by facilitating access to primary law as well as state-specific law, records, forms and treatises.

Best Case Solutions is the leading bankruptcy software product to the bankruptcy industry. It provides software and workflow tools to flawlessly streamline petition preparation and the electronic filing process, while timely incorporating ever-changing court requirements.

ftwilliam.com offers employee benefits professionals the highest quality plan documents (retirement, welfare and non-qualified) and government forms (5500/PBGC, 1099 and IRS) software at highly competitive prices.

MediRegs products provide integrated health care compliance content and software solutions for professionals in healthcare, higher education and life sciences, including professionals in accounting, law and consulting.

Wolters Kluwer Law & Business, a division of Wolters Kluwer, is headquartered in New York. Wolters Kluwer is a market-leading global information services company focused on professionals.

Contents

Table of Cases		*xi*
Table of Authorities		*xiii*

**CHAPTER 1. THE ROLE OF THE SUPREME
COURT IN THE CONSTITUTIONAL ORDER**   **1**

D.	The Sources of Judicial Decisions: Text, "Representation Reinforcement," and Natural Law	1
	District of Columbia v. Heller	1
F.	"Case or Controversy" Requirements and the Passive Virtues	38

**CHAPTER 2. FEDERALISM AT WORK:
CONGRESS AND THE NATIONAL ECONOMY**   **43**

A.	The Values of Federalism and Some Techniques for Implementing Them	43
C.	The Evolution of Commerce Clause Doctrine	45
D.	State Regulation of Interstate Commerce	46

**CHAPTER 3. THE SCOPE OF CONGRESS'S
POWERS: TAXING AND SPENDING, WAR
POWERS, INDIVIDUAL RIGHTS, AND STATE
AUTONOMY**   **49**

A.	Regulation through Taxing, Spending, and the War Power	49
B.	Congress's Enforcement Power Under the Reconstruction Amendments	53
C.	The Tenth Amendment as a Federalism-Based Limitation on Congressional Power	54
	Bond v. United States	57

**CHAPTER 4.   THE DISTRIBUTION OF
NATIONAL POWERS**   **61**

A.   Introduction   61
B.   A Case Study: Presidential Seizure   62
C.   Foreign Affairs   62
D.   Domestic Affairs   67
     *Free Enterprise Fund v. Public Company Accounting
     Oversight Board*   68

**CHAPTER 5.   EQUALITY AND THE
CONSTITUTION**   **81**

C.   Equal Protection Methodology: Heightened Scrutiny
     and the Problem of Race   81
D.   Equal Protection Methodology: Heightened Scrutiny and
     the Problem of Gender   82
E.   Equal Protection Methodology: The Problem of Sexual
     Orientation   83

CHAPTER 6.   IMPLIED FUNDAMENTAL RIGHTS   **87**

A.   Introduction   87
C.   The Incorporation Controversy   88
     McDonald v. City of Chicago   88
D.   Substantive Due Process: The Protection of
     Economic Interests and the Question of Redistribution   110
F.   Modern Substantive Due Process: Privacy,
     Personhood, and Family   111
G.   Procedural Due Process   113
H.   The Contracts and Takings Clauses   117

CHAPTER 7.   FREEDOM OF EXPRESSION   **121**

A.   Introduction   121
B.   Content-Based Restrictions: Dangerous Ideas
     and Information   122
     Snyder v. Phelps   131
D.   Content-Based Restrictions: "Low" Value Speech   134
     Sorrell v. IMS Health, Inc.   140
     United States v. Stevens   143
     Brown v. Entertainment Merchants Ass'n   150

E.   Content-Neutral Restrictions   160
     Christian Legal Society Chapter v. Martinez   162
     Pleasant Grove City, Utah v. Summum   168
     McConnell v. Federal Election Comm'n   176
     Arizona Free Enterprise Club's Freedom Club PAC v.
     Bennett   180
     Citizens United v. Federal Election Commission   191
F.   Freedom of the Press   210

CHAPTER 8.   THE CONSTITUTION AND RELIGION   **213**

A.   Introduction: Historical and Analytic Overview   213
B.   The Establishment Clause   214
D.   Permissible Accommodation   217

**CHAPTER 9.   STATE ACTION, BASELINES, AND
THE PROBLEM OF PRIVATE POWER**   **219**

B.   Pure Inaction and the Theory of Governmental
     Neutrality   219

Table of Cases

Italics indicate principal and intermediate cases.
All references are to page numbers in the main text.

American Electric Power Co. v. Connecticut, 140
Arizona Christian School Tuition Org. v. Winn, 120
Arizona Free Enterprise Club's Freedom Club PAC v. Bennett, *1360*
Ashcroft v. al-Kidd, 408
Bond v. United States, 172, 349, *354*
Borough of Duryea, Pennsylvania v. Guarnieri, 1382
Brown v. Entertainment Merchants' Ass'n, *1201*
Caperton v. A.T. Massey Coal Co., 140, 960
Christian Legal Society Chapter v. Martinez, *1305*, 1393
Citizens United v. Federal Election Commission, 1360, *1363*
Comstock, United States v., 228, 353
District Attorney's Office for the Third Judicial District v. Osborne, 951
Doe v. Reed, 1345, 1360, 1376
FCC v. Fox Television Stations, 1214, 1426
Flores-Villar v. United States, 652
Free Enterprise Fund v. Public Company Accounting Oversight Board, *436*
Harper v. Canada, 1357
Haywood v. Drown, 349
Holder v. Humanitarian Law Project, 1066, 1334
McConnell v. FEC, *1360*, 1363
McDonald v. City of Chicago, *734*
Nevada Comm'n on Ethics v. Carrigan, 1345
Pleasant Grove City, Utah v. Summum, *1317*, 1488
Ricci v. DeStefano, 619
Salazar v. Buono, 1483
Snyder v. Phelps, *1091*
Sorrell v. IMS Health, Inc., *1169*
Stevens, United States v., *1201*
Stop the Beach Renourishment v. Florida Dept. of Environmental Protection, 759, 1009
Strauss v. Horton 682
Summers v. Earth Island Institute, 117
Thomas More Law Center v. Obama, 294
Turner v. Rogers, 957

Varnum v. Brien, 678
White, United States v., 1066
Ysursa v. Pocatello Education Association, 1299
Zana v. Turkey, 1066

Table of Authorities

Ackerman & Hathaway, Limited War and the Constitution: Iraq and the Crisis of Presidential Legality, 109 Mich. L. Rev. 447 (2011), 397

Adelman & Deitrich, Extremist Speech and the Internet: The Continuing Importance of Brandenburg, 4 Harv. L. & Pol. Rev. 361 (2010), 1440

Ammori, Beyond Content-Neutrality: Understanding Content-Based Promotion of Democratic Speech, 61 Fed. Comm. L. J. 273 (2009), 1291

Balkin, The Constitutionality of the Individual Mandate for Health Insurance, 362 New England J. Med. 482 (2010), 294

Balkin, The Reconstruction Power, 85 N.Y.U. L. Rev. 1801 (2010), 307

Bebchuk & Jackson, Corporate Political Speech: Who Decides?, 124 Harv. L. Rev. 83 (2010), 1363

Bell, The Hangman's Noose and the Lynch Mob: Hate Speech and the Jena Six, 44 Har. Civ. Rts.-Civ. Lib. L. Rev. 329 (2009), 1249

Bell, Restraining the Heartless: Racist Speech and Minority Rights, 84 Ind. L. J. 963 (2009), 1226

BeVier, Full of Surprises — And More to Come: Randall v. Sorrell, The First Amendment, and Campaign Finance Regulation, 2006 Supreme Court Review 173, 1363

BeVier & Harrison, The State Action Principle and Its Critics, 96 Va. L. Rev. 1767 (2010), 1556

Bezanson, Art and the Constitution 93 Iowa L. Rev. 1593 (2008), 1175

Bollinger, L., Uninhibited, Robust, and Wide-Open: A Free Press for a New Century (2010), 1135, 1440

Bulman-Pozen & Gerken, Uncooperative Federalism, 118 Yale L.J. 1256 (2009), 172

Chander, Youthful Indiscretion in an Internet Age, in Levmore & Nussbaum, eds., The Offensive Internet (2010), 1152

Citron, Cyber Civil Rights, 80 B.U. L. Rev. 61 (2009), 1253

Citron, Law's Expressive Value in Combating Cyber Gender Harassment, 108 Mich. L. Rev. 373 (2009), 1253

Clark, Separation of Powers as a Safeguard of Federalism, 79 Tex. L. Rev. 1321 (2001), 357

Colby & Smith, Living Originalism, 59 Duke L. J. 239 (2009), 713

Collins & Chaltain, We Must Not Be Afraid to be Free (2011), 1106

Corbin, Ceremonial Deism and the Reasonable Religious Outsider, 57 UCLA L. Rev. 1545 (2010), 1481

Corbin, The First Amendment Right Against Compelled Listening, 89 B.U. L. Rev. 939 (2009), 1314

Debate, A Healthy Debate: The Constitutionality of an Individual Mandate, 158 U. Pa. L. Rev. PENNumbra 93 (2009), 294

Denning, Reconstructing the Dormant Commerce Clause Doctrine, 50 Wm. & Mary L. Rev. 417 (2008), 238

Developments in the Law — State Action and the Public/Private Distinction, 123 Harv. L. Rev. 1248 (2010), 1565

Devins, Talk Loudly and Carry a Small Stick: The Supreme Court and Enemy Combatants, 12 U. Pa. J. Const. L. 491 (2010), 392

Erbsen, Horizontal Federalism, 93 Minn. L. Rev. 493 (2008), 234

Fairman, C., FUCK: Word Taboo and Protecting Our First Amendment Liberties (2009), 1206

Fallon, The Supreme Court, Habeas Corpus, and the War on Terror: An Essay on Law and Political Science, 110 Colum. L. Rev. 352 (2010), 392

Feeley, M. and Rubin, E. Federalism: Political Identity and Tragic Compromise (2009), 172

Galle, Federal Grants, State Decisions, 88 B.U. L. Rev. 875 (2008), 297

Garnett, A Hands-Off Approach to Religious Doctrine, 84 Notre Dame L. Rev. 837 (2009), 1454

Gellman & Looper-Friedman, Thou Shalt Use the Equal Protection Clause for Religion Cases (Not Just the Establishment Clause), 10 U. Pa. J. Const'l L. 666 (2008), 1537

Gersen, Unbundled Powers, 96 Va. L. Rev. 301 (2010), 357

Greene, The So-Called Right to Privacy, 43 U.C. Davis. L. Rev. 715 (2010), 842

Hathaway, Presidential Power over International Law: Restoring the Balance, 119 Yale L. J. 140 (2009), 400

Healy, Brandenburg in a Time of Terror, 84 Notre Dame L. Rev. 655 (2009), 1042

Heyman, The Dark Side of the Force: The Legacy of Justice Holmes for First Amendment Jurisprudence, 19 Wm. & Mary Bill Rts. J 661 (2011), 1228

Humbach, "Sexting" and the First Amendment, 37 Hastings Const. L. Q. 433 (2010), 1198

Huq, The Signaling Function of Religious Speech in Domestic Counter-terrorism, 89 Tex. L. Rev. 833 (2011), 1507

Jones, Avalanche or Undue Alarm? An Empirical Study of Subpoenas Received by the New Media, 93 Minn. L. Rev. 585 (2008), 1406

Koppelman, Corruption of Religion and the Establishment Clause, 50 Wm. & Mary L. Rev. 1831 (2009), 1450

Knake, Attorney Advice and the First Amendment, 68 Wash. & Lee L. Rev. 639 (2011), 1066

Krotoszynski, The Return of Seditious Libel, 55 UCLA L. Rev. 1239 (2008), 1274

Lendler, The Time to Kill a Snake: *Gitlow v. New York* and the Bad-Tendency Doctrine, 36 J. Sup. Ct. Hist. 11 (No. 1) (2011), 1046

Lidsky, Nobody's Fools: The Rational Audience as First Amendment Ideal, 2010 U. Ill. L. Rev. 299, 1023

Luban, Lawfare and Legal Ethics in Guantanamo, 60 Stan. L. Rev. 1981 (2008), 392

Lund, The Congressional Chaplaincies, 17 Wm. & Mary Bill of Rts. J. 1171 (2009), 1482

Lund, Legislative Prayer and the Secret Costs of Religious Endorsements, 94 Minn. L. Rev. 972 (2010), 1482

McConnell, State Action and the Supreme Court's Emerging Consensus on the Line between Establishment and Private Religious Expression, 28 Pepp. L. Rev. 681 (2001), 1565

Norton, The Measure of Government Speech: Identifying Expression's Source, 88 B.U. L. Rev. 587 (2008), 1313

Nourse & Figura, Toward a Representational Theory of the Executive, 91 B.U. L. Rev. 2733 (2011), 436

Nussbaum, M., From Disgust to Humanity (2010), 1189

Nzelibe & Stephenson, Complementary Constraints: Separation of Powers, Rational Voting, and Constitutional Design, 123 Harv. L. Rev. 617 (2010), 357

Pildes, Free Enterprise Fund, Boundary Enforcing Decisions, and the Unitary Executive Branch Theory of Government Administration, 6 Duke J. Const. L. & Publ. Pol'y 1 (2010), 436

Primus, When Should Original Meaning Matter?, 107 Mich. L. Rev. 165 (2008), 713

Rao, A Modest Proposal: Abolishing Agency Independence in Free Enterprise Fund v. PCAOB, 79 Ford. L. Rev. 2541 (2011), 436

Richards, Intellectual Privacy, 87 Tex. L. Rev. 387 (2008), 1067

Rivkin & Casey, Health Care Purchase Mandate: Unconstitutional and Likely to Be Struck Down by the Courts, 158 U. Pa. L. Rev. PENNumbra 94 (2009), 294

Roberts, The Dialectic of Privacy and Punishment in the Gendered Regulation of Parenting, 5 Stan. J. Civ. Rts. & Civ. Lib. 191 (2009), 910

Rosenthal, First Amendment Investigations and the Inescapable Pragmatism of the Common Law of Free Speech, 86 Ind. L. J. 1 (2011), 1067

Schauer, Facts and the First Amendment, 57 U.C.L.A. L. Rev. 897 (2010), 1145

Siegel, N., Dole's Future: A Strategic Analysis, 16 S. Ct. Econ. Rev. 165 (2008), 295

Solove & Richards, Rethinking Free Speech and Civil Liability, 109 Colum. L. Rev. 1650 (2009), 1152

Solove, Speech, Privacy, and Reputation on the Internet, in Levmore & Nussbaum, eds., The Offensive Internet (2010), 1152

Stone, Privacy, the First Amendment, and the Internet, in Levmore & Nussbaum, eds., The Offensive Internet (2010)

Strauss, D., The Living Constitution (2010), 1440

Suk, The Trajectory of Trauma: Bodies and Minds of Abortion Discourse, 110 Colum. L. Rev. 1193 (2010), 898

Sullivan, Two Concepts of Freedom of Speech, 124 Harv. L. Rev. 123 (2010), 1363

Symposium, Return to Missouri v. Holland: Federalism and International Law, 73 Mo. L. Rev. 921 (2008), 332

Taylor, Free Expression and Expressness, 33 N.Y.U. Rev. L & Soc. Ch. 375 (2009), 1249

Tushnet, M., *Heller* and the New Originalism, 69 Ohio St. L.J. 609 (2008), 715

Tushnet, M., The Inevitable Globalization of Constitutional Law, 49 Va. J. Int'l L. 985 (2009), 370

Vazquez, Missouri v. Holland's Second Holding, 73 Mo. L. Rev. 939 (2008), 332

Vazquez, The Separation of Powers as a Safeguard of Nationalism, 83 Notre Dame L. Rev. 1601 (2008), 357

Volokh, Symbolic Expression and the Original Meaning of the First Amendment, 97 Geo. L.J. 1057 (2009), 1325

Waldron, Dignity and Defamation: The Visibility of Hate, 123 Harv. L. Rev. 1597 (2010), 1229

Wells, Privacy and Funeral Protests, 87 N.C. L. Rev. 151 (2008), 1273

Werhan, The Classical Athenian Ancestry of American Freedom of Speech, 2008 Sup. Ct. Rev. 293, 1027

Williams, Feminist Theory and Freedom of Speech, 84 Ind. L. J. 999 (2009), 1023

Williams & Denning, The "New Protectionism" and the American Common Market, 85 Notre Dame L. Rev. 247 (2009), 248

1

THE ROLE OF THE SUPREME COURT IN THE CONSTITUTIONAL ORDER

D. The Sources of Judicial Decisions: Text, "Representation Reinforcement," and Natural Law

Page 78. Before Section E, add the following:

DISTRICT OF COLUMBIA v. HELLER

554 U.S. 570 (2008)

JUSTICE SCALIA delivered the opinion of the Court.

We consider whether a District of Columbia prohibition on the possession of usable handguns in the home violates the Second Amendment to the Constitution....

II

A

The Second Amendment provides: "A well regulated Militia, being necessary to the security of a free State, the right of the people to keep and bear Arms, shall not be infringed." In interpreting this text, we are guided by the principle that "[t]he Constitution was written to be understood by the voters; its words and phrases were used in their normal and ordinary as distinguished from technical meaning." ...

The two sides in this case have set out very different interpretations of the Amendment. Petitioners and today's dissenting Justices believe that it protects only the right to possess and carry a firearm in connection with militia service.

Respondent argues that it protects an individual right to possess a firearm unconnected with service in a militia, and to use that arm for traditionally lawful purposes, such as self-defense within the home.

The Second Amendment is naturally divided into two parts: its prefatory clause and its operative clause. The former does not limit the latter grammatically, but rather announces a purpose....

Logic demands that there be a link between the stated purpose and the command. The Second Amendment would be nonsensical if it read, "A well regulated Militia, being necessary to the security of a free State, the right of the people to petition for redress of grievances shall not be infringed." [But a] prefatory clause does not limit or expand the scope of the operative clause. [Therefore,] while we will begin our textual analysis with the operative clause, we will return to the prefatory clause to ensure that our reading of the operative clause is consistent with the announced purpose.

1.   Operative Clause.

a. "Right of the People."   The first salient feature of the operative clause is that it codifies a "right of the people." The unamended Constitution and the Bill of Rights use the phrase "right of the people" two other times, in the First Amendment's Assembly-and-Petition Clause and in the Fourth Amendment's Search-and-Seizure Clause. The Ninth Amendment uses very similar terminology. [All] three of these instances unambiguously refer to individual rights, not "collective" rights, or rights that may be exercised only through participation in some corporate body....

What is more, in all six other provisions of the Constitution that mention "the people," the term unambiguously refers to all members of the political community, not an unspecified subset....

This contrasts markedly with the phrase "the militia" in the prefatory clause. As we will describe below, the "militia" in colonial America consisted of a subset of "the people" — those who were male, able bodied, and within a certain age range. Reading the Second Amendment as protecting only the right to "keep and bear Arms" in an organized militia therefore fits poorly with the operative clause's description of the holder of that right as "the people."

We start therefore with a strong presumption that the Second Amendment right is exercised individually and belongs to all Americans.

b. "Keep and Bear Arms." We move now from the holder of the right — "the people" — to the substance of the right: "to keep and bear Arms."

Before addressing the verbs "keep" and "bear," we interpret their object: "Arms." The 18th-century meaning is no different from the meaning today. The 1773 edition of Samuel Johnson's dictionary defined "arms" as "weapons of offence, or armour of defence." Timothy Cunningham's important 1771 legal

2

dictionary defined "arms" as "any thing that a man wears for his defence, or takes into his hands, or useth in wrath to cast at or strike another."

The term was applied, then as now, to weapons that were not specifically designed for military use and were not employed in a military capacity. For instance, Cunningham's legal dictionary gave as an example of usage: "Servants and labourers shall use bows and arrows on Sundays, &c. and not bear other arms." [Although] one founding-era thesaurus limited "arms" (as opposed to "weapons") to "instruments of offence *generally* made use of in war," even that source stated that all firearms constituted "arms."

Some have made the argument, bordering on the frivolous, that only those arms in existence in the 18th century are protected by the Second Amendment. We do not interpret constitutional rights that way. Just as the First Amendment protects modern forms of communications, and the Fourth Amendment applies to modern forms of search, the Second Amendment extends, prima facie, to all instruments that constitute bearable arms, even those that were not in existence at the time of the founding.

We turn to the phrases "keep arms" and "bear arms." Johnson defined "keep" as, most relevantly, "[t]o retain; not to lose," and "[t]o have in custody." Webster defined it as "[t]o hold; to retain in one's power or possession." No party has apprised us of an idiomatic meaning of "keep Arms." Thus, the most natural reading of "keep Arms" in the Second Amendment is to "have weapons."

The phrase "keep arms" was not prevalent in the written documents of the founding period that we have found, but there are a few examples, all of which favor viewing the right to "keep Arms" as an individual right unconnected with militia service. William Blackstone, for example, wrote that Catholics convicted of not attending service in the Church of England suffered certain penalties, one of which was that they were not permitted to "keep arms in their houses." ["Keep] arms" was simply a common way of referring to possessing arms, for militiamen *and everyone else.*

At the time of the founding, as now, to "bear" meant to "carry." When used with "arms," however, the term has a meaning that refers to carrying for a particular purpose — confrontation. [Although] the phrase implies that the carrying of the weapon is for the purpose of "offensive or defensive action," it in no way connotes participation in a structured military organization.

From our review of founding-era sources, we conclude that this natural meaning was also the meaning that "bear arms" had in the 18th century. In numerous instances, "bear arms" was unambiguously used to refer to the carrying of weapons outside of an organized militia. The most prominent examples are those most relevant to the Second Amendment: Nine state constitutional provisions written in the 18th century or the first two decades of the 19th, which enshrined a right of citizens to "bear arms in defense of themselves

3

and the state" or "bear arms in defense of himself and the state." It is clear from those formulations that "bear arms" did not refer only to carrying a weapon in an organized military unit. Justice James Wilson interpreted the Pennsylvania Constitution's arms-bearing right, for example, as a recognition of the natural right of defense "of one's person or house" — what he called the law of "self preservation." That was also the interpretation of those state constitutional provisions adopted by pre-Civil War state courts....

The phrase "bear Arms" also had at the time of the founding an idiomatic meaning that was significantly different from its natural meaning: "to serve as a soldier, do military service, fight" or "to wage war." But it *unequivocally* bore that idiomatic meaning only when followed by the preposition "against," which was in turn followed by the target of the hostilities. (That is how, for example, our Declaration of Independence § 28, used the phrase: "He has constrained our fellow Citizens taken Captive on the high Seas to bear Arms against their Country.... ")....

In any event, the meaning of "bear arms" that petitioners and Justice Stevens propose is *not even* the (sometimes) idiomatic meaning. Rather, they manufacture a hybrid definition, whereby "bear arms" connotes the actual carrying of arms (and therefore is not really an idiom) but only in the service of an organized militia. No dictionary has ever adopted that definition, and we have been apprised of no source that indicates that it carried that meaning at the time of the founding. But it is easy to see why petitioners and the dissent are driven to the hybrid definition. Giving "bear Arms" its idiomatic meaning would cause the protected right to consist of the right to be a soldier or to wage war — an absurdity that no commentator has ever endorsed. Worse still, the phrase "keep and bear Arms" would be incoherent. The word "Arms" would have two different meanings at once: "weapons" (as the object of "keep") and (as the object of "bear") one-half of an idiom. It would be rather like saying "He filled and kicked the bucket" to mean "He filled the bucket and died." Grotesque....

Justice Stevens places great weight on James Madison's inclusion of a conscientious-objector clause in his original draft of the Second Amendment: "but no person religiously scrupulous of bearing arms, shall be compelled to render military service in person." He argues that this clause establishes that the drafters of the Second Amendment intended "bear Arms" to refer only to military service. It is always perilous to derive the meaning of an adopted provision from another provision deleted in the drafting process. In any case, what Justice Stevens would conclude from the deleted provision does not follow. It was not meant to exempt from military service those who objected to going to war but had no scruples about personal gunfights. Quakers opposed the use of arms not just for militia service, but for any violent purpose whatsoever — so much so that Quaker frontiersmen were forbidden to use arms to defend their families, even though "[i]n such circumstances the temptation to seize a hunting rifle or knife in self-defense... must sometimes have been almost overwhelming." [Thus], the most natural interpretation of Madison's deleted text is that those opposed to carrying weapons for potential violent confrontation would not be "compelled to render military service," in which such carrying would be required.

Finally, Justice Stevens suggests that "keep and bear Arms" was some sort of term of art, presumably akin to "hue and cry" or "cease and desist." [Justice] Stevens believes that the unitary meaning of "keep and bear Arms" is established by the Second Amendment's calling it a "right" (singular) rather than "rights" (plural). There is nothing to this. State constitutions of the founding period routinely grouped multiple (related) guarantees under a singular "right," and the First Amendment protects the "right [singular] of the people peaceably to assemble, and to petition the Government for a redress of grievances."....

c. Meaning of the Operative Clause.   Putting all of these textual elements together, we find that they guarantee the individual right to possess and carry weapons in case of confrontation. This meaning is strongly confirmed by the historical background of the Second Amendment. We look to this because it has always been widely understood that the Second Amendment, like the First and Fourth Amendments, codified a *pre-existing* right. The very text of the Second Amendment implicitly recognizes the pre-existence of the right and declares only that it "shall not be infringed." As we said in *United States v. Cruikshank*, 92 U.S. 542, 553 (1876), "[t]his is not a right granted by the Constitution. Neither is it in any manner dependent upon that instrument for its existence. The Second amendment declares that it shall not be infringed...."

Between the Restoration and the Glorious Revolution, the Stuart Kings Charles II and James II succeeded in using select militias loyal to them to suppress political dissidents, in part by disarming their opponents. [These] experiences caused Englishmen to be extremely wary of concentrated military forces run by the state and to be jealous of their arms. They accordingly obtained an assurance from William and Mary, in the Declaration of Right (which was codified as the English Bill of Rights), that Protestants would never be disarmed: "That the subjects which are Protestants may have arms for their defense suitable to their conditions and as allowed by law." This right has long been understood to be the predecessor to our Second Amendment. It was clearly an individual right, having nothing whatever to do with service in a militia. To be sure, it was an individual right not available to the whole population, given that it was restricted to Protestants, and like all written English rights it was held only against the Crown, not Parliament. But it was secured to them as individuals, according to "libertarian political principles," not as members of a fighting force.

5

By the time of the founding, the right to have arms had become fundamental for English subjects. Blackstone, whose works, we have said, "constituted the preeminent authority on English law for the founding generation," cited the arms provision of the Bill of Rights as one of the fundamental rights of Englishmen. [It] was, he said, "the natural right of resistance and self-preservation," and "the right of having and using arms for self-preservation and defence." Thus, the right secured in 1689 as a result of the Stuarts' abuses was by the time of the founding understood to be an individual right protecting against both public and private violence.

And, of course, what the Stuarts had tried to do to their political enemies, George III had tried to do to the colonists. In the tumultuous decades of the 1760's and 1770's, the Crown began to disarm the inhabitants of the most rebellious areas. [The colonists] understood the right to enable individuals to defend themselves. As the most important early American edition of Blackstone's Commentaries (by the law professor and former Antifederalist St. George Tucker) made clear in the notes to the description of the arms right, Americans understood the "right of self-preservation" as permitting a citizen to "repe[l] force by force" when "the intervention of society in his behalf, may be too late to prevent an injury."

There seems to us no doubt, on the basis of both text and history, that the Second Amendment conferred an individual right to keep and bear arms. Of course the right was not unlimited, just as the First Amendment's right of free speech was not. Thus, we do not read the Second Amendment to protect the right of citizens to carry arms for *any sort* of confrontation, just as we do not read the First Amendment to protect the right of citizens to speak for *any purpose*. Before turning to limitations upon the individual right, however, we must determine whether the prefatory clause of the Second Amendment comports with our interpretation of the operative clause.

2. Prefatory Clause.

The prefatory clause reads: "A well regulated Militia, being necessary to the security of a free State.... "

a. "Well-Regulated Militia." In *United States v. Miller*, 307 U.S. 174, 179 (1939), we explained that "the Militia comprised all males physically capable of acting in concert for the common defense." That definition comports with founding-era sources.

Petitioners take a seemingly narrower view of the militia, stating that "[m]ilitias are the state- and congressionally-regulated military forces described in the Militia Clauses (art. I, § 8, cls. 15-16)." [We] believe that petitioners identify the wrong thing, namely, the organized militia. Unlike armies and navies, which Congress is given the power to create ("to raise... Armies"; "to provide... a Navy," Art. I, § 8, cls. 12-13), the militia is assumed by Article

I already to be *in existence*. [and to consist of] all able-bodied men. [Although] the militia consists of all able-bodied men, the federally organized militia may consist of a subset of them.

Finally, the adjective "well-regulated" implies nothing more than the imposition of proper discipline and training.

b. "Security of a Free State." . . .

There are many reasons why the militia was thought to be "necessary to the security of a free state." First, of course, it is useful in repelling invasions and suppressing insurrections. Second, it renders large standing armies unnecessary. [Third,] when the able-bodied men of a nation are trained in arms and organized, they are better able to resist tyranny.

3.   Relationship between Prefatory Clause and Operative Clause

We reach the question, then: Does the preface fit with an operative clause that creates an individual right to keep and bear arms? It fits perfectly, once one knows the history that the founding generation knew and that we have described above. That history showed that the way tyrants had eliminated a militia consisting of all the able-bodied men was not by banning the militia but simply by taking away the people's arms, enabling a select militia or standing army to suppress political opponents. This is what had occurred in England that prompted codification of the right to have arms in the English Bill of Rights.

[During] the 1788 ratification debates, the fear that the federal government would disarm the people in order to impose rule through a standing army or select militia was pervasive in Antifederalist rhetoric. . . .

It is therefore entirely sensible that the Second Amendment's prefatory clause announces the purpose for which the right was codified: to prevent elimination of the militia. The prefatory clause does not suggest that preserving the militia was the only reason Americans valued the ancient right; most undoubtedly thought it even more important for self-defense and hunting. But the threat that the new Federal Government would destroy the citizens' militia by taking away their arms was the reason that right — unlike some other English rights — was codified in a written Constitution. . . .

B

Our interpretation is confirmed by analogous arms-bearing rights in state constitutions that preceded and immediately followed adoption of the Second Amendment. . . .

Between 1789 and 1820, nine States adopted Second Amendment analogues. Four of them [referred] to the right of the people to "bear arms in defence of themselves and the State." Another three States [used] the even more individualistic phrasing that each citizen has the "right to bear arms in defence of himself and the State." Finally, two States [used] "common defence" language. . . .

D

We now address how the Second Amendment was interpreted from immediately after its ratification through the end of the 19th century. Before proceeding, however, we take issue with Justice Stevens' equating of these sources with postenactment legislative history, a comparison that betrays a fundamental misunderstanding of a court's interpretive task. [That phrase] most certainly does not refer to the examination of a variety of legal and other sources to determine *the public understanding* of a legal text in the period after its enactment or ratification. That sort of inquiry is a critical tool of constitutional interpretation. As we will show, virtually all interpreters of the Second Amendment in the century after its enactment interpreted the amendment as we do.

1.   Post-ratification Commentary

Three important founding-era legal scholars interpreted the Second Amendment in published writings. All three understood it to protect an individual right unconnected with militia service....

2.   Pre-Civil War Case Law

The 19th-century cases that interpreted the Second Amendment universally support an individual right unconnected to militia service....

Many early 19th-century state cases indicated that the Second Amendment right to bear arms was an individual right unconnected to militia service, though subject to certain restrictions. A Virginia case in 1824 holding that the Constitution did not extend to free blacks explained that "numerous restrictions imposed on [blacks] in our Statute Book, many of which are inconsistent with the letter and spirit of the Constitution, both of this State and of the United States as respects the free whites, demonstrate, that, here, those instruments have not been considered to extend equally to both classes of our population. We will only instance the restriction upon the migration of free blacks into this State, and upon their right to bear arms." *Aldridge v. Commonwealth*, 4 Va. 447 (Gen. Ct.). [An] 1829 decision by the Supreme Court of Michigan said: "The constitution of the United States also grants to the citizen the right to keep and bear arms. But the grant of this privilege cannot be construed into the right in him who keeps a gun to destroy his neighbor. No rights are intended to be granted by the constitution for an unlawful or unjustifiable purpose."

In *Nunn v. State*, 1 Ga. 243, 251 (1846), the Georgia Supreme Court construed the Second Amendment as protecting the *"natural* right of self-defence" and therefore struck down a ban on carrying pistols openly....

Likewise, in *State v. Chandler*, 5 La. Ann. 489, 490 (1850), the Louisiana Supreme Court held that citizens had a right to carry arms openly: "This is the right guaranteed by the Constitution of the United States, and which is calculated to incite men to a manly and noble defence of themselves, if necessary, and of their country, without any tendency to secret advantages and unmanly assassinations."...

3.   Post-Civil War Legislation

In the aftermath of the Civil War, there was an outpouring of discussion of the Second Amendment in Congress and in public discourse, as people debated whether and how to secure constitutional rights for newly free slaves. Since those discussions took place 75 years after the ratification of the Second Amendment, they do not provide as much insight into its original meaning as earlier sources. Yet those born and educated in the early 19th century faced a widespread effort to limit arms ownership by a large number of citizens; their understanding of the origins and continuing significance of the Amendment is instructive.

Blacks were routinely disarmed by Southern States after the Civil War. Those who opposed these injustices frequently stated that they infringed blacks' constitutional right to keep and bear arms. Needless to say, the claim was not that blacks were being prohibited from carrying arms in an organized state militia. [A] joint congressional Report decried:

> in some parts of [South Carolina], armed parties are, without proper authority, engaged in seizing all fire-arms found in the hands of the freemen. Such conduct is in clear and direct violation of their personal rights as guaranteed by the Constitution of the United States, which declares that "the right of the people to keep and bear arms shall not be infringed." The freedmen of South Carolina have shown by their peaceful and orderly conduct that they can safely be trusted with fire-arms, and they need them to kill game for subsistence, and to protect their crops from destruction by birds and animals....

Congress enacted the Freedmen's Bureau Act on July 16, 1866. Section 14 stated:

> [T]he right... to have full and equal benefit of all laws and proceedings concerning personal liberty, personal security, and the acquisition, enjoyment, and disposition of estate, real and personal, including the constitutional right to bear arms, shall be secured to and enjoyed by all the citizens... without respect to race or color, or previous condition of slavery....

The understanding that the Second Amendment gave freed blacks the right to keep and bear arms was reflected in congressional discussion of the bill....

Similar discussion attended the passage of the Civil Rights Act of 1871 and the Fourteenth Amendment....

9

4.   Post-Civil War Commentators.

Every late-19th-century legal scholar that we have read interpreted the Second Amendment to secure an individual right unconnected with militia service. The most famous was the judge and professor Thomas Cooley, who wrote a massively popular 1868 Treatise on Constitutional Limitations. Concerning the Second Amendment it said:

> Among the other defences to personal liberty should be mentioned the right of the people to keep and bear arms.... The alternative to a standing army is "a well-regulated militia," but this cannot exist unless the people are trained to bearing arms. How far it is in the power of the legislature to regulate this right, we shall not undertake to say, as happily there has been very little occasion to discuss that subject by the courts....

E

We now ask whether any of our precedents forecloses the conclusions we have reached about the meaning of the Second Amendment.

United States v. Cruikshank, in the course of vacating the convictions of members of a white mob for depriving blacks of their right to keep and bear arms, held that the Second Amendment does not by its own force apply to anyone other than the Federal Government. [The] limited discussion of the Second Amendment in *Cruikshank* supports, if anything, the individual-rights interpretation. There was no claim in *Cruikshank* that the victims had been deprived of their right to carry arms in a militia; indeed, the Governor had disbanded the local militia unit the year before the mob's attack....

Presser v. Illinois, 116 U.S. 252 (1886), held that the right to keep and bear arms was not violated by a law that forbade "bodies of men to associate together as military organizations, or to drill or parade with arms in cities and towns unless authorized by law." This does not refute the individual-rights interpretation of the Amendment; no one supporting that interpretation has contended that States may not ban such groups....

Justice Stevens places overwhelming reliance upon this Court's decision in *United States v. Miller*, 307 U.S. 174 (1939). "[H]undreds of judges," we are told, "have relied on the view of the amendment we endorsed there," and "[e]ven if the textual and historical arguments on both side of the issue were evenly balanced, respect for the well-settled views of all of our predecessors on this Court, and for the rule of law itself... would prevent most jurists from endorsing such a dramatic upheaval in the law." And what is, according to Justice Stevens, the holding of *Miller* that demands such obeisance? That the Second Amendment "protects the right to keep and bear arms for certain military purposes, but that it does not curtail the legislature's power to regulate the nonmilitary use and ownership of weapons."

Nothing so clearly demonstrates the weakness of Justice Stevens' case. *Miller* did not hold that and cannot possibly be read to have held that. The judgment in the case upheld against a Second Amendment challenge two men's federal convictions for transporting an unregistered short-barreled shotgun in interstate commerce, in violation of the National Firearms Act. It is entirely clear that the Court's basis for saying that the Second Amendment did not apply was *not* that the defendants were "bear[ing] arms" not "for... military purposes" but for "nonmilitary use." Rather, it was that the *type of weapon at issue* was not eligible for Second Amendment protection....

This holding is not only consistent with, but positively suggests, that the Second Amendment confers an individual right to keep and bear arms (though only arms that "have some reasonable relationship to the preservation or efficiency of a well regulated militia"). Had the Court believed that the Second Amendment protects only those serving in the militia, it would have been odd to examine the character of the weapon rather than simply note that the two crooks were not militiamen....

It is particularly wrongheaded to read *Miller* for more than what it said, because the case did not even purport to be a thorough examination of the Second Amendment. Justice Stevens claims that the opinion reached its conclusion "[a]fter reviewing many of the same sources that are discussed at greater length by the Court today." Not many, which was not entirely the Court's fault. The respondent made no appearance in the case, neither filing a brief nor appearing at oral argument; the Court heard from no one but the Government (reason enough, one would think, not to make that case the beginning and the end of this Court's consideration of the Second Amendment). [This] is the mighty rock upon which the dissent rests its case.[1]

We may as well consider at this point (for we will have to consider eventually) *what* types of weapons *Miller* permits. Read in isolation, *Miller*'s phrase "part of ordinary military equipment" could mean that only those weapons useful in warfare are protected. That would be a startling reading of the opinion, since it would mean that the National Firearms Act's restrictions on machineguns (not challenged in *Miller*) might be unconstitutional, machineguns being useful in warfare in 1939. We think that *Miller*'s "ordinary military equipment" language must be read in tandem with what comes after: "[O]rdinarily when

---

1. As for the "hundreds of judges" who have relied on the view of the Second Amendment Justice Stevens claims we endorsed in *Miller*: If so, they overread *Miller*. And their erroneous reliance upon an uncontested and virtually unreasoned case cannot nullify the reliance of millions of Americans (as our historical analysis has shown) upon the true meaning of the right to keep and bear arms. In any event, it should not be thought that the cases decided by these judges would necessarily have come out differently under a proper interpretation of the right.

11

called for [militia] service [able-bodied] men were expected to appear bearing arms supplied by themselves and of the kind in common use at the time." The traditional militia was formed from a pool of men bringing arms "in common use at the time" for lawful purposes like self-defense. "In the colonial and revolutionary war era, [small-arms] weapons used by militiamen and weapons used in defense of person and home were one and the same." [We] therefore read *Miller* to say only that the Second Amendment does not protect those weapons not typically possessed by law-abiding citizens for lawful purposes, such as short-barreled shotguns. That accords with the historical understanding of the scope of the right, see Part III, *infra.* . . .

We conclude that nothing in our precedents forecloses our adoption of the original understanding of the Second Amendment. It should be unsurprising that such a significant matter has been for so long judicially unresolved. For most of our history, the Bill of Rights was not thought applicable to the States, and the Federal Government did not significantly regulate the possession of firearms by law-abiding citizens. Other provisions of the Bill of Rights have similarly remained unilluminated for lengthy periods. This Court first held a law to violate the *First Amendment's* guarantee of freedom of speech in 1931, almost 150 years after the Amendment was ratified, see *Near v. Minnesota ex rel. Olson*, 283 U.S. 697 (1931), and it was not until after World War II that we held a law invalid under the Establishment Clause, see *Illinois ex rel. McCollum v. Bd. of Educ.*, 333 U.S. 203 (1948). . . .

III

Like most rights, the right secured by the Second Amendment is not unlimited. From Blackstone through the 19th-century cases, commentators and courts routinely explained that the right was not a right to keep and carry any weapon whatsoever in any manner whatsoever and for whatever purpose. For example, the majority of the 19th-century courts to consider the question held that prohibitions on carrying concealed weapons were lawful under the Second Amendment or state analogues. Although we do not undertake an exhaustive historical analysis today of the full scope of the Second Amendment, nothing in our opinion should be taken to cast doubt on longstanding prohibitions on the possession of firearms by felons and the mentally ill, or laws forbidding the carrying of firearms in sensitive places such as schools and government buildings, or laws imposing conditions and qualifications on the commercial sale of arms.[26]

---

26. We identify these presumptively lawful regulatory measures only as examples; our list does not purport to be exhaustive.

We also recognize another important limitation on the right to keep and carry arms. *Miller* said, as we have explained, that the sorts of weapons protected were those "in common use at the time." We think that limitation is fairly supported by the historical tradition of prohibiting the carrying of "dangerous and unusual weapons."

It may be objected that if weapons that are most useful in military service — M-16 rifles and the like — may be banned, then the Second Amendment right is completely detached from the prefatory clause. But as we have said, the conception of the militia at the time of the Second Amendment's ratification was the body of all citizens capable of military service, who would bring the sorts of lawful weapons that they possessed at home to militia duty. It may well be true today that a militia, to be as effective as militias in the 18th century, would require sophisticated arms that are highly unusual in society at large. Indeed, it may be true that no amount of small arms could be useful against modern-day bombers and tanks. But the fact that modern developments have limited the degree of fit between the prefatory clause and the protected right cannot change our interpretation of the right.

IV

We turn finally to the law at issue here. As we have said, the law totally bans handgun possession in the home. It also requires that any lawful firearm in the home be disassembled or bound by a trigger lock at all times, rendering it inoperable.

As the quotations earlier in this opinion demonstrate, the inherent right of self-defense has been central to the Second Amendment right. The handgun ban amounts to a prohibition of an entire class of "arms" that is overwhelmingly chosen by American society for that lawful purpose. The prohibition extends, moreover, to the home, where the need for defense of self, family, and property is most acute. Under any of the standards of scrutiny that we have applied to enumerated constitutional rights,[27] banning from the home "the most preferred

---

27. Justice Breyer correctly notes that this law, like almost all laws, would pass rational-basis scrutiny. But rational-basis scrutiny is a mode of analysis we have used when evaluating laws under constitutional commands that are themselves prohibitions on irrational laws. In those cases, "rational basis" is not just the standard of scrutiny, but the very substance of the constitutional guarantee. Obviously, the same test could not be used to evaluate the extent to which a legislature may regulate a specific, enumerated right, be it the freedom of speech, the guarantee against double jeopardy, the right to counsel, or the right to keep and bear arms. See *United States v. Carolene Products Co.*, 304 U.S. 144, 152, n. 4 (1938) ("There may be narrower scope for operation of the presumption of constitutionality [*i.e.*, narrower than that provided by rational-basis review] when legislation appears

firearm in the nation to 'keep' and use for protection of one's home and family," would fail constitutional muster. . . .

It is no answer to say [that] it is permissible to ban the possession of handguns so long as the possession of other firearms (*i.e.*, long guns) is allowed. It is enough to note, as we have observed, that the American people have considered the handgun to be the quintessential self-defense weapon. There are many reasons that a citizen may prefer a handgun for home defense: It is easier to store in a location that is readily accessible in an emergency; it cannot easily be redirected or wrestled away by an attacker; it is easier to use for those without the upper-body strength to lift and aim a long gun; it can be pointed at a burglar with one hand while the other hand dials the police. Whatever the reason, handguns are the most popular weapon chosen by Americans for self-defense in the home, and a complete prohibition of their use is invalid. . . .

Justice Breyer has devoted most of his separate dissent to the handgun ban. He says that, even assuming the Second Amendment is a personal guarantee of the right to bear arms, the District's prohibition is valid. He first tries to establish this by founding-era historical precedent, pointing to various restrictive laws in the colonial period. [A] 1783 Massachusetts law forbade the residents of Boston to "take into" or "receive into" "any Dwelling House, Stable, Barn, Out-house, Ware-house, Store, Shop or other Building" loaded firearms, and permitted the seizure of any loaded firearms that "shall be found" there. That statute's text and its prologue, which makes clear that the purpose of the prohibition was to eliminate the danger to firefighters posed by the "depositing of loaded Arms" in buildings, give reason to doubt that colonial Boston authorities would have enforced that general prohibition against someone who temporarily loaded a firearm to confront an intruder (despite the law's application in that case). In any case, we would not stake our interpretation of the Second Amendment upon a single law, in effect in a single city, that contradicts the overwhelming weight of other evidence regarding the right to keep and bear arms for defense of the home. The other laws Justice Breyer cites are gunpowder-storage laws that he concedes did not clearly prohibit loaded weapons, but required only that excess gunpowder be kept in a special container or on the top floor of the home. Nothing about those fire-safety laws undermines our analysis; they do not remotely burden the right of self-defense as much as an absolute ban on handguns. Nor, correspondingly, does our analysis suggest the invalidity of laws regulating the storage of firearms to prevent accidents. . . .

---

on its face to be within a specific prohibition of the Constitution, such as those of the first ten amendments . . . "). If all that was required to overcome the right to keep and bear arms was a rational basis, the Second Amendment would be redundant with the separate constitutional prohibitions on irrational laws, and would have no effect.

Justice Breyer moves on to make a broad jurisprudential point: He criticizes us for declining to establish a level of scrutiny for evaluating Second Amendment restrictions. He proposes, explicitly at least, none of the traditionally expressed levels (strict scrutiny, intermediate scrutiny, rational basis), but rather a judge-empowering "interest-balancing inquiry" that "asks whether the statute burdens a protected interest in a way or to an extent that is out of proportion to the statute's salutary effects upon other important governmental interests." After an exhaustive discussion of the arguments for and against gun control, Justice Breyer arrives at his interest-balanced answer: because handgun violence is a problem, because the law is limited to an urban area, and because there were somewhat similar restrictions in the founding period (a false proposition that we have already discussed), the interest-balancing inquiry results in the constitutionality of the handgun ban. QED.

We know of no other enumerated constitutional right whose core protection has been subjected to a freestanding "interest-balancing" approach. The very enumeration of the right takes out of the hands of government — even the Third Branch of Government — the power to decide on a case-by-case basis whether the right is *really worth* insisting upon. A constitutional guarantee subject to future judges' assessments of its usefulness is no constitutional guarantee at all. Constitutional rights are enshrined with the scope they were understood to have when the people adopted them, whether or not future legislatures or (yes) even future judges think that scope too broad. We would not apply an "interest-balancing" approach to the prohibition of a peaceful neo-Nazi march through Skokie. See *National Socialist Party of America v. Skokie*, 432 U.S. 43 (1977) (per curiam). The First Amendment contains the freedom-of-speech guarantee that the people ratified, which included exceptions for obscenity, libel, and disclosure of state secrets, but not for the expression of extremely unpopular and wrong-headed views. The Second Amendment is no different. Like the First, it is the very *product* of an interest-balancing by the people — which Justice Breyer would now conduct for them anew. And whatever else it leaves to future evaluation, it surely elevates above all other interests the right of law-abiding, responsible citizens to use arms in defense of hearth and home.

Justice Breyer chides us for leaving so many applications of the right to keep and bear arms in doubt, and for not providing extensive historical justification for those regulations of the right that we describe as permissible. But since this case represents this Court's first in-depth examination of the Second Amendment, one should not expect it to clarify the entire field, any more than *Reynolds v. United States*, 98 U.S. 145 (1879), our first in-depth Free Exercise Clause case, left that area in a state of utter certainty. And there will be time enough to expound upon the historical justifications for the exceptions we have mentioned if and when those exceptions come before us....

* * *

15

We are aware of the problem of handgun violence in this country, and we take seriously the concerns raised by the many *amici* who believe that prohibition of handgun ownership is a solution. The Constitution leaves the District of Columbia a variety of tools for combating that problem, including some measures regulating handguns. But the enshrinement of constitutional rights necessarily takes certain policy choices off the table. These include the absolute prohibition of handguns held and used for self-defense in the home. Undoubtedly some think that the Second Amendment is outmoded in a society where our standing army is the pride of our Nation, where well-trained police forces provide personal security, and where gun violence is a serious problem. That is perhaps debatable, but what is not debatable is that it is not the role of this Court to pronounce the Second Amendment extinct....

JUSTICE STEVENS, with whom JUSTICE SOUTER, JUSTICE GINSBURG, and JUSTICE BREYER join, dissenting.

The question presented by this case is not whether the Second Amendment protects a "collective right" or an "individual right." Surely it protects a right that can be enforced by individuals. But a conclusion that the Second Amendment protects an individual right does not tell us anything about the scope of that right.

Guns are used to hunt, for self-defense, to commit crimes, for sporting activities, and to perform military duties. The Second Amendment plainly does not protect the right to use a gun to rob a bank; it is equally clear that it *does* encompass the right to use weapons for certain military purposes. Whether it also protects the right to possess and use guns for nonmilitary purposes like hunting and personal self-defense is the question presented by this case. The text of the Amendment, its history, and our decision in *United States v. Miller*, 307 U.S. 174 (1939), provide a clear answer to that question.

The Second Amendment was adopted to protect the right of the people of each of the several States to maintain a well-regulated militia. It was a response to concerns raised during the ratification of the Constitution that the power of Congress to disarm the state militias and create a national standing army posed an intolerable threat to the sovereignty of the several States. Neither the text of the Amendment nor the arguments advanced by its proponents evidenced the slightest interest in limiting any legislature's authority to regulate private civilian uses of firearms. Specifically, there is no indication that the Framers of the Amendment intended to enshrine the common-law right of self-defense in the Constitution.

In 1934, Congress enacted the National Firearms Act, the first major federal firearms law. Upholding a conviction under that Act, this Court held that, "[i]n the absence of any evidence tending to show that possession or use of a 'shotgun having a barrel of less than eighteen inches in length' at this time has some reasonable relationship to the preservation or efficiency of a well regulated militia, we cannot say that the Second Amendment guarantees the right to keep and bear such an instrument." The view of the Amendment we took in *Miller*— that it protects the right to keep and bear arms for certain military purposes, but that it does not curtail the Legislature's power to regulate the nonmilitary use and ownership of weapons — is both the most natural reading of the Amendment's text and the interpretation most faithful to the history of its adoption.

Since our decision in *Miller,* hundreds of judges have relied on the view of the Amendment we endorsed there; we ourselves affirmed it in 1980. See *Lewis v. United States*, 445 U.S. 55 (1980).[3] No new evidence has surfaced since 1980 supporting the view that the Amendment was intended to curtail the power of Congress to regulate civilian use or misuse of weapons. Indeed, a review of the drafting history of the Amendment demonstrates that its Framers *rejected* proposals that would have broadened its coverage to include such uses.

The opinion the Court announces today fails to identify any new evidence supporting the view that the Amendment was intended to limit the power of Congress to regulate civilian uses of weapons. Unable to point to any such evidence, the Court stakes its holding on a strained and unpersuasive reading of the Amendment's text; significantly different provisions in the 1689 English Bill of Rights, and in various 19th-century State Constitutions; postenactment commentary that was available to the Court when it decided *Miller;* and, ultimately, a feeble attempt to distinguish *Miller* that places more emphasis on the Court's decisional process than on the reasoning in the opinion itself.

Even if the textual and historical arguments on both sides of the issue were evenly balanced, respect for the well-settled views of all of our predecessors on this Court, and for the rule of law itself, would prevent most jurists from endorsing such a dramatic upheaval in the law. As Justice Cardozo observed years ago, the "labor of judges would be increased almost to the breaking point if every past decision could be reopened in every case, and one could not lay one's own course of bricks on the secure foundation of the courses laid by others who had gone before him." The Nature of the Judicial Process 149 (1921)....

I

[T]hree portions of [the Second Amendment's] text merit special focus: the introductory language defining the Amendment's purpose, the class of persons encompassed within its reach, and the unitary nature of the right that it protects.

---

3. Our discussion in *Lewis* was brief but significant. Upholding a conviction for receipt of a firearm by a felon, we wrote: "These legislative restrictions on the use of firearms are neither based upon constitutionally suspect criteria, nor do they entrench upon any constitutionally protected liberties. See *United States v. Miller* . . . ."

"A well regulated Militia, being necessary to the security of a free State"

The preamble to the Second Amendment makes three important points. It identifies the preservation of the militia as the Amendment's purpose; it explains that the militia is necessary to the security of a free State; and it recognizes that the militia must be "well regulated."....

[The] Second Amendment's omission of any statement of purpose related to the right to use firearms for hunting or personal self-defense, is especially striking in light of the fact that the Declarations of Rights of Pennsylvania and Vermont did expressly protect such civilian uses at the time. [The] contrast between those two declarations and the Second Amendment reinforces the clear statement of purpose announced in the Amendment's preamble. It confirms that the Framers' single-minded focus in crafting the constitutional guarantee "to keep and bear arms" was on military uses of firearms, which they viewed in the context of service in state militias....

The Court today tries to denigrate the importance of this clause of the Amendment by beginning its analysis with the Amendment's operative provision and returning to the preamble merely "to ensure that our reading of the operative clause is consistent with the announced purpose." That is not how this Court ordinarily reads such texts, and it is not how the preamble would have been viewed at the time the Amendment was adopted....

"The right of the people"

The centerpiece of the Court's textual argument is its insistence that the words "the people" as used in the Second Amendment must have the same meaning, and protect the same class of individuals, as when they are used in the First and Fourth Amendments. [But] the Court *itself* reads the Second Amendment to protect a "subset" significantly narrower than the class of persons protected by the First and Fourth Amendments; when it finally drills down on the substantive meaning of the Second Amendment, the Court limits the protected class to "law-abiding, responsible citizens." But the class of persons protected by the First and Fourth Amendments is *not* so limited; for even felons (and presumably irresponsible citizens as well) may invoke the protections of those constitutional provisions. The Court offers no way to harmonize its conflicting pronouncements.

The Court also overlooks the significance of the way the Framers used the phrase "the people" in these constitutional provisions. In the First Amendment, [it] is only the right peaceably to assemble, and to petition the Government for a redress of grievances, that is described as a right of "the people." These rights contemplate collective action. While the right peaceably to assemble protects the individual rights of those persons participating in the assembly, its concern is with action engaged in by members of a group, rather than any single individual.

Likewise, although the act of petitioning the Government is a right that can be exercised by individuals, it is primarily collective in nature....

Similarly, the words "the people" in the Second Amendment refer back to the object announced in the Amendment's preamble. They remind us that it is the collective action of individuals having a duty to serve in the militia that the text directly protects and, perhaps more importantly, that the ultimate purpose of the Amendment was to protect the States' share of the divided sovereignty created by the Constitution.

[I]t is true that the Fourth Amendment describes a right that need not be exercised in any collective sense. But that observation does not settle the meaning of the phrase "the people" when used in the Second Amendment. For, as we have seen, the phrase means something quite different in the Petition and Assembly Clauses of the First Amendment....

"To keep and bear Arms"

Although the Court's discussion of these words treats them as two "phrases" — as if they read "to keep" and "to bear" — they describe a unitary right: to possess arms if needed for military purposes and to use them in conjunction with military activities....

The term "bear arms" is a familiar idiom; when used unadorned by any additional words, its meaning is "to serve as a soldier, do military service, fight." One 18th-century dictionary defined "arms" as "weapons of offence, or armour of defence," and another contemporaneous source explained that "[b]y *arms*, we understand those instruments of offence generally made use of in war; such as firearms, swords, & c. By *weapons,* we more particularly mean instruments of other kinds (exclusive of fire-arms), made use of as offensive, on special occasions." Had the Framers wished to expand the meaning of the phrase "bear arms" to encompass civilian possession and use, they could have done so by the addition of phrases such as "for the defense of themselves," as was done in the Pennsylvania and Vermont Declarations of Rights. The *unmodified* use of "bear arms," by contrast, refers most naturally to a military purpose, as evidenced by its use in literally dozens of contemporary texts....

The Amendment's use of the term "keep" in no way contradicts the military meaning conveyed by the phrase "bear arms" and the Amendment's preamble. To the contrary, a number of state militia laws in effect at the time of the Second Amendment's drafting used the term "keep" to describe the requirement that militia members store their arms at their homes, ready to be used for service when necessary....

This reading is confirmed by the fact that the clause protects only one right, rather than two. [The] single right that it does describe is both a duty and a right to have arms available and ready for military service, and to use them for military purposes when necessary.[13] Different language surely would have been used to protect nonmilitary use and possession of weapons from regulation if such an intent had played any role in the drafting of the Amendment....

II

The proper allocation of military power in the new Nation was an issue of central concern for the Framers. The compromises they ultimately reached, reflected in Article I's Militia Clauses and the Second Amendment, represent quintessential examples of the Framers' "splitting the atom of sovereignty."

Two themes relevant to our current interpretive task ran through the debates on the original Constitution. "On the one hand, there was a widespread fear that a national standing Army posed an intolerable threat to individual liberty and to the sovereignty of the separate States." [On] the other hand, the Framers recognized the dangers inherent in relying on inadequately trained militia members "as the primary means of providing for the common defense"; during the Revolutionary War, "[t]his force, though armed, was largely untrained, and its deficiencies were the subject of bitter complaint." In order to respond to those twin concerns, a compromise was reached: Congress would be authorized to raise and support a national Army and Navy, and also to organize, arm, discipline, and provide for the calling forth of "the Militia." U.S. Const., Art. I, § 8, cls. 12-16. The President, at the same time, was empowered as the "Commander in Chief of the Army and Navy of the United States, and of the Militia of the several States, when called into the actual Service of the United States." Art. II, § 2. But, with respect to the militia, a significant reservation was made to the States: Although Congress would have the power to call forth, organize, arm, and discipline the militia, as well as to govern "such Part of them as may be employed in the Service of the United States," the States respectively would retain the right to appoint the officers and to train the militia in accordance with the discipline prescribed by Congress. Art. I, § 8, cl. 16.

But the original Constitution's retention of the militia and its creation of divided authority over that body did not prove sufficient to allay fears about the dangers posed by a standing army. For it was perceived by some that Article I contained a significant gap: While it empowered Congress to organize, arm, and discipline the militia, it did not prevent Congress from providing for the militia's *dis*armament....

---

13. The Court notes that the *First Amendment* protects two separate rights with the phrase "the 'right [singular] of the people peaceably to assemble, and to petition the Government for a redress of grievances.'" *Ante*, at 18. But this only proves the point: In contrast to the language quoted by the Court, the Second Amendment does not protect a "right to keep *and to* bear arms," but rather a "right to keep and bear arms." The state constitutions cited by the Court are distinguishable on the same ground.

[This risk] was one of the primary objections to the original Constitution voiced by its opponents. The Anti-Federalists were ultimately unsuccessful in persuading state ratification conventions to condition their approval of the Constitution upon the eventual inclusion of any particular amendment. But a number of States did propose to the first Federal Congress amendments reflecting a desire to ensure that the institution of the militia would remain protected under the new Government. [While some proposals] were exclusively concerned with standing armies and conscientious objectors, [others] would have protected a more broadly worded right, less clearly tied to service in a state militia. Faced with all of these options, it is telling that James Madison chose to craft the Second Amendment as he did....

Madison's decision to model the Second Amendment on the distinctly military [proposal] is therefore revealing, since it is clear that he considered and rejected formulations that would have unambiguously protected civilian uses of firearms. When Madison prepared his first draft, and when that draft was debated and modified, it is reasonable to assume that all participants in the drafting process were fully aware of the other formulations that would have protected civilian use and possession of weapons and that their choice to craft the Amendment as they did represented a rejection of those alternative formulations.

Madison's initial inclusion of an exemption for conscientious objectors sheds revelatory light on the purpose of the Amendment. It confirms an intent to describe a duty as well as a right, and it unequivocally identifies the military character of both....

III

Although it gives short shrift to the drafting history of the Second Amendment, the Court dwells at length on four other sources: the 17th-century English Bill of Rights; Blackstone's Commentaries on the Laws of England; postenactment commentary on the Second Amendment; and post-Civil War legislative history. All of these sources shed only indirect light on the question before us, and in any event offer little support for the Court's conclusion.

The English Bill of Rights

The Court's reliance on Article VII of the 1689 English Bill of Rights — which, like most of the evidence offered by the Court today, was considered in *Miller* — is misguided both because Article VII was enacted in response to different concerns from those that motivated the Framers of the Second Amendment, and because the guarantees of the two provisions were by no means coextensive. Moreover, the English text contained no preamble or other provision identifying a narrow, militia-related purpose.

21

The English Bill of Rights responded to abuses by the Stuart monarchs; among the grievances set forth in the Bill of Rights was that the King had violated the law "[b]y causing several good Subjects being Protestants to be disarmed at the same time when Papists were both armed and Employed contrary to Law." Article VII of the Bill of Rights was a response to that selective disarmament; it guaranteed that "the Subjects which are Protestants may have Armes for their defence, Suitable to their condition and as allowed by Law." This grant did not establish a general right of all persons, or even of all Protestants, to possess weapons. Rather, the right was qualified in two distinct ways: First, it was restricted to those of adequate social and economic status ("suitable to their Condition"); second, it was only available subject to regulation by Parliament ("as allowed by Law").

The Court may well be correct that the English Bill of Rights protected the right of *some* English subjects to use *some* arms for personal self-defense free from restrictions by the Crown (but not Parliament). But that right — adopted in a different historical and political context and framed in markedly different language — tells us little about the meaning of the Second Amendment.

Blackstone's Commentaries

The Court's reliance on Blackstone's Commentaries on the Laws of England is unpersuasive for the same reason as its reliance on the English Bill of Rights. Blackstone's invocation of "'the natural right of resistance and self-preservation,'" and "'the right of having and using arms for self-preservation and defence'" referred specifically to Article VII in the English Bill of Rights. The excerpt from Blackstone offered by the Court, therefore, is, like Article VII itself, of limited use in interpreting the very differently worded, and differently historically situated, Second Amendment.

What *is* important about Blackstone is the instruction he provided on reading the sort of text before us today. Blackstone described an interpretive approach that gave far more weight to preambles than the Court allows.... "[T]he proeme, or preamble, is often called in to help the construction of an act of parliament."

Postenactment Commentary

The Court also excerpts, without any real analysis, commentary by a number of additional scholars, some near in time to the framing and others post-dating it by close to a century. Those scholars are for the most part of limited relevance in construing the guarantee of the Second Amendment: Their views are not altogether clear, they tended to collapse the Second Amendment with Article VII of the English Bill of Rights, and they appear to have been unfamiliar with the drafting history of the Second Amendment....

Post-Civil War Legislative History

The Court suggests that by the post-Civil War period, the Second Amendment was understood to secure a right to firearm use and ownership for purely private purposes like personal self-defense. While it is true that some of the legislative history on which the Court relies supports that contention, such sources are entitled to limited, if any, weight. All of the statements the Court cites were made long after the framing of the Amendment and cannot possibly supply any insight into the intent of the Framers; and all were made during pitched political debates, so that they are better characterized as advocacy than good-faith attempts at constitutional interpretation.

What is more, much of the evidence the Court offers is decidedly less clear than its discussion allows. The Court notes that "[b]lacks were routinely disarmed by Southern States after the Civil War. Those who opposed these injustices frequently stated that they infringed blacks' constitutional right to keep and bear arms." The Court hastily concludes that "[n]eedless to say, the claim was not that blacks were being prohibited from carrying arms in an organized state militia." But some of the claims of the sort the Court cites may have been just that. In some Southern States, Reconstruction-era Republican governments created state militias in which both blacks and whites were permitted to serve. Because "[t]he decision to allow blacks to serve alongside whites meant that most southerners refused to join the new militia," the bodies were dubbed "Negro militia[s]." . . . .

IV. . . .

[The Second] Amendment played little role in any legislative debate about the civilian use of firearms for most of the 19th century, and it made few appearances in the decisions of this Court. Two 19th-century cases, however, bear mentioning.

In *United States v. Cruikshank*, 92 U.S. 542 (1876), the Court sustained a challenge to respondents' convictions under the Enforcement Act of 1870 for conspiring to deprive any individual of "'any right or privilege granted or secured to him by the constitution or laws of the United States.'" The Court wrote, as to counts 2 and 10 of respondents' indictment:"

> The right there specified is that of "'bearing arms for a lawful purpose."
> This is not a right granted by the Constitution. Neither is it in any manner
> dependent on that instrument for its existence. The Second amendment
> declares that it shall not be infringed; but this, as has been seen, means
> no more than that it shall not be infringed by Congress. This is one of the
> amendments that has no other effect than to restrict the powers of the
> national government.

The majority's assertion that the Court in *Cruikshank* "described the right protected by the Second Amendment as '"bearing arms for a lawful purpose,"'" is not accurate. The *Cruikshank* Court explained that the defective *indictment* contained such language, but the Court did not itself describe the right, or endorse the indictment's description of the right....

Only one other 19th-century case in this Court, *Presser v. Illinois*, 116 U.S. 252 (1886), engaged in any significant discussion of the Second Amendment. The petitioner in *Presser* was convicted of violating a state statute that prohibited organizations other than the Illinois National Guard from associating together as military companies or parading with arms. Presser challenged his conviction, asserting, as relevant, that the statute violated both the Second and the Fourteenth Amendments....

[In upholding the conviction,] *Presser,* therefore, both affirmed *Cruikshank's* holding that the Second Amendment posed no obstacle to regulation by state governments, and suggested that in any event nothing in the Constitution protected the use of arms outside the context of a militia "authorized by law" and organized by the State or Federal Government....

[The] dominant understanding of the Second Amendment's inapplicability to private gun ownership continued well into the 20th century. The first two federal laws directly restricting civilian use and possession of firearms — the 1927 Act prohibiting mail delivery of "pistols, revolvers, and other firearms capable of being concealed on the person," and the 1934 Act prohibiting the possession of sawed-off shotguns and machine guns — were enacted over minor Second Amendment objections dismissed by the vast majority of the legislators who participated in the debates. Members of Congress clashed over the wisdom and efficacy of such laws as crime-control measures. But since the statutes did not infringe upon the military use or possession of weapons, for most legislators they did not even raise the specter of possible conflict with the Second Amendment.

Thus, for most of our history, the invalidity of Second-Amendment-based objections to firearms regulations has been well settled and uncontroversial.[38]

---

38. The majority appears to suggest that even if the meaning of the Second Amendment has been considered settled by courts and legislatures for over two centuries, that settled meaning is overcome by the "reliance of millions of Americans" "upon the true meaning of the right to keep and bear arms." Presumably by this the Court means that many Americans own guns for self-defense, recreation, and other lawful purposes, and object to government interference with their gun ownership. I do not dispute the correctness of this observation. But it is hard to see how Americans have "relied," in the usual sense of the word, on the existence of a constitutional right that, until 2001, had been rejected by every federal court to take up the question. Rather, gun owners have "relied" on the laws passed by democratically elected legislatures, which have generally adopted only limited gun-control measures.

Indeed, the Second Amendment was not even mentioned in either full House of Congress during the legislative proceedings that led to the passage of the 1934 Act. Yet enforcement of that law produced the judicial decision that confirmed the status of the Amendment as limited in reach to military usage. After reviewing many of the same sources that are discussed at greater length by the Court today, the *Miller* Court unanimously concluded that the Second Amendment did not apply to the possession of a firearm that did not have "some reasonable relationship to the preservation or efficiency of a well regulated militia."

The key to that decision did not, as the Court belatedly suggests, turn on the difference between muskets and sawed-off shotguns; it turned, rather, on the basic difference between the military and nonmilitary use and possession of guns. Indeed, if the Second Amendment were not limited in its coverage to military uses of weapons, why should the Court in *Miller* have suggested that some weapons but not others were eligible for Second Amendment protection? If use for self-defense were the relevant standard, why did the Court not inquire into the suitability of a particular weapon for self-defense purposes?

Perhaps in recognition of the weakness of its attempt to distinguish *Miller*, the Court argues in the alternative that *Miller* should be discounted because of its decisional history. It is true that the appellee in *Miller* did not file a brief or make an appearance, although the court below had held that the relevant provision of the National Firearms Act violated the Second Amendment (albeit without any reasoned opinion). But, as our decision in *Marbury v. Madison*, 5 U.S. 137, in which only one side appeared and presented arguments, demonstrates, the absence of adversarial presentation alone is not a basis for refusing to accord *stare decisis* effect to a decision of this Court....

The majority cannot seriously believe that the *Miller* Court did not consider any relevant evidence; the majority simply does not approve of the conclusion the *Miller* Court reached on that evidence. Standing alone, that is insufficient reason to disregard a unanimous opinion of this Court, upon which substantial reliance has been placed by legislators and citizens for nearly 70 years.

Indeed, reliance interests surely cut the other way: Even apart from the reliance of judges and legislators who properly believed, until today, that the Second Amendment did not reach possession of firearms for purely private activities, "millions of Americans," have relied on the power of government to protect their safety and well-being, and that of their families. With respect to the case before us, the legislature of the District of Columbia has relied on its ability to act to "reduce the potentiality for gun-related crimes and gun-related deaths from occurring within the District of Columbia," H. Con. Res. 694, 94th Cong., 2d Sess., 25 (1976); so, too have the residents of the District.

V

The Court concludes its opinion by declaring that it is not the proper role of this Court to change the meaning of rights "enshrine[d]" in the Constitution. But the right the Court announces was not "enshrined" in the Second Amendment by the Framers; it is the product of today's law-changing decision. The majority's exegesis has utterly failed to establish that as a matter of text or history, "the right of law-abiding, responsible citizens to use arms in defense of hearth and home" is "elevate[d] above all other interests" by the Second Amendment.

Until today, it has been understood that legislatures may regulate the civilian use and misuse of firearms so long as they do not interfere with the preservation of a well-regulated militia. The Court's announcement of a new constitutional right to own and use firearms for private purposes upsets that settled understanding, but leaves for future cases the formidable task of defining the scope of permissible regulations. Today judicial craftsmen have confidently asserted that a policy choice that denies a "law-abiding, responsible citize[n]" the right to keep and use weapons in the home for self-defense is "off the table." Given the presumption that most citizens are law abiding, and the reality that the need to defend oneself may suddenly arise in a host of locations outside the home, I fear that the District's policy choice may well be just the first of an unknown number of dominoes to be knocked off the table.[39]

[Today's decision] will surely give rise to a far more active judicial role in making vitally important national policy decisions than was envisioned at any time in the 18th, 19th, or 20th centuries.

The Court properly disclaims any interest in evaluating the wisdom of the specific policy choice challenged in this case, but it fails to pay heed to a far more important policy choice — the choice made by the Framers themselves. The Court would have us believe that over 200 years ago, the Framers made a choice to limit the tools available to elected officials wishing to regulate civilian

---

39. It was just a few years after the decision in *Miller* that Justice Frankfurter (by any measure a true judicial conservative) warned of the perils that would attend this Court's entry into the "political thicket" of legislative districting. *Colegrove v. Green*, 328 U.S. 549 (1946) (plurality opinion). The equally controversial political thicket that the Court has decided to enter today is qualitatively different from the one that concerned Justice Frankfurter: While our entry into that thicket was justified because the political process was manifestly unable to solve the problem of unequal districts, no one has suggested that the political process is not working exactly as it should in mediating the debate between the advocates and opponents of gun control. What impact the Court's unjustified entry into *this* thicket will have on that ongoing debate — or indeed on the Court itself — is a matter that future historians will no doubt discuss at length. It is, however, clear to me that adherence to a policy of judicial restraint would be far wiser than the bold decision announced today.

uses of weapons, and to authorize this Court to use the common-law process of case-by-case judicial lawmaking to define the contours of acceptable gun control policy. Absent compelling evidence that is nowhere to be found in the Court's opinion, I could not possibly conclude that the Framers made such a choice.

For these reasons, I respectfully dissent.

JUSTICE BREYER, with whom JUSTICE STEVENS, JUSTICE SOUTER, and JUSTICE GINSBURG join, dissenting....

I

The majority's conclusion is wrong for two independent reasons. The first reason is that set forth by Justice Stevens — namely, that the Second Amendment protects militia-related, not self-defense-related, interests....

The second independent reason is that the protection the Amendment provides is not absolute. The Amendment permits government to regulate the interests that it serves. Thus, irrespective of what those interests are — whether they do or do not include an independent interest in self-defense — the majority's view cannot be correct unless it can show that the District's regulation is unreasonable or inappropriate in Second Amendment terms. This the majority cannot do....

II....

[Colonial] history itself offers important examples of the kinds of gun regulation that citizens would then have thought compatible with the "right to keep and bear arms," whether embodied in Federal or State Constitutions, or the background common law. And those examples include substantial regulation of firearms in urban areas, including regulations that imposed obstacles to the use of firearms for the protection of the home....

This historical evidence demonstrates that a self-defense assumption is the *beginning*, rather than the *end*, of any constitutional inquiry. That the District law impacts self-defense merely raises *questions* about the law's constitutionality. [There] are no purely logical or conceptual answers to such questions. All of which to say that to raise a self-defense question is not to answer it.

III

I therefore begin by asking a process-based question: How is a court to determine whether a particular firearm regulation (here, the District's restriction on handguns) is consistent with the Second Amendment? What kind of constitutional standard should the court use? How high a protective hurdle does the Amendment erect?

The question matters. The majority is wrong when it says that the District's law is unconstitutional "[u]nder any of the standards of scrutiny that we have applied to enumerated constitutional rights." How could that be? It certainly would not be unconstitutional under, for example, a "rational basis" standard, which requires a court to uphold regulation so long as it bears a "rational relationship" to a "legitimate governmental purpose." The law at issue here, which in part seeks to prevent gun-related accidents, at least bears a "rational relationship" to that "legitimate" life-saving objective....

Respondent proposes that the Court adopt a "strict scrutiny" test, which would require reviewing with care each gun law to determine whether it is "narrowly tailored to achieve a compelling governmental interest." But the majority implicitly, and appropriately, rejects that suggestion by broadly approving a set of laws — prohibitions on concealed weapons, forfeiture by criminals of the Second Amendment right, prohibitions on firearms in certain locales, and governmental regulation of commercial firearm sales — whose constitutionality under a strict scrutiny standard would be far from clear.

Indeed, adoption of a true strict-scrutiny standard for evaluating gun regulations would be impossible. That is because almost every gun-control regulation will seek to advance (as the one here does) a "primary concern of every government — a concern for the safety and indeed the lives of its citizens." *United States v. Salerno*, 481 U.S. 739 (1987). The Court has deemed that interest, as well as "the Government's general interest in preventing crime," to be "compelling," and the Court has in a wide variety of constitutional contexts found such public-safety concerns sufficiently forceful to justify restrictions on individual liberties, *see e.g., Brandenburg v. Ohio*, 395 U.S. 444 (1969) (per curiam) (First Amendment free speech rights); *Sherbert v. Verner*, 374 U.S. 398 (1963) (First Amendment religious rights); *Brigham City v. Stuart*, 547 U.S. 398 (2006) (Fourth Amendment protection of the home); *New York v. Quarles*, 467 U.S. 649 (1984) (Fifth Amendment rights under *Miranda v. Arizona*); *Salerno*, *supra* (Eighth Amendment bail rights). Thus, any attempt *in theory* to apply strict scrutiny to gun regulations will *in practice* turn into an interest-balancing inquiry, with the interests protected by the Second Amendment on one side and the governmental public-safety concerns on the other, the only question being whether the regulation at issue impermissibly burdens the former in the course of advancing the latter.

I would simply adopt such an interest-balancing inquiry explicitly....

In applying this kind of standard the Court normally defers to a legislature's empirical judgment in matters where a legislature is likely to have greater expertise and greater institutional factfinding capacity....

The above-described approach seems preferable to a more rigid approach here for a further reason. Experience as much as logic has led the Court to decide that in one area of constitutional law or another the interests are likely to prove stronger on one side of a typical constitutional case than on the other. Here, we have little prior experience. Courts that *do* have experience in these matters have uniformly taken an approach that treats empirically-based legislative judgment with a degree of deference....

IV....

[Justice Breyer turns now to the constitutionality of the District's ban on handguns.]

A

No one doubts the constitutional importance of the statute's basic objective, saving lives. But there is considerable debate about whether the District's statute helps to achieve that objective. I begin by reviewing the statute's tendency to secure that objective from the perspective of (1) the legislature (namely, the Council of the District of Columbia) that enacted the statute in 1976, and (2) a court that seeks to evaluate the Council's decision today.

1

First, consider the facts as the legislature saw them when it adopted the District statute. As stated by the local council committee that recommended its adoption, the major substantive goal of the District's handgun restriction is "to reduce the potentiality for gun-related crimes and gun-related deaths from occurring within the District of Columbia." The committee concluded, on the basis of "extensive public hearings" and "lengthy research," that "[t]he easy availability of firearms in the United States has been a major factor contributing to the drastic increase in gun-related violence and crime over the past 40 years." It reported to the Council "startling statistics," regarding gun-related crime, accidents, and deaths, focusing particularly on the relation between handguns and crime and the proliferation of handguns within the District.

The committee informed the Council that guns were "responsible for 69 deaths in this country each day," for a total of "[a]pproximately 25,000 gun-deaths... each year," along with an additional 200,000 gun-related injuries. Three thousand of these deaths, the report stated, were accidental. A quarter of the victims in those accidental deaths were children under the age of 14. And according to the committee, "[f]or every intruder stopped by a homeowner with a firearm, there are 4 gun-related accidents within the home."

In respect to local crime, the committee observed that there were 285 murders in the District during 1974 — a record number. The committee also stated that, "[c]ontrary to popular opinion on the subject, firearms are more frequently involved in deaths and violence among relatives and friends than in premeditated criminal activities." Citing an article from the American Journal of Psychiatry, the committee reported that "[m]ost murders are committed by previously law-abiding citizens, in situations where spontaneous violence is generated by anger, passion or intoxication, and where the killer and victim are acquainted." "Twenty-five percent of these murders," the committee informed the Council, "occur within families."

The committee report furthermore presented statistics strongly correlating handguns with crime. Of the 285 murders in the District in 1974, 155 were committed with handguns. This did not appear to be an aberration, as the report revealed that "handguns [had been] used in roughly 54% of all murders" (and 87% of murders of law enforcement officers) nationwide over the preceding several years. Nor were handguns only linked to murders, as statistics showed that they were used in roughly 60% of robberies and 26% of assaults. "A crime committed with a pistol," the committee reported, "is 7 times more likely to be lethal than a crime committed with any other weapon." ...

The District's special focus on handguns thus reflects the fact that the committee report found them to have a particularly strong link to undesirable activities in the District's exclusively urban environment. The District did not seek to prohibit possession of other sorts of weapons deemed more suitable for an "urban area."

2

Next, consider the facts as a court must consider them looking at the matter as of today. Petitioners, and their *amici,* have presented us with more recent statistics that tell much the same story that the committee report told 30 years ago. At the least, they present nothing that would permit us to second-guess the Council in respect to the numbers of gun crimes, injuries, and deaths, or the role of handguns.

From 1993 to 1997, there were 180,533 firearm-related deaths in the United States, an average of over 36,000 per year. Fifty-one percent were suicides, 44% were homicides, 1% were legal interventions, 3% were unintentional accidents, and 1% were of undetermined causes. Over that same period there were an additional 411,800 nonfatal firearm-related injuries treated in U.S. hospitals, an average of over 82,000 per year. Of these, 62% resulted from assaults, 17% were unintentional, 6% were suicide attempts, 1% were legal interventions, and 13% were of unknown causes.

The statistics are particularly striking in respect to children and adolescents. In over one in every eight firearm-related deaths in 1997, the victim was someone under the age of 20. Firearm-related deaths account for 22.5% of all injury deaths between the ages of 1 and 19. More male teenagers die from firearms than from all natural causes combined.

Handguns are involved in a majority of firearm deaths and injuries in the United States. From 1993 to 1997, 81% of firearm-homicide victims were killed by handgun. In the same period, for the 41% of firearm injuries for which the weapon type is known, 82% of them were from handguns. And among children under the age of 20, handguns account for approximately 70% of all unintentional firearm-related injuries and deaths....

Handguns also appear to be a very popular weapon among criminals. In a 1997 survey of inmates who were armed during the crime for which they were incarcerated, 83.2% of state inmates and 86.7% of federal inmates said that they were armed with a handgun. And handguns are not only popular tools for crime, but popular objects of it as well: the FBI received on average over 274,000 reports of stolen guns for each year between 1985 and 1994, and almost 60% of stolen guns are handguns. Department of Justice studies have concluded that stolen handguns in particular are an important source of weapons for both adult and juvenile offenders.

Statistics further suggest that urban areas, such as the District, have different experiences with gun-related death, injury, and crime, than do less densely populated rural areas. A disproportionate amount of violent and property crimes occur in urban areas, and urban criminals are more likely than other offenders to use a firearm during the commission of a violent crime....

3

Respondent and his many *amici* for the most part do not disagree about the *figures* set forth in the preceding subsection, but they do disagree strongly with the District's *predictive judgment* that a ban on handguns will help solve the crime and accident problems that those figures disclose....

First, they point out that, since the ban took effect, violent crime in the District has increased, not decreased. Indeed, a comparison with 49 other major cities reveals that the District's homicide rate is actually substantially *higher* relative to these other cities than it was before the handgun restriction went into effect.

Second, respondent's *amici* point to a statistical analysis that regresses murder rates against the presence or absence of strict gun laws in 20 European nations. That analysis concludes that strict gun laws are correlated with *more* murders, not fewer. They further argue that handgun bans do not reduce suicide rates, or rates of accidents, even those involving children.

Third, they point to evidence indicating that firearm ownership does have a beneficial self-defense effect. Based on a 1993 survey, the authors of one study estimated that there were 2.2-to-2.5 million defensive uses of guns (mostly brandishing, about a quarter involving the actual firing of a gun) annually. Another study estimated that for a period of 12 months ending in 1994, there were 503,481 incidents in which a burglar found himself confronted by an armed homeowner, and that in 497,646 (98.8%) of them, the intruder was successfully scared away. A third study suggests that gun-armed victims are substantially less likely than non-gun-armed victims to be injured in resisting robbery or assault. And additional evidence suggests that criminals are likely to be deterred from burglary and other crimes if they know the victim is likely to have a gun.

Fourth, respondent's *amici* argue that laws criminalizing gun possession are self-defeating, as evidence suggests that they will have the effect only of restricting law-abiding citizens, but not criminals, from acquiring guns....

These empirically based arguments may have proved strong enough to convince many legislatures, as a matter of legislative policy, not to adopt total handgun bans. But the question here is whether they are strong enough to destroy judicial confidence in the reasonableness of a legislature that rejects them. And that they are not. For one thing, they can lead us more deeply into the uncertainties that surround any effort to reduce crime, but they cannot prove either that handgun possession diminishes crime or that handgun bans are ineffective. The statistics do show a soaring District crime rate. And the District's crime rate went up after the District adopted its handgun ban. But, as students of elementary logic know, *after it* does not mean *because of it.* What would the District's crime rate have looked like without the ban? Higher? Lower? The same? Experts differ; and we, as judges, cannot say.

What about the fact that foreign nations with strict gun laws have higher crime rates? Which is the cause and which the effect? The proposition that strict gun laws *cause* crime is harder to accept than the proposition that strict gun laws in part grow out of the fact that a nation already has a higher crime rate. And we are then left with the same question as before: What would have happened to crime without the gun laws — a question that respondent and his *amici* do not convincingly answer.

Further, suppose that respondent's *amici* are right when they say that householders' possession of loaded handguns help to frighten away intruders. On that assumption, one must still ask whether that benefit is worth the potential death-related cost. And that is a question without a directly provable answer.

Finally, consider the claim of respondent's *amici* that handgun bans *cannot* work; there are simply too many illegal guns already in existence for a ban on legal guns to make a difference. In a word, they claim that, given the urban sea of pre-existing legal guns, criminals can readily find arms regardless. Nonetheless, a legislature might respond, we want to make an effort to try to dry up that urban sea, drop by drop. And none of the studies can show that effort is not worthwhile.

In a word, the studies to which respondent's *amici* point raise policy-related questions. They succeed in proving that the District's predictive judgments are controversial. But they do not by themselves show that those judgments are incorrect; nor do they demonstrate a consensus, academic or otherwise, supporting that conclusion.

Thus, it is not surprising that the District and its *amici* support the District's handgun restriction with studies of their own. One in particular suggests that, statistically speaking, the District's law has indeed had positive life-saving effects. Others suggest that firearm restrictions as a general matter reduce homicides, suicides, and accidents in the home. Still others suggest that the defensive uses of handguns are not as great in number as respondent's *amici* claim....

The upshot is a set of studies and counterstudies that, at most, could leave a judge uncertain about the proper policy conclusion. But from respondent's perspective any such uncertainty is not good enough. That is because legislators, not judges, have primary responsibility for drawing policy conclusions from empirical fact. And, given that constitutional allocation of decisionmaking responsibility, the empirical evidence presented here is sufficient to allow a judge to reach a firm *legal* conclusion....

[T]he District's decision represents the kind of empirically based judgment that legislatures, not courts, are best suited to make. In fact, deference to legislative judgment seems particularly appropriate here, where the judgment has been made by a local legislature, with particular knowledge of local problems and insight into appropriate local solutions....

B

I next assess the extent to which the District's law burdens the interests that the Second Amendment seeks to protect....

1

The District's statute burdens the Amendment's first and primary objective [of protecting the militia] hardly at all....

To begin with, the present case has nothing to do with *actual* military service. [I] am aware of no indication that the District either now or in the recent past has called up its citizenry to serve in a militia, that it has any inkling of doing so anytime in the foreseeable future, or that this law must be construed to prevent the use of handguns during legitimate militia activities....

[The] District's law does not seriously affect military training interests. The law permits residents to engage in activities that will increase their familiarity with firearms. They may register (and thus possess in their homes) weapons other than handguns, such as rifles and shotguns. See D. C. Code §§ 7-2502.01, 7-2502.02(a) (only weapons that cannot be registered are sawed-off shotguns, machine guns, short-barreled rifles, and pistols not registered before 1976)....

And while the District law prevents citizens from training with handguns *within the District*, the District consists of only 61.4 square miles of urban area. The adjacent States do permit the use of handguns for target practice, and those States are only a brief subway ride away....

Of course, a subway rider must buy a ticket, and the ride takes time. It also costs money to store a pistol, say, at a target range, outside the District. But given the costs already associated with gun ownership and firearms training, I cannot say that a subway ticket and a short subway ride (and storage costs) create more than a minimal burden. Compare *Crawford v. Marion County Election Bd.*, 553 U.S. ___ (2008) (Breyer, J., dissenting) (acknowledging travel burdens on indigent persons in the context of voting where public transportation options were limited)....

2

The majority briefly suggests that the "right to keep and bear Arms" might encompass an interest in hunting. But in enacting the present provisions, the District sought "to take nothing away from sportsmen." And any inability of District residents to hunt near where they live has much to do with the jurisdiction's exclusively urban character and little to do with the District's firearm laws....

3

The District's law does prevent a resident from keeping a loaded handgun in his home. And it consequently makes it more difficult for the householder to use the handgun for self-defense in the home against intruders, such as burglars. [Statistics] suggest that handguns are the most popular weapon for self-defense. And there are some legitimate reasons why that would be the case. [To] that extent the law burdens to some degree an interest in self-defense that for present purposes I have assumed the Amendment seeks to further.

C

In weighing needs and burdens, we must take account of the possibility that there are reasonable, but less restrictive alternatives. Are there *other* potential measures that might similarly promote the same goals while imposing lesser restrictions? Here I see none.

The reason there is no clearly superior, less restrictive alternative to the District's handgun ban is that the ban's very objective is to reduce significantly the number of handguns in the District, say, for example, by allowing a law enforcement officer immediately to assume that *any* handgun he sees is an *illegal* handgun. And there is no plausible way to achieve that objective other than to ban the guns....

[Any] measure less restrictive in respect to the use of handguns for self-defense will, to that same extent, prove less effective in preventing the use of handguns for illicit purposes. If a resident has a handgun in the home that he can use for self-defense, then he has a handgun in the home that he can use to commit suicide or engage in acts of domestic violence....

Licensing restrictions would not similarly reduce the handgun population, and the District may reasonably fear that even if guns are initially restricted to law-abiding citizens, they might be stolen and thereby placed in the hands of criminals....

The absence of equally effective alternatives to a complete prohibition finds support in the empirical fact that other States and urban centers prohibit particular types of weapons....

D

The upshot is that the District's objectives are compelling; its predictive judgments as to its law's tendency to achieve those objectives are adequately supported; the law does impose a burden upon any self-defense interest that the Amendment seeks to secure; and there is no clear less restrictive alternative. I turn now to the final portion of the "permissible regulation" question: Does the District's law *disproportionately* burden Amendment-protected interests? Several considerations, taken together, convince me that it does not.

First, the District law is tailored to the life-threatening problems it attempts to address. The law concerns one class of weapons, handguns, leaving residents free to possess shotguns and rifles, along with ammunition. The area that falls within its scope is totally urban.

Second, the self-defense interest in maintaining loaded handguns in the home to shoot intruders is not the *primary* interest, but at most a subsidiary interest, that the Second Amendment seeks to serve....

Further, any self-defense interest at the time of the Framing could not have focused exclusively upon urban-crime related dangers. Two hundred years ago, most Americans, many living on the frontier, would likely have thought of self-defense primarily in terms of outbreaks of fighting with Indian tribes, rebellions such as Shays' Rebellion, marauders, and crime-related dangers to travelers on the roads, on footpaths, or along waterways. Insofar as the Framers focused at all on the tiny fraction of the population living in large cities, they would have been aware that these city dwellers were subject to firearm restrictions that their rural counterparts were not. They are unlikely then to have thought of a right to keep loaded handguns in homes to confront intruders in urban settings as *central*....

Nor, for that matter, am I aware of any evidence that *handguns* in particular were central to the Framers' conception of the Second Amendment. The lists of militia-related weapons in the late 18th-century state statutes appear primarily to refer to other sorts of weapons, muskets in particular....

Third, irrespective of what the Framers *could have thought,* we know what they *did think.* Samuel Adams, who lived in Boston, advocated a constitutional amendment that would have precluded the Constitution from ever being "construed" to "prevent the people of the United States, who are peaceable citizens, from keeping their own arms." Samuel Adams doubtless knew that the Massachusetts Constitution contained somewhat similar protection. And he doubtless knew that Massachusetts law prohibited Bostonians from keeping loaded guns in the house. So how could Samuel Adams have advocated such protection *unless* he thought that the protection was *consistent* with local regulation that seriously impeded urban residents from using their arms against intruders? It seems unlikely that he meant to deprive the Federal Government of power (to enact Boston-type weapons regulation) that he know Boston had and (as far as we know) he would have thought constitutional under the Massachusetts Constitution. . . .

Fourth, a contrary view, as embodied in today's decision, will have unfortunate consequences. The decision will encourage legal challenges to gun regulation throughout the Nation. Because it says little about the standards used to evaluate regulatory decisions, it will leave the Nation without clear standards for resolving those challenges. And litigation over the course of many years, or the mere specter of such litigation, threatens to leave cities without effective protection against gun violence and accidents during that time. . . .

V

The majority derides my approach as "judge-empowering." I take this criticism seriously, but I do not think it accurate. . . .

The majority's methodology is, in my view, substantially less transparent than mine. At a minimum, I find it difficult to understand the reasoning that seems to underlie certain conclusions that it reaches.

The majority spends the first 54 pages of its opinion attempting to rebut Justice Stevens' evidence that the Amendment was enacted with a purely militia-related purpose. In the majority's view, the Amendment also protects an interest in armed personal self-defense, at least to some degree. But the majority does not tell us precisely what that interest is. "Putting all of [the Second Amendment's] textual elements together," the majority says, "we find that they guarantee the individual right to possess and carry weapons in case of confrontation." Then, three pages later, it says that "we do not read the Second Amendment to permit citizens to carry arms for *any sort* of confrontation." Yet, with one critical exception, it does not explain which confrontations count. It simply leaves that question unanswered.

The majority does, however, point to one type of confrontation that counts, for it describes the Amendment as "elevat[ing] above all other interests the

36

right of law-abiding, responsible citizens to use arms in defense of hearth and home." What is its basis for finding that to be the core of the Second Amendment right? The only historical sources identified by the majority that even appear to touch upon that specific matter consist of an 1866 newspaper editorial discussing the Freedmen's Bureau Act, two quotations from that 1866 Act's legislative history, and a 1980 state court opinion saying that in colonial times the same were used to defend the home as to maintain the militia. How can citations such as these support the far-reaching proposition that the Second Amendment's primary concern is not its stated concern about the militia, but rather a right to keep loaded weapons at one's bedside to shoot intruders?

Nor is it at all clear to me how the majority decides *which* loaded "arms" a homeowner may keep. The majority says that that Amendment protects those weapons "typically possessed by law-abiding citizens for lawful purposes." This definition conveniently excludes machineguns, but permits handguns, which the majority describes as "the most popular weapon chosen by Americans for self-defense in the home." But what sense does this approach make? According to the majority's reasoning, if Congress and the States lift restrictions on the possession and use of machineguns, and people buy machineguns to protect their homes, the Court will have to reverse course and find that the Second Amendment *does*, in fact, protect the individual self-defense-related right to possess a machinegun. On the majority's reasoning, if tomorrow someone invents a particularly useful, highly dangerous self-defense weapon, Congress and the States had better ban it immediately, for once it becomes popular Congress will no longer possess the constitutional authority to do so. In essence, the majority determines what regulations are permissible by looking to see what existing regulations permit. There is no basis for believing that the Framers intended such circular reasoning.

I am similarly puzzled by the majority's list, in Part III of its opinion, of provisions that in its view would survive Second Amendment scrutiny. These consist of (1) "prohibitions on carrying concealed weapons"; (2) "prohibitions on the possession of firearms by felons"; (3) "prohibitions on the possession of firearms by ... the mentally ill"; (4) "laws forbidding the carrying of firearms in sensitive places such as schools and government buildings"; and (5) government "conditions and qualifications" attached "to the commercial sale of arms." Why these? Is it that similar restrictions existed in the late 18th century? The majority fails to cite any colonial analogues....

At the same time the majority ignores a more important question: Given the purposes for which the Framers enacted the Second Amendment, how should it be applied to modern-day circumstances that they could not have anticipated? Assume, for argument's sake, that the Framers did intend the Amendment to offer a degree of self-defense protection. Does that mean that the Framers also intended to guarantee a right to possess a loaded gun near swimming pools, parks, and playgrounds? That they would not have cared about the children who might pick up a loaded gun on their parents' bedside table? That they (who certainly showed concern for the risk of fire) would have lacked concern for the risk of accidental deaths or suicides that readily accessible loaded handguns in urban areas might bring? Unless we believe that they intended future generations to ignore such matters, answering questions such as the questions in this case requires judgment — judicial judgment exercised within a framework for constitutional analysis that guides that judgment and which makes its exercise transparent. One cannot answer those questions by combining inconclusive historical research with judicial *ipse dixit*....

F.   *"Case or Controversy" Requirements and the Passive Virtues*

Page 117.   At the end of section 3a of the Note, add the following:

Compare *Sierra Club* and *SCRAP* to Summers v. Earth Island Institute, 555 U.S. 488 (2009). Plaintiffs, a group of environmental organizations, challenged the failure of the United States Forest Service to enforce regulations requiring it to establish notice, comment, and appeal procedures for proposed actions implementing land and resource management plans. The Forest Service regulations provided for a categorical exemption from this requirement for fire-rehabilitation activities in relatively small areas that did not cause significant environmental impact.

Plaintiff's original action challenged the Forest Service's failure to provide for notice and comment with regard to a particular project. Soon after the District Court granted a preliminary injunction with regard to that project, the dispute over it was settled. Despite the fact that no other particular project was before the Court, the trial court held that the Forest Service regulations pertaining to that project were unlawful, and the Court of Appeals affirmed. In a five-to-four decision, the Supreme Court, in an opinion written by Justice Scalia, reversed.

The Court acknowledged that plaintiff organizations had standing to challenge the particular project, but rejected the proposition that when a "plaintiff has sued to challenge the lawfulness of certain action or threatened action but has settled that suit, he retains standing to challenge the basis for that action (here the regulation in the abstract), apart from any concrete application that threatens imminent harm to his interests." The plaintiffs lacked standing because they "have identified no other application of the invalidated regulations that threatens imminent and concrete harm to the interests of their members."

The Court held that an affidavit submitted by a member of one of the plaintiff organizations, alleging that he "has visited many National Forests and plans to visit several unnamed National Forests in the future" did not suffice. The affidavit failed

> to allege that *any* particular timber sale or other project claimed to be unlawfully subject to the regulations will impede a specific and concrete plan of [the affiant's] to enjoy the National Forests. The National Forests occupy more than 190 million acres, an area larger than Texas. There may be a chance, but it is hardly a likelihood, that [affiant's] wanderings will bring him to a parcel about to be affected by a project unlawfully subject to the regulations. Indeed, without further specification, it is impossible to tell *which* projects are (in respondents' view) unlawfully subject to regulations.

The Court also rejected plaintiffs' argument that they had standing to complain of the procedural injury caused by their inability to file comments on Forest Service actions. "[A] deprivation of a procedural right without some concrete interest that is affected by the deprivation—a procedural right *in vacuo*—is insufficient to create Article III standing." Nor was it relevant that the procedural right was created by Congress, since "the requirement of injury in fact is a hard floor of Article III jurisdiction that cannot be removed by statute."

In a short concurring opinion, Justice Kennedy joined the opinion of the Court, but noted that the case "would present different considerations if Congress had sought to provide redress for a concrete injury 'giv[ing] rise to a case or controversy where none existed before.'"

Justice Breyer filed a dissenting opinion that was joined by Justices Stevens, Souter, and Ginsburg. He observed that the plaintiff organizations had "hundreds of thousands of members who use forests regularly across the nation." The members' activities led him to this analogy: "To know, virtually for certain, that snow will fall in New England this winter is not to know the name of each particular town where it is bound to arrive. The law of standing does not require the latter kind of specificity."

Page 120.   At the end of the page, add the following:

In Arizona Christian School Tuition Org. v. Winn, 131 S. Ct. 1436 (2011), the Supreme Court distinguished between taxpayer standing to challenge government expenditures and taxpayer standing to challenge tax credits given to other taxpayers. The Court reasoned that in cases challenging government expenditures, the taxpayer-plaintiff was effectively alleging that his tax money was being extracted and spent in violation of the Constitution. By contrast, the Court declined to treat a tax credit as an exaction of funds from dissenting taxpayers. Rather, tax credits simply permitted other private taxpayers to direct their own funds to an organization of their choice. Responding to prior cases where the Court had reached the merits of Establishment Clause challenges to tax benefit programs brought by dissenting taxpayers, the Court declared that "those cases do not mention standing and so are not contrary to the conclusion reached here. When a potential jurisdictional defect is neither noted nor discussed in a federal decision, the decision does not stand for the proposition that no defect existed.... The Court would risk error if it relied on assumptions that have gone unstated and unexamined." The Court also suggested that in many challenges to tax credits, "the disadvantaged party would not have to rely on *Flast* to obtain redress for a resulting injury," because he would be directly disadvantaged by an inability to obtain the benefit. The dissenting Justices, by contrast, argued that "[c]ash grants and targeted tax breaks are means of accomplishing the same government objective — to provide financial support to select individuals or organizations. Taxpayers who oppose state aid of religion have equal reason to protest whether that aid flows from the one form of subsidy or the other. Either way, the government has financed the religious activity. And so either way, taxpayers should be able to challenge the subsidy."

Page 140.   At the end of section 3 of the Note, add the following:

In Caperton v. A. T. Massey Coal Co., 129 S. Ct. 2252 (2009), the Supreme Court addressed the question whether the due process clause required a state supreme court justice to recuse himself from a case involving an individual who had spent roughly $3 million in support of the justice's election. In recent years, a number of litigants had raised questions regarding the propriety of elected judges — and more than forty states elect at least some of their judges — sitting on cases involving individuals who had made substantial expenditures in judicial election campaigns. The Supreme Court, by a five-to-four vote, held that under the circumstances of the case, due process required recusal. (The due process clause holding is described in more detail *infra* in the Supplement to page 960.)

Justice Kennedy's opinion for the Court concluded that recusal is required when "there is a serious risk of actual bias — based on objective and reasonable perceptions — [that] a person with a personal stake in a particular case had a significant and disproportionate influence in placing the judge on the case by raising funds or directing the judge's election campaign when the case was pending or imminent. The inquiry centers on the contribution's relative size in comparison to the total amount of money contributed to the campaign, the total amount spent in the election, and the apparent effect such contribution had on the outcome of the election." In the case before the Court, the Court found that Massey's chairman's efforts had had such influence. "His contributions eclipsed the total amount spent by all other [supporters] and exceeded by 300% the amount spent by [the justice's own] campaign committee."

The Court explained that:

> Our decision today addresses an extraordinary situation where the Constitution requires recusal. Massey and its *amici* predict that various adverse consequences will follow from recognizing a constitutional violation here — ranging from a flood of recusal motions to unnecessary interference with judicial elections. We disagree. The facts now before us are extreme by any measure. The parties point to no other instance involving judicial campaign contributions that presents a potential for bias comparable to the circumstances in this case.
>
> It is true that extreme cases often test the bounds of established legal principles, and sometimes no administrable standard may be available to address the perceived wrong. But it is also true that extreme cases are more likely to cross constitutional limits, requiring this Court's intervention and formulation of objective standards. This is particularly true when due process is violated. *See, e.g., County of Sacramento v. Lewis*, 523 U.S. 833 (1998) (reiterating the due-process prohibition on "executive abuse of power... which shocks the conscience"); id., at 858 (KENNEDY, J., concurring) (explaining that "objective considerations, including history and precedent, are the controlling principle" of this due process standard).

It concluded that because states' own codes of judicial conduct often required recusal under a wider range of circumstances and thus "provide more protection than due process requires, most disputes over disqualification will be resolved without resort to the Constitution. Application of the constitutional standard implicated in this case will thus be confined to rare instances."

In dissent, Chief Justice Roberts questioned whether the Court had identified any manageable standards for requiring recusal. He charged that "the standard the majority articulates [fails] to provide clear, workable guidance for future cases," and provided a numbered list of forty questions he claimed the Court's opinion left open, such as "How much money is too much money?," "Must the judge recuse in cases involving individuals or groups who spent large amounts of money trying unsuccessfully to defeat him?," and "If causation is a pertinent factor, how do we know whether the contribution or expenditure had any effect on the outcome of the election?" He concluded: "The Court's inability to formulate a 'judicially discernible and manageable standard' strongly counsels against the recognition of a novel constitutional right. See *Vieth v. Jubelirer*, 541 U.S. 267, 306 (2004) (plurality opinion) (holding political gerrymandering claims nonjusticiable based on the lack of workable standards); id., at 317 (KENNEDY, J., concurring in judgment) ('the failings of the many proposed standards for measuring the burden a gerrymander imposes... make our intervention improper.') The need to consider these and countless other questions helps explain why the common law and this Court's constitutional jurisprudence have never required disqualification on such vague grounds as 'probability' or 'appearance' of bias."

In American Electric Power Co. v. Connecticut, ____ U.S. ____ (2011), the Supreme Court affirmed, by an equally divided Court, a court of appeals decision finding justiciable a lawsuit brought by eight states against major electric power corporations operating fossil-fuel-fired power plants seeking abatement of the plants' contributions to global warming under a federal common law of nuisance theory. The district court had held that the plaintiffs' claims were nonjusticiable because the "'initial policy determination addressing global climate change' was an undertaking for the political branches, which were charged with the 'identification and balancing of economic, environmental, foreign policy, and national security interests.'" The court of appeals disagreed, holding that the plaintiffs' complaint raised a straightforward federal common law of nuisance claim of the sort traditionally decided by courts. Ultimately, the Supreme Court unanimously held, on the merits, that the plaintiffs' federal common law claim was displaced by the Clean Air Act and the action authorized by the Act. In the course of reaching that conclusion, the Court found in the Act a congressional preference for expert agency decision-making followed by deferential judicial review because "informed assessment of competing interests is required" and "[f]ederal judges lack the scientific, economic, and technological resources."

2

FEDERALISM AT WORK: CONGRESS AND THE NATIONAL ECONOMY

A. The Values of Federalism and Some Techniques for Implementing Them

Page 172. At the end of section 5 of the Note, add the following:

Consider Bulman-Pozen & Gerken, Uncooperative Federalism, 118 Yale L.J. 1256 (2009), which argues that states may use their power to resist federal policy even in areas where the Constitution uncontroversially grants Congress regulatory power. The authors identify "licensed dissent" where states engage in experimentation authorized by Congress, dissent "made possible by a regulatory gap" as in some aspects of environmental regulation, and "civil disobedience" exemplified by local actions declaring opposition to federal policies. Are these activities aspects of federalism properly understood?

5a. *Protecting liberty.* Bond v. United States, ___U.S. ___ (2011):

Federalism secures the freedom of the individual. It allows States to respond, through the enactment of positive law, to the initiative of those who seek a voice in shaping the destiny of their own times without having to rely solely upon the political processes that control a remote central power. [Federalism] also protects the liberty of all persons within a State by ensuring that laws enacted in excess of delegated governmental power cannot direct or control their actions. By denying any one government complete jurisdiction over all the concerns of public life, federalism protects the liberty of the individual from arbitrary power. When government acts in excess of its lawful powers, that liberty is at stake.

Note two themes. (a) State-level *legislation* can affirmatively promote freedom. (b) Legislation "in excess of delegated power" threatens liberty. How can that be so with respect to national-level legislation of a sort that states could permissibly adopt without violating (state- or national-level) protections of liberty?

Page 172.   After section 6 of the Note, add the following:

6a. *A skeptical view of federalism's values.* Malcolm M. Feeley and Edward Rubin, Federalism: Political Identity and Tragic Compromise 15, 16 (2009), argue that federalism "serves as a means of modulating, or varying, political identity. [If] people's political identity is associated with some region that has been subsumed into a larger polity, federalism provides a means by which the disjunction between their political identity and their territorial mode of governance can be reduced. [Federalism] will only be appealing to people if the region itself [relates] to their sense of political identity." On this understanding, is federalism an appropriate form of governance for the United States?

Feely and Rubin distinguish federalism from decentralization and local democracy. Decentralization "is a managerial strategy by which a centralized regime can achieve the results it desires in a more effective manner." Id. at 20. So, for example, "if one wants to implement a program of ensuring and increasing participation in the democratic process, increasing the number of decentralized decisions may well be a valid way to proceed, but this would be a national policy, not a result of federalism. [Federalism] does not necessarily increase participation; it simply authorizes a set of specified political subunits to decide for themselves how much participation is desirable. Some might choose to encourage participation, but others might choose to suppress it." Id. at 22. They note that national policymakers could "achiev[e] the same goal [by] hiring community organizers, funding local organizations, and requiring approvals for government decisions from different sectors of the population," and that "[in] a truly federal regime, some states might opt for elections, while others might not." Id. at 22, 23. "Federalism reserves particular issues to subnational governmental units, regardless of the political process that exists within these units, whereas local democracy establishes a particular political process in the subnational units without granting those units any particular area of authority." Id. at 31. Similarly, experimentation is "a happy incident of managerial decentralization. [Divergent] goals will typically render instrumental experimentation irrelevant." Id. at 26.

On the argument that federalism promotes economic efficiency, Feeley and Rubin argue that "[federalism] allows a multiplicity of norms, not simply a multiplicity of rules. In a truly federal system, some subunits might not be interested in economic efficiency; [they] might be primarily motivated by the desire to preserve an agrarian lifestyle, to protect the environment, or to encourage individual spirituality. [They] might lose out in the competition for factories and corporate executives [but] rather than perceiving their losses as a chastening lesson [they] might perceive them as a necessary cost or as a positive advantage." Id. at 24.

On "the idea that people can choose among jurisdictions on the basis of the services that they provide," Feeley and Rubin argue that this "will be true [if] the national government imposes certain uniform standards [to] ensure that citizens can live as comfortably in one as in another [region] or [if] the nation is so culturally homogeneous that most of its citizens are comfortable in any of its regions." In the latter case, they argue, federalism "is unnecessary and thus likely to be vestigial." Id. at 24-25.

C. The Evolution of Commerce Clause Doctrine

Page 228.   At the end of section 3 of the Note, add the following:

3a. *The necessary and proper clause and congressional power.* United States v. Comstock, 130 S. Ct. 1949 (2010), upheld the constitutionality of a federal statute authorizing the civil commitment of mentally ill, sexually dangerous federal prisoners after the dates they would otherwise be released, finding the statute supported by the necessary and proper clause. Justice Breyer's opinion for the Court "base[d] this conclusion on five considerations, taken together." (1) "[T]he Necessary and Proper Clause grants Congress broad authority to enact federal legislation. [In] determining whether the Necessary and Proper Clause grants Congress the legislative authority to enact a particular federal statute, we look to see whether the statute constitutes a means that is rationally related to the implementation of a constitutionally enumerated power." (2) "[T]he civil-commitment statute before us constitutes a modest addition to a set of federal prison-related mental-health statutes that have existed for many decades. [Even] a longstanding history of related federal action does not demonstrate a statute's constitutionality. A history of involvement, however, can nonetheless be 'helpful in reviewing the substance of a congressional statutory scheme,' [*Raich*] and, in particular, the reasonableness of the relation between the new statute and pre-existing federal interests. Here, Congress has long been involved in the delivery of mental health care to federal prisoners, and has long provided for their civil commitment." (3) "Congress reasonably extended its longstanding civil-commitment system to cover

45

mentally ill and sexually dangerous persons who are already in federal custody, even if doing so detains them beyond the termination of their criminal sentence. For one thing, the Federal Government is the custodian of its prisoners. As federal custodian, it has the constitutional power to act in order to protect nearby (and other) communities from the danger federal prisoners may pose." (4) "[T]he statute properly accounts for state interests. [It] requires *accommodation* of state interests," by requiring that relevant state authorities be informed of the civil commitment and requiring the release from federal custody of those for whom a state is willing to accept responsibility. (5) "[T]he links between [the statute] and an enumerated Article I power are not too attenuated. Neither is the statutory provision too sweeping in its scope."

Justice Kennedy concurred in the result, observing that "[t]he terms 'rationally related' and 'rational basis' must be employed with care, particularly if either is to be used as a stand-alone test. [The] opinion of the Court should not be interpreted to hold that the only, or even the principal, constraints on the exercise of congressional power are the Constitution's express prohibitions. The Court's discussion of the Tenth Amendment invites the inference that restrictions flowing from the federal system are of no import when defining the limits of the National Government's power, as it proceeds by first asking whether the power is within the National Government's reach, and if so it discards federalism concerns entirely." Justice Alito also concurred in the result, finding that the statute "is a necessary and proper means of carrying into execution the enumerated powers that support the federal criminal statutes under which the affected prisoners were convicted."

Justice Thomas, joined by Justice Scalia, dissented. "Must each of the five considerations exist before the Court sustains future federal legislation as proper exercises of Congress' Necessary and Proper Clause authority? What if the facts of a given case support a finding of only four considerations? Or three? And if three or four will suffice, *which* three or four are imperative?"

D. State Regulation of Interstate Commerce

Page 234. At the end of section 1a of the Note, add the following:

See also Erbsen, Horizontal Federalism, 93 Minn. L. Rev. 493, 503 (2008), which treats the dormant commerce doctrine as one of "a set of constitutional mechanisms for preventing or mitigating interstate friction that may arise from the out-of-state effects of in-state decisions." The full faith and credit clause and the article III provision for diversity jurisdiction are textual provisions in that set; the due process clause limitations on the assertion of state-court jurisdiction over out-of-state activity exemplify a doctrinal member of the set.

Page 238.   At the end of section 3 of the Note, add the following:

See also Denning, Reconstructing the Dormant Commerce Clause Doctrine, 50 Wm. & Mary L. Rev. 417 (2008).

Page 248.   Before section 3 of the Note, add the following:

2a. *A "new protectionism"?* Do the Court's decisions in *United Haulers* and *Davis* represent the development of a "new protectionism" that favors *public* enterprise? Does such protectionism undermine the nation-wide common market that Justice Jackson argued was one of the primary aims served by the dormant commerce clause? See Williams & Denning, The "New Protectionism" and the American Common Market, 85 Notre Dame L. Rev. 247 (2009).

3

THE SCOPE OF CONGRESS'S POWERS: TAXING AND SPENDING, WAR POWERS, INDIVIDUAL RIGHTS, AND STATE AUTONOMY

A. Regulation through Taxing, Spending, and the War Power

Page 294.   After section 2 of the Note, add the following:

2a. *Health care reform and the individual mandate.* Congress recently enacted, as part of comprehensive health care reform legislation, a requirement, beginning in 2014, that most individuals maintain a specified level of health insurance. See Patient Protection and Affordable Care Act of 2010, § 1501(b). Congress prefaced this requirement with a series of findings designed to support its conclusion that the individual responsibility requirement is "commercial and economic in nature," and thus that Congress acted within its commerce clause powers in enacting the mandate.

The mandate is enforced through a penalty to be included with the individual's tax return for any year in which he does not maintain the required coverage. A number of states and individuals have filed suit challenging the individual mandate. One of their arguments is that Congress cannot use its commerce power to impose a penalty on individuals who refuse to buy a product or service. See Congressional Research Service, Requiring Individuals to Obtain Health Insurance: A Constitutional Analysis 3 (2009) (discussing this question).

In addition to arguing that Congress acted within its commerce power, the Department of Justice has also defended the law as a constitutional exercise of Congress's taxing power because the law would impose an income tax penalty on those who do not obtain insurance.

Does the individual mandate represent a constitutional exercise of Congress's taxing power? With respect to this argument, consider Balkin, The Constitutionality of the Individual Mandate for Health Insurance, 362 New England J. Med. 482 (2010):

> The constitutional test is whether Congress could reasonably conclude that its taxing and spending programs promote the general welfare of the country. This test is easily satisfied. The new health care reform bill insures more people and prevents them from being denied insurance coverage because of preexisting conditions. Successful reform requires that uninsured persons — most of whom are younger and healthier than average — join the national risk pool; this will help to lower the costs of health insurance premiums nationally.
>
> Taxing uninsured people helps to pay for the costs of the new regulations. The tax gives uninsured people a choice. If they stay out of the risk pool, they effectively raise other people's insurance costs, and Congress taxes them to recoup some of the costs. If they join the risk pool, they do not have to pay the tax. A good analogy would be a tax on polluters who fail to install pollution-control equipment: they can pay the tax or install the equipment.
>
> [T]he textual argument for Congress's authority under the General Welfare Clause is obvious and powerful. . . .
>
> If the individual mandate falls within Congress's power to tax and spend, no other constitutional authority is necessary. . . .

For a contrasting view, see Rivkin & Casey, Health Care Purchase Mandate: Unconstitutional and Likely to Be Struck Down by the Courts, 158 U. Pa. L. Rev. PENNumbra 94, 100 (2009):

> [Although the Supreme] Court's interpretation of the Commerce Clause's breadth certainly has changed since [*Bailey*], it has not repudiated the fundamental principle that Congress cannot use a tax to regulate conduct that is otherwise indisputably beyond its regulatory power. . . .
>
> It is worth reemphasizing that the problem with basing the mandate on Congress's taxing power is not that such power cannot be used in a regulatory fashion; indeed, the Court has specifically authorized taxing schemes with regulatory effects. *See, e.g., Sonzinsky v. United States,*

300 U.S. 506 (1937). The problem is that this particular regulatory scheme — the health insurance purchase mandate — exceeds Congress's regulatory power. ... [T]he Constitution inherently limits the reach of the Taxing and Spending Clause, just as it does the Commerce Clause, and that exertions of congressional power that exceed the proper scope of these clauses are void. The fact that they may not violate any provisions of the Bill of Rights is irrelevant.

Balkin's debate with Rivkin and Casey is reprinted in A Healthy Debate: The Constitutionality of an Individual Mandate, 158 U. Pa. L. Rev. PENNumbra 93 (2009).

In Thomas More Law Center v. Obama, ___ F.3d ___ (6th Cir. 2011), the court rejected the claim that the individual mandate could be sustained as an exercise of the taxing power:

"Congress might have raised taxes on everyone in an amount equivalent to the current penalty, then offered credits to those with minimum essential insurance. Or it might have imposed a lower tax rate on people with health insurance than those without it. But Congress did neither of these things, and that makes a difference. ...

"The individual mandate is a regulatory penalty, not a revenue-raising tax, for several reasons. *First*, that is what Congress said. It called the sanction for failing to obtain medical insurance a 'penalty,' not a tax. Words matter, and it is fair to assume that Congress knows the difference between a tax and a penalty, between its taxing and commerce powers, making it appropriate to take Congress at its word. ...

"*Second*, the legislative findings in the Act show that Congress invoked its commerce power, not its taxing authority. ... The findings say nothing about, or even suggestive of, the taxing power.

"*Third*, Congress showed throughout the Act that it understood the difference between these terms and concepts, using 'tax' in some places and 'penalty' in others. The statute not only says that the consequence of failing to obtain healthcare coverage leads to a "penalty," but it also proceeds to use the word at least 17 other times in the individual mandate provision, and by our rough count 180 or so times in the rest of the Act. In other parts of the law, Congress imposed 'taxes,' using that word 620 or so times. Congress respected the distinction between the words throughout the Act, and so should we.

"*Fourth*, the central function of the mandate was *not* to raise revenue. It was to change individual behavior by requiring all qualified Americans to obtain medical insurance. ... [T]he Act generally requires uninsured individuals to buy *private* insurance, a requirement that will not raise *any* revenue for the government. ... The penalty provision, to be sure, will raise revenue. But it strains credulity to say that the proponents of the Act will call it a success if the individuals affected by the mandate simply pay penalties rather than buy private insurance. . . .

"*Fifth*, case law supports this conclusion. The Act operates by starting with a substantive provision that "adopt[s] the criteria of wrongdoing," *Child Labor Tax Case*, 259 U.S. at 20. . . .

"The Act then spells out the 'principal consequence on those who transgress its standard,' *Child Labor Tax Case*, 259 U.S. at 38, which is to impose a penalty . . . , giving the minimum-coverage mandate the 'characteristics of regulation and punishment,' *Dep't of Revenue v. Kurth Ranch*, 511 U.S. 767, 779 (1994), not taxation . . . .

"That Congress has a 'comprehensive' and 'plenary' power to tax, U.S. Br. at 58, shows that, *if* the legislature had used taxes in this part of the Affordable Care Act, the Act likely would be constitutional. But that does not tell us whether Congress invoked this power or whether the penalty is a 'Tax[]' under Article I of the Constitution. It did not, and it is not.

"That the constitutionality of a law 'does not depend on recitals of the power which it undertakes to exercise,' *Woods v. Cloyd W. Miller Co.*, 333 U.S. 138, 144 (1948), changes nothing. In enumerated-power cases, there often will be a question whether Congress invoked its powers under the Commerce Clause, § 5 of the Fourteenth Amendment, the Spending Clause or the Taxing Clause, and *Woods* establishes that congressional recitals provide sufficient grounds for invoking a power but not the exclusive means for doing so. None of this alters the reality that each power has distinct substantive predicates and distinct substantive terms, and the courts may not simply label a law something it is not."

Page 295.   After section 4c of the Note, add the following:

To what extent do the limitations on Congress's powers under the commerce clause or the enforcement clauses of the Reconstruction-era amendments (particularly section 5 of the fourteenth amendment) carry over to the spending power? Consider N. Siegel, Dole's Future: A Strategic Analysis, 16 S. Ct. Econ. Rev. 165 (2008). Siegel identifies three different models of limitations on use of the spending clause. Under "substance federalism," the Court "conceives of the activity as concerning a matter that the Constitution leaves to the states." Id. at 191. Under "form federalism," the Court might "believ[e] a given regulation exceeds a particular congressional power, but would have no objection if Congress sought to accomplish the same goal through a different, legitimate source of authority. The Court, on that account, understands different constitutional 'hooks' for federal legislation to implicate distinct substantive values." Id. By contrast, under "form-plus-pique federalism," the Court might be "provoked by use of the Spending Clause after analogous use of the Commerce Clause or Section Five had been struck down, even though the Court would not have been concerned about such use of the Spending Clause if a previous Commerce Clause or Section Five decision had not been rendered." Id. at 192. Siegel suggests that the members of the Roberts Court are potentially split among these positions:

> (1) Fewer than five votes exist for the view that advocates little or no judicially enforced federalism; (2) fewer than five votes likely exist for the substance federalism commitment; (3) fewer than five votes likely exist for the form federalism position; and (4) it is unclear how many Justices are appropriately characterized as form-plus-pique jurists. Because of (4), it is unclear (a) whether five votes exist for a combination of "no judicially enforced federalism" and form federalism, or (b) whether and when five votes likely exist for a combination of substance federalism and form plus pique.

Id. at 199.

Page 297. At the end of section 6 of the Note, add the following:

For a different view, see Galle, Federal Grants, State Decisions, 88 B.U.L. Rev. 875, 934 (2008) (arguing that the clear statement rule is indefensible in light of a variety of theoretical and empirical reasons to believe that state officials are not in fact constrained to accept federal grants and that the rule "displaces the expressed preferences of political actors, including both federal grant-offerors and state and local grant-acceptors").

B. Congress's Enforcement Power Under the Reconstruction Amendments

Page 307. At the end of section 2 of the Note, add the following:

Consider also Balkin, The Reconstruction Power, 85 N.Y.U. L. Rev. 1801, 1831 (2010), suggesting that

Courts should uphold legislation based on distinctive congressional inter-pretations if (1) Congress could achieve the same result through remedial legislation if it accepted the Supreme Court's view; (2) Congress's interpretation is within a range of reasonable answers to the constitutional question; or (3) the differences between Congress's and the Court's inter-pretation can be explained by Congress's different institutional situation and strengths.

C. The Tenth Amendment as a Federalism-Based Limitation on Congressional Power

Page 332. At the bottom of the page, after the first paragraph of section 3 of the Note, add the following:

See Vazquez, Missouri v. Holland's Second Holding, 73 Mo. L. Rev. 939, 967 (2008) (suggesting that Congress's treaty-making power may raise feder-alism concerns when Congress enters into "aspirational" treaties that concern matters that would otherwise lie outside Congress's Article I powers and suggesting a distinction between "obligatory treaties" and "aspirational" ones such that "the former treaties may be implemented by Congress even if they concern matters beyond Congress's legislative power under Article I, but the latter treaties may be implemented by Congress only if they concern matters within the Article I legislative power"). For a variety of views about the relationship between Congress's treaty power and the tenth amendment, see Symposium, Return to Missouri v. Holland: Federalism and International Law, 73 Mo. L. Rev. 921 (2008).

Page 349. At the end of section 1b of the Note, add the following:

In Haywood v. Drown, 129 S. Ct. 2108 (2009), the Supreme Court held that a New York statute that divested state courts of general jurisdiction of their power to hear damages actions under 42 U.S.C. § 1983 against state corrections officers — replacing those actions with the ability instead to sue the state itself in the New York Court of Claims, where the prisoner would not be entitled to attorney's fees, damages, or injunctive relief—violated the supremacy clause. The Court noted that under Testa v. Katt, a state could refuse jurisdiction on the basis of neutral rules regarding judicial administration, but found that New York's policy contradicted the congressional "judgment that *all* persons who violate federal rights while acting under color of state law shall be held liable for damages. As we have unanimously recognized, '[a] State may not ... relieve congestion in its courts by declaring a whole category of federal claims to be frivolous.'"

c. *Legislation limiting state sovereignty and legislation beyond Congress's enumerated powers.* Bond v. United States, ___ U.S. ___ (2011), expressly rejected a proposed distinction between federal legislation that "interferes with a specific aspect of state sovereignty," as illustrated by the anti-commandeering cases, and legislation that "Congress could not enact [under] its enumerated powers," as illustrated by *Lopez*, chapter II (C) above: "The principles of limited national powers and state sovereignty are intertwined. While neither originates in the Tenth Amendment, both are expressed by it. Impermissible interference with state sovereignty is not within the enumerated powers of the National Government, and action that exceeds the National Government's enumerated powers undermines the sovereign interests of States."

Page 353.   At the end of section 5 of the Note, add the following:

5a. *The tenth amendment and areas of traditional state control.* In United States v. Comstock, 130 S. Ct. 1949 (2010), discussed in detail in the supplement to page 228 of the main volume, the Court addressed the constitutionality of a federal statute that authorized the civil commitment of mentally ill, sexually dangerous federal prisoners beyond the release date for their criminal sentence. Writing for the Court, Justice Breyer rejected the argument that the federal statute impermissibly invades a traditional province of state sovereignty:

"[T]he Tenth Amendment's text is clear: 'The powers *not delegated to the United States* by the Constitution, nor prohibited by it to the States, are reserved to the States respectively, or to the people.' (Emphasis added.) The powers 'delegated to the United States by the Constitution' include those specifically enumerated powers listed in Article I along with the implementation authority granted by the Necessary and Proper Clause. Virtually by definition, these powers are not powers that the Constitution 'reserved to the States.'"

Justice Breyer rejected Justice Thomas's claim in dissent that the statute improperly limited states' powers to deal with potentially dangerous individuals:

"To the contrary, it requires *accommodation* of state interests: The Attorney General must inform the State in which the federal prisoner 'is domiciled or was tried' that he is detaining someone with respect to whom those States may wish to assert their authority, and he must encourage those States to assume custody of the individual. He must also immediately 'release' that person 'to the appropriate official of' either State 'if such State will assume [such] responsibility.' And either State has the right, at any time, to assert its authority over the individual, which will prompt the individual's immediate transfer to State custody." Once such a transfer occurs, the state can determine whether to continue detaining the individual.

In his concurrence in the judgment, Justice Kennedy expressed concern with the Court's tenth amendment analysis:

"I had thought it a basic principle that the powers reserved to the States consist of the whole, undefined residuum of power remaining after taking account of powers granted to the National Government. The Constitution delegates limited powers to the National Government and then reserves the remainder for the States (or the people), not the other way around, as the Court's analysis suggests. And the powers reserved to the States are so broad that they remain undefined. Residual power, sometimes referred to (perhaps imperfectly) as the police power, belongs to the States and the States alone.

"It is correct in one sense to say that if the National Government has the power to act under the Necessary and Proper Clause then that power is not one reserved to the States. But the precepts of federalism embodied in the Constitution inform which powers are properly exercised by the National Government in the first place. It is of fundamental importance to consider whether essential attributes of state sovereignty are compromised by the assertion of federal power under the Necessary and Proper Clause; if so, that is a factor suggesting that the power is not one properly within the reach of federal power.

"The opinion of the Court should not be interpreted to hold that the only, or even the principal, constraints on the exercise of congressional power are the Constitution's express prohibitions. The Court's discussion of the Tenth Amendment invites the inference that restrictions flowing from the federal system are of no import when defining the limits of the National Government's power, as it proceeds by first asking whether the power is within the National Government's reach, and if so it discards federalism concerns entirely.

"These remarks explain why the Court ignores important limitations stemming from federalism principles. Those principles are essential to an understanding of the function and province of the States in our constitutional structure."

In dissent, Justice Thomas, joined by Justice Scalia, disagreed with the Court's conclusion that the statutory requirement that the Attorney General offer the states the right to take custody of soon-to-be released federal inmates satisfied the tenth amendment:

"This right of first refusal is mere window dressing. Tr. of Oral Arg. 5 ('It is not the usual course that the State does take responsibility'). More importantly, it is an altogether hollow assurance that § 4248 preserves the principle of dual sovereignty. ... For once it is determined that Congress has the authority to provide for the civil detention of sexually dangerous persons, Congress 'is acting within the powers granted it under the Constitution,' and 'may impose its will on the States.' Section 4248's right of first refusal is thus not a matter of constitutional necessity, but an act of legislative grace.

"Nevertheless, 29 States appear as *amici* and argue that § 4248 is constitutional. They tell us that they do not object to Congress retaining custody of 'sexually dangerous persons' after their criminal sentences expire because the cost of detaining such persons is 'expensive'–approximately $64,000 per year– and these States would rather the Federal Government bear this expense.

"Congress' power, however, is fixed by the Constitution; it does not expand merely to suit the States' policy preferences, or to allow State officials to avoid difficult choices regarding the allocation of state funds. By assigning the Federal Government power over 'certain enumerated objects only,' the Constitution 'leaves to the several States a residuary and inviolable sovereignty over all other objects.' The Federalist No. 39, at 285 (J. Madison). ... The Constitution gives States no more power to decline this responsibility than it gives them to infringe upon those liberties in the first instance.

"Absent congressional action that is in accordance with, or necessary and proper to, an enumerated power, the duty to protect citizens from violent crime, including acts of sexual violence, belongs solely to the States."

Page 354.   Before the Note, add the following.

BOND v. UNITED STATES, ___ **U.S.** ___ **(2011).** A provision in the Chemical Weapons Convention Implementation Act of 1998 criminalizes knowing possession or use of any chemical that "can cause death, temporary incapacitation or permanent harm to humans or animals" where not intended for a "peaceful purpose." Bond was indicted under this statute when she placed a caustic substance on various objects her husband's paramour was likely to touch, causing burns to the other woman's hand. Bond challenged the constitutionality of the provision on the grounds that it exceeded Congress's power, citing, among other authorities, the tenth amendment. The court of appeals held that Bond lacked standing to raise a tenth amendment challenge, relying on a sentence from the Supreme Court's opinion in *Tennessee Elec. Power Co. v. TVA*, 306 U.S. 118 (1939), a case brought by utility companies challenging the TVA's generation and sale of electrical power: "As we have seen there is no objection to the Authority's operations by the states, and, if this were not so, the appellants, absent the states or their officers, have no standing in this suit to raise any question under the amendment." In an opinion by Justice Kennedy, the Supreme Court unanimously reversed.

The Court noted that Article III itself posed no barrier to Bond's standing to assert her tenth amendment defenses in the district court. She was a defendant in a criminal case initiated by the government which sought to convict and imprison her, and thus there was a live case or controversy in which she had a sufficient stake to establish the required "concrete adverseness."

Turning to the question of prudential standing, the Court rejected the argument that Bond lacked prudential standing because she was asserting "the legal rights and interests of States and States alone":

"That, however, is not so. . . . Bond seeks to vindicate her own constitutional interests. The individual, in a proper case, can assert injury from governmental action taken in excess of the authority that federalism defines. Her rights in this regard do not belong to a State. . . .

"The Framers concluded that allocation of powers between the National Government and the States enhances freedom, first by protecting the integrity of the governments themselves, and second by protecting the people, from whom all governmental powers are derived.

"Federalism has more than one dynamic. It is true that the federal structure serves to grant and delimit the prerogatives and responsibilities of the States and the National Government vis-a-vis one another. The allocation of powers in our federal system preserves the integrity, dignity, and residual sovereignty of the States. The federal balance is, in part, an end in itself, to ensure that States function as political entities in their own right.

"But that is not its exclusive sphere of operation. Federalism is more than an exercise in setting the boundary between different institutions of government for their own integrity. 'State sovereignty is not just an end in itself: "Rather, federalism secures to citizens the liberties that derive from the diffusion of sovereign power."' *New York v. United States*, 505 U.S. 144, 181 (1992) . . . .

"Federalism secures the freedom of the individual. It allows States to respond, through the enactment of positive law, to the initiative of those who seek a voice in shaping the destiny of their own times without having to rely solely upon the political processes that control a remote central power. True, of course, these objects cannot be vindicated by the Judiciary in the absence of a proper case or controversy; but the individual liberty secured by federalism is not simply derivative of the rights of the States.

"Federalism also protects the liberty of all persons within a State by ensuring that laws enacted in excess of delegated governmental power cannot direct or control their actions. . . .

"The limitations that federalism entails are not therefore a matter of rights belonging only to the States. States are not the sole intended beneficiaries of federalism. An individual has a direct interest in objecting to laws that upset the constitutional balance between the National Government and the States when the enforcement of those laws causes injury that is concrete, particular, and redressable. Fidelity to principles of federalism is not for the States alone to vindicate.

"The recognition of an injured person's standing to object to a violation of a constitutional principle that allocates power within government is illustrated, in an analogous context, by cases in which individuals sustain discrete, justiciable injury from actions that transgress separation-of-powers limitations. Separation-of-powers principles are intended, in part, to protect each branch of government from incursion by the others. Yet the dynamic between and among the branches is not the only object of the Constitution's concern. The structural principles secured by the separation of powers protect the individual as well. . . .

"If the constitutional structure of our Government that protects individual liberty is compromised, individuals who suffer otherwise justiciable injury may object.

"Just as it is appropriate for an individual, in a proper case, to invoke separation-of-powers or checks-and-balances constraints, so too may a litigant, in a proper case, challenge a law as enacted in contravention of constitutional principles of federalism. That claim need not depend on the vicarious assertion of a State's constitutional interests, even if a State's constitutional interests are also implicated."

The Court also rejected the government's argument that a private party would have standing to raise only tenth amendment claims that Congress had exceeded its enumerated powers, and not claims that a statute interfered with a "specific aspect of state sovereignty":

"There is no basis to support the Government's proposed distinction between different federalism arguments for purposes of prudential standing rules. The principles of limited national powers and state sovereignty are intertwined. While neither originates in the Tenth Amendment, both are expressed by it. Impermissible interference with state sovereignty is not within the enumerated powers of the National Government, and action that exceeds the National Government's enumerated powers undermines the sovereign interests of States."

Justice Ginsburg, in a concurrence joined by Justice Breyer, observed that because unconstitutional criminal laws are void and every defendant "has a personal right not to be convicted under a constitutionally invalid law," a court must address the defendant's constitutional challenge "even where the constitutional provision that would render the conviction void is directed at protecting a party not before the Court."

4
THE DISTRIBUTION OF NATIONAL POWERS

A. Introduction

Page 357. At the end of section 2 of the Note, add the following:

Consider the possibility that by making the enactment of federal law difficult, separation of powers provisions serve to protect the values of federalism discussed in Chapters Two and Three, supra. For an argument along these lines, see Clark, Separation of Powers as a Safeguard of Federalism, 79 Tex. L. Rev. 1321 (2001). Compare Vazquez, The Separation of Powers as a Safeguard of Nationalism, 83 Notre Dame L. Rev. 1601, 1606 (2008) (arguing that "because the process of repealing a federal law is the same as for creating it in the first place, the requirements of bicameralism and presentment [can] make it difficult to restore legislative power [to] the states.")

Page 357. At the end of section 3 of the Note, add the following:

In Nzelibe & Stephenson, Complementary Constraints: Separation of Powers, Rational Voting, and Constitutional Design, 123 Harv. L. Rev. 617 (2010), the authors raise doubts about the conventional view that separation of powers causes "gridlock." When a President can act alone, he has greater flexibility, but voters may harshly penalize presidential failure. In contrast, when the President acts in concert with Congress, voters may feel less need to punish him for policy failure. This relaxation of an electoral deterrent might actually increase the President's willingness to initiate policy change. Relatedly, the authors argue that "voters may be better off under a system of separated powers in which the agenda-setting political actor (for example, the President) has the option to seek the approval of another branch (for example, Congress) than under a regime in which such joint approval is required." Id. at 622.

Would the purposes of separation of powers be better served by institutions with blended functions, but separated according to policy domains? Consider Gersen, Unbundled Powers, 96 Va. L. Rev. 301, 303-304 (2010):

> [Imagine] three new branches of the national government: one controlling war, one controlling economic policy, and one controlling education. [Each] political institution would have plenary policy-making authority within its policy domain, but no authority outside it. . . .
>
> Passages in the Supreme Court's separation of powers cases often read as implicit claims of uniqueness or optimality. Separation of powers produces liberty, accountability, and effective government; other regimes do not. Separation of functions, however, is neither the only, nor clearly the best, way to achieve these laudable goals. [Separation] of functions [might be compared to] the "unbundled powers alternative": Multiple branches exercising combined functions in topically limited domains. Functional separation is certainly sometimes preferable, but there is no good reason to think it is better as a global matter; and there are many reasons to think it is not.

B. A Case Study: Presidential Seizure

Page 370. At the end of section 2e of the Note, add the following:

Compare M. Tushnet, The Inevitable Globalization of Constitutional Law, 49 Va. J. Int'l L. 985, 988 (2009) (arguing that "because the globalization of domestic constitutional law is inevitable, notions of separation of powers — or of legislative supremacy qualified by the existence of judicial review — will need to accommodate themselves to that globalization.")

C. Foreign Affairs

Page 392. Before the Note, add the following:

Consider the following evaluation:

[Bush-era] enemy combatant decisions were anything but counter-majoritarian. These decisions tracked larger social and political forces. These decisions, moreover, were hugely popular with newspapers, academics, and other elite audiences (audiences that matter a great deal to centrist Justices). [Contrary] to media and academic portrayals of these cases as bold, decisive, and consequential, Bush-era decisions were truly incremental. The 2004 and 2006 decisions placed few meaningful demands on the administration; *Boumediene* was decided at a moment in time when the Court had good reason to think that the political process was well on its way to closing Guantanamo (so that constitutionally mandated habeas hearings would be symbolically consequential but of little practical import). [Today's] Court has no institutional incentive to place meaningful limits on Obama administration policymaking. [There] is no reason to think that it will check the President in ways that will severely constrain elected branch [priorities].

Devins, Talk Loudly and Carry a Small Stick: The Supreme Court and Enemy Combatants, 12 U. Pa. J. Const. L. 491, 495 (2010).

See also Fallon, The Supreme Court, Habeas Corpus, and the War on Terror: An Essay on Law and Political Science, 110 Colum. L. Rev. 352 (2010) (arguing that "the Supreme Court has operated mostly on the margins of the nation's War on Terror policy, but has grown more assertive [in] recognition of a changing political climate and a lessening sense of the urgency of the terrorist threat." However, "[should] the War on Terror become significantly more terrifying, all bets would be off."); Pushaw, Creating Legal Rights for Suspected Terrorists: Is the Court Being Courageous or Politically Pragmatic, 84 Notre Dame L. Rev. 1975, 1978 (2009) (expressing skepticism about the "conventional wisdom that a uniquely brave Supreme Court, motivated by its steadfast commitment to the rule of law, successfully foiled the military policies of a singularly evil President," and arguing that "five pragmatic Justices, animated by their personal and political disagreements with the Bush administration, capitalized on the relatively rare opportunity to give a legal lecture to a politically unpopular (but not especially bellicose) President and Congress at a time when a national security crisis had safely passed.")

For a survey of the obstacles imposed on defense lawyers representing Guantanamo detainees, including "policies designed to reduce their access to their clients; policies that create knotty ethical difficulties; [and] practices that ['are] designed to drive a wedge between lawyers and their clients,'" see Luban, Lawfare and Legal Ethics in Guantanamo, 60 Stan. L. Rev. 1981, 1983 (2008).

Page 396.   At the end of section 3 of the Note, add the following:

Consider the legal problems posed by American involvement in Libya. After conflict broke out between the rebels and the Libyan regime, the United Nations Security Council adopted a resolution authorizing "member States... to take all necessary measures... to protect civilians and civilian populated areas under threat of attack" and to establish a "no-fly zone" in Libya.

Two days later, on March 19, 2011, the United States, in conjunction with its NATO allies, began air strikes in Libya. Within 48 hours of the beginning of the air strikes, President Obama sent a letter to the Speaker of the House and President pro tempore of the Senate "as part of my efforts to keep Congress fully informed, consistent with the War Powers Resolution." The letter stated that U.S. military forces had begun air strikes for purpose of preparing a no-fly zone and that "[United] States forces are conducting a limited and well-defined mission in support of international efforts to protect civilians and prevent a humanitarian disaster."

On April 1, 2011, the Justice Department's Office of Legal Counsel (OLC) released a memorandum determining that the President had constitutional authority to use military force in Libya without prior congressional approval. Relying on prior OLC opinions in the Clinton Administration, particularly those opinions on the unilateral presidential deployments to Haiti (1994) and Bosnia (1995), the memorandum asserted that the President's legal authority to direct military force in Libya

> turned on two questions: first, whether the United States operations in Libya would serve sufficiently important national interests to permit the President's action as Commander in Chief and Chief Executive and pursuant to his authority to conduct U.S. foreign relations; and second, whether the military operations that the President anticipated ordering would be sufficiently extensive in "nature, scope, and duration" to constitute a "war requiring prior, specific congressional approval under the Declaration of War Clause.

According to the memorandum, this understanding of presidential power "reflects not only the express assignment of powers and responsibilities to the President and Congress in the Constitution, but also [the] 'historical gloss' placed on the Constitution by two centuries of practice."

As to the first question OLC concluded that "the combination of at least two national interests that the President reasonably determined were at stake here" — preserving stability in the Middle East and "supporting the [United Nation's Security Council's] credibility and effectiveness" — provided a sufficient basis for the President's exercise of his constitutional authority to order the use of military force.

Turning to the second question, the memorandum acknowledged that presidential authority to deploy military force even in the serve of such national security interests might be limited if the engagement constituted a "war" within the meaning of the Declaration of War clause — such as in Vietnam, the first and second Gulf Wars, and, presumably, Korea. (In this way, the opinion differed from the view OLC had articulated in the George W. Bush Administration, which was that the President is authorized to initiate actions of this sort without congressional approval.) The memorandum nonetheless concluded that

> the historical practice of presidential military action without congressional approval precludes any suggestion that Congress's authority to declare war covers every military [engagement]. This standard generally will be satisfied only by prolonged and substantial military engagements, typically involving exposure of U.S. military personnel to significant risk over a substantial period.

On April 4, 2011, the United States transferred responsibility for the military operations to NATO, and U.S. involvement assumed a supporting role that included logistical and search and rescue assistance, suppression and destruction of Libyan air defenses, and strikes by unmanned aerial vehicles against particular targets. Although the 60-day period specified in the War Powers Resolution appeared to expire on May 20, 2011, and although Congress failed to pass a measure authorizing United States involvement, the involvement continued. At first, the Administration offered no defense of its refusal to end the operation in compliance with the Resolution, but on June 15, 2011 the Administration sent a letter to congressional leaders. The letter asserted that

> The current U.S. military operations [are] consistent with the War Powers Resolution and do not under that law require further congressional authorization, because U.S. military operations are distinct from the kind of "hostilities" contemplated by the Resolution's 60-day termination provision. U.S. forces are playing a constrained and supporting role in a multination coalition, whose operations are both legitimated by and limited to the terms of a United States Security Council resolution that authorizes the use of force solely to protect civilians and civilian populated areas under attack or threat of attack and to enforce a no-fly zone and an arms embargo. U.S. operations do not involve sustained fighting or active exchanges of fire with hostile forces, nor do they involve the presence of U.S. ground troops, U.S. casualties or a serious threat thereof, or any significant chance of escalation into a conflict characterized by those factors.

Is the Libyan operation constitutional in the absence of congressional author-ization? Is it in compliance with the War Powers Resolution? Why is the fact that the U.S. is playing a "supporting role" and that the operations are pursuant to a Security Council resolution relevant to the question whether there are "hostilities"? Does the memorandum mean that "hostilities" do not exist so long as the U.S. does not use ground troops and attacks a foe that is unable to respond?

Notice that the Obama Administration's interpretation of inherent executive authority together with its interpretation of the word "hostilities" in the Resolu-tion may leave only a narrow band of cases where the 60-day provision of the Resolution is applicable. If the fighting is too substantial, then it is a "war" and cannot be initiated even for 60 days without Congressional approval. But if it is not substantial enough — if there is no "serious threat" of U.S. casualties or significant chance of escalation — then it does not constitute "hostilities" and therefore is also not covered by the 60-day rule.

Page 397.   Before section 5 of the Note, add the following:

Consider the following proposed reform:

Traditional doctrine divides America's wars into two categories: unlimited wars, like World War II, and momentary interventions, like Grenada. But the recent conflicts in Iraq and Afghanistan fit into neither of these neat boxes. They are of limited duration and purpose, but far from momentary. [These] modern conflicts challenge the conventional understanding of power-sharing arrangements between the president and Congress over the use of military force. . . .

This diagnosis suggests the need for an institutional remedy. . . .

Under our proposed "Rules for Limited War," all future authorizations will be valid for only two years unless the House or Senate sets a different time-limit — or declares that the war should continue, without limit, until victory is achieved. But unless Congress makes this decision explicit in its initial authorizing resolution, the two-year term will serve as a default rule. The new rules will be enforced through a prohibition on all war appropria-tions after the congressional deadline except for money needed to wind down the mission over the course of one year.

Ackerman & Hathaway, Limited War and the Constitution: Iraq and the Crisis of Presidential Legality, 109 Mich. L. Rev. 447, 448, 451 (2011).

Page 400.   At the end of the Note, add the following:

In Hathaway, Presidential Power over International Law: Restoring the Balance, 119 Yale L.J. 140 (2009), the author proposes reforming international lawmaking by a statute that would organize it around two separate tracks–administrative and legislative. Executive agreements would be handled administratively through a notice and comment model similar to that created by the Administrative Procedure Act for domestic legislation. The purpose of this change would be to make the agreements more open and subject to more public participation. Other agreements would be subject to the existing legislative track and would either be treaties (approved by the Senate) or congressional-executive agreements approved by both Houses of Congress. Would a statute imposing administrative procedure-like constraints on Presidential international lawmaking be constitutional?

D.   Domestic Affairs

Page 405.   Before subsection c of the Note, add the following:

Lower level officials do, however, enjoy "qualified immunity." These officials can be held liable for damages only if they violate law that was "clearly established" at the time of the violation. Harlow v. Fitzgerald, 457 U.S., at 818.

For an interesting application of the qualified immunity doctrine, see Ashcroft v. Al-Kidd, 131 S. Ct. 2074 (2011). In his complaint, Al-Kidd alleged that in the aftermath of the World Trade Center attack, then-Attorney General Ashcroft authorized the pretextual use of the material witness statute. The statute authorizes the detention of individuals when their testimony is required for a criminal prosecution and when detention is necessary to assure their availability at trial. Al-Kidd alleged that the statute was used to detain him because the government suspected him of involvement in terrorist activities but lacked probable cause justifying arrest for any offense. A native-born American citizen, he was detained as he checked in for a flight to Saudi Arabia based upon a material witness warrant. The affidavit filed in support of the warrant asserted that his testimony was "crucial" to the prosecution of another individual and that without his detention, the testimony would be lost. The affidavit did not mention that Al-Kidd's parents, wife, and children were all citizens and residents of the United States and stated that he had purchased a one-way ticket, when in fact the ticket was round trip. Al-Kidd remained in federal custody for sixteen days and on supervised release for fourteen months. He was never called as a witness and never charged with any offense.

In a 6-3 decision, the Court, in an opinion by Justice Scalia, held that on the merits, Al-Kidd had failed to allege a Fourth Amendment violation because the subjective motive of government officials was irrelevant to the lawfulness of arrests and detentions. The Court then went on to hold that, assuming arguendo that the Fourth Amendment had been violated, Ashcroft was nonetheless entitled to qualified immunity. The Court pointed out that "[at] the time of al-Kidd's arrest, not a single judicial opinion had held pretext could render an objectively reasonable arrest pursuant to a material-witness warrant unconstitutional." While a district court opinion had suggested that such warrants were illegitimate in "footnoted dictum devoid of supporting citation... a district judge's *ipse dixit* [falls] far short of what is necessary absent controlling authority." Nor was it sufficient to find clearly established law "lurking in the broad 'history and purposes of the Fourth Amendment.' We have repeatedly told courts [not] to define clearly established law at a high level of generality." In short, "[when] properly applied, [qualified immunity] protects 'all but the plainly incompetent or those who knowingly violate the law.' Ashcroft deserves neither [label]."

In a concurring opinion, Justice Kennedy argued that "[the] fact that the Attorney General holds a high office in the Government must inform what law is clearly established for the purposes of this case." He pointed out that an "official with responsibilities in many jurisdictions may face ambiguous and sometimes inconsistent sources of decisional law." National office holders should therefore "be given some deference for qualified immunity purposes, at least if they implement policies consistent with the governing law of the jurisdiction where the action is taken."

Justice Ginsburg, joined by Justices Breyer and Sotomayor, and Justice Sotomayor, joined by Justices Ginsburg and Breyer, filed opinions concurring in the judgment.

Page 436.   At the bottom of the page, add the following:

FREE ENTERPRISE FUND v. PUBLIC COMPANY ACCOUNTING OVERSIGHT BOARD

130 S. Ct. 3138 (2010)

CHIEF JUSTICE ROBERTS delivered the opinion of the Court.

Our Constitution divided the "powers of the new Federal Government into three defined categories, Legislative, Executive, and Judicial." *INS* v. *Chadha.* Article II vests "[t]he executive Power... in a President of the United States of America," who must "take Care that the Laws be faithfully executed." In light of "[t]he impossibility that one man should be able to perform all the great business of the State," the Constitution provides for executive officers to "assist the supreme Magistrate in discharging the duties of his trust." 30 Writings of George Washington 334 (J. Fitzpatrick ed. 1939).

Since 1789, the Constitution has been understood to empower the President to keep these officers accountable — by removing them from office, if necessary. See generally [*Myers*]. This Court has determined, however, that this authority is not without limit. In [*Humphrey's Executor*,] we held that Congress can, under certain circumstances, create independent agencies run by principal officers appointed by the President, whom the President may not remove at will but only for good cause. [The] parties do not ask us to reexamine any of these precedents, and we do not do so.

We are asked, however, to consider a new situation not yet encountered by the Court. The question is whether these separate layers of protection may be combined. May the President be restricted in his ability to remove a principal officer, who is in turn restricted in his ability to remove an inferior officer, even though that inferior officer determines the policy and enforces the laws of the United States?

We hold that such multilevel protection from removal is contrary to Article II's vesting of the executive power in the President. The President cannot "take Care that the Laws be faithfully executed" if he cannot oversee the faithfulness of the officers who execute them. Here the President cannot remove an officer who enjoys more than one level of good-cause protection, even if the President determines that the officer is neglecting his duties or discharging them improperly. That judgment is instead committed to another officer, who may or may not agree with the President's determination, and whom the President cannot remove simply because that officer disagrees with him. This contravenes the President's "constitutional obligation to ensure the faithful execution of the laws."

I

A

[The Sarbanes-Oxley Act of 2002, 116 Stat. 745, creates a Public Company Accounting Oversight Board composed of five members appointed by the Securities and Exchange Commission. The Board is a private nonprofit corporation, and its members are not considered government employees for statutory purposes. Nonetheless, the Board has broad authority to oversee the accounting industry. The Commission can remove members of the Board only for "good cause shown."]

The parties agree that the Commissioners cannot themselves be removed by the President except under the *Humphrey's Executor* standard of "inefficiency, neglect of duty, or malfeasance in office, and we decide the case with that understanding.

[Petitioners are an accounting firm and a nonprofit organization to which the firm belongs. The Board released a report critical of the firm and began a formal investigation. Petitioners then sued the Board, claiming that it was unconstitutional and seeking an injunction preventing it from exercising its powers]....

III

We hold that the dual for-cause limitations on the removal of Board members contravene the Constitution's separation of powers....

B

[We] have previously upheld limited restrictions on the President's removal power. In those cases, however, only one level of protected tenure separated the President from an officer exercising executive power. It was the President — or a subordinate he could remove at will — who decided whether the officer's conduct merited removal under the good-cause standard. The Act before us does something quite different. It not only protects Board members from removal except for good cause, but withdraws from the President any decision on whether that good cause exists. That decision is vested instead in other tenured officers — the Commissioners — none of whom is subject to the President's direct control. The result is a Board that is not accountable to the President, and a President who is not responsible for the Board. The added layer of tenure protection makes a difference. Without a layer of insulation between the Commission and the Board, the Commission could remove a Board member at any time, and therefore would be fully responsible for what the Board does. The President could then hold the Commission to account for its supervision of the Board, to the same extent that he may hold the Commission to account for everything else it does. A second level of tenure protection changes the nature of the President's review. Now the Commission cannot remove a Board member at will. The President therefore cannot hold the Commission fully accountable for the Board's conduct, to the same extent that he may hold the Commission accountable for everything else that it does....

[If] allowed to stand, this dispersion of responsibility could be multiplied. If Congress can shelter the bureaucracy behind two layers of good-cause tenure, why not a third? At oral argument, the Government was unwilling to concede that even *five* layers between the President and the Board would be too many. The officers of such an agency — safely encased within a Matryoshka doll of tenure protections—would be immune from Presidential oversight, even as they exercised power in the people's name....

By granting the Board executive power without the Executive's oversight, this Act subverts the President's ability to ensure that the laws are faithfully executed—as well as the public's ability to pass judgment on his efforts. The Act's restrictions are incompatible with the Constitution's separation of powers.

C....

According to the dissent, Congress may impose multiple levels of for cause tenure between the President and his subordinates when it "rests agency independence upon the need for technical expertise." The Board's mission is said to demand both "technical competence" and "apolitical expertise," and its powers may only be exercised by "technical professional experts." In this respect the statute creating Board is, we are told, simply one example of the "vast numbers of statutes governing vast numbers of subjects, concerned with vast numbers of different problems, [that] provide for, or foresee, their execution or administration through the work of administrators organized within many different kinds of administrative structures, exercising different kinds of administrative authority, to achieve their legislatively mandated objectives."

No one doubts Congress's power to create a vast and varied federal bureaucracy. But where, in all this, is the role for oversight by an elected President? The Constitution requires that a President chosen by the entire Nation oversee the execution of the laws....

One can have a government that functions without being ruled by functionaries, and a government that benefits from expertise without being ruled by experts. Our Constitution was adopted to enable the people to govern themselves, through their elected leaders. The growth of the Executive Branch, which now wields vast power and touches almost every aspect of daily life, heightens the concern that it may slip from the Executive's control, and thus from that of the people. This concern is largely absent from the dissent's paean to the administrative state....

D

The parties have identified only a handful of isolated positions in which inferior officers might be protected by two levels of good-cause tenure....

The dissent here suggests that other such positions might exist, and complains that we do not resolve their status in this opinion. The dissent itself, however, stresses the very size and variety of the Federal Government, and those features discourage general pronouncements on matters neither briefed nor argued here. In any event, the dissent fails to support its premonitions of doom; none of the positions it identifies are similarly situated to the Board.

For example, many civil servants within independent agencies would not qualify as "Officers of the United States," who "exercis[e] significant authority pursuant to the laws of the United States," [*Buckley*]. We do not decide the status of other Government employees, nor do we decide whether "lesser functionaries subordinate to officers of the United States" must be subject to the same sort of control as those who exercise "significant authority pursuant to the laws." [*Buckley*]. Nor do the employees referenced by the dissent enjoy the same significant and unusual protections from Presidential oversight as members of the Board. . . .

Finally, the dissent wanders far afield when it suggests that today's opinion might increase the President's authority to remove military officers. Without expressing any view whatever on the scope of that authority, it is enough to note that we see little analogy between our Nation's armed services and the Public Company Accounting Oversight Board. Military officers are broadly subject to Presidential control through the chain of command and through the President's powers as Commander in Chief. The President and his subordinates may also convene boards of inquiry or courts-martial to hear claims of misconduct or poor performance by those officers. Here, by contrast, the President has no authority to initiate a Board member's removal for cause. . . .

IV

Petitioners' complaint argued that the Board's "freedom from Presidential oversight and control" rendered it "and all power and authority exercised by it" in violation of the Constitution. We reject such a broad holding. Instead, we agree with the Government that the unconstitutional tenure provisions are severable from the remainder of the statute. . . .

V

Petitioners raise three more challenges to the Board under the Appointments Clause. None has merit. [The Court rejects petitioners' argument that Board members are principal officers requiring Presidential appointment with the advice and consent of the Senate]. Given that the Commission is properly viewed, under the Constitution, as possessing the power to remove Board members at will, and given the Commission's other oversight authority, we have no hesitation in concluding that [the] Board members are inferior officers whose appointment Congress may permissibly vest in a "Hea[d] of Departmen[t]."

But, petitioners argue, the Commission is not a "Departmen[t]." . . .

Because the Commission is a freestanding component of the Executive Branch, not subordinate to or contained within any other such component, it constitutes a "Departmen[t]" for the purposes of the Appointments Clause.

But petitioners are not done yet. They argue that the full Commission cannot constitutionally appoint Board members, because only the Chairman of the Commission is the Commission's "Hea[d]." The Commission's powers, however, are generally vested in the Commissioners jointly, not the Chairman alone. . . .

As a constitutional matter, we see no reason why a multimember body may not be the "Hea[d]" of a "Departmen[t]" that it governs. . . .

In light of the foregoing, petitioners are not entitled to broad injunctive relief against the Board's continued operations. But they are entitled to declaratory relief sufficient to ensure that the reporting requirements and auditing standards to which they are subject will be enforced only by a constitutional agency accountable to the Executive.

* * *

The Constitution that makes the President accountable to the people for executing the laws also gives him the power to do so. That power includes, as a general matter, the authority to remove those who assist him in carrying out his duties. Without such power, the President could not be held fully accountable for discharging his own responsibilities; the buck would stop somewhere else. [While] we have sustained in certain cases limits on the President's removal power, the Act before us imposes a new type of restriction — two levels of protection from removal for those who nonetheless exercise significant executive power. Congress cannot limit the President' authority in this way. . . .

JUSTICE BREYER, with whom JUSTICE STEVENS, JUSTICE GINSBURG, and JUSTICE SOTOMAYOR join, dissenting. . . .

I agree that the Accounting Board members are inferior officers. But in my view the statute does not significantly interfere with the President's "executive Power." It violates no separation-of-powers principle. And the Court's contrary holding threatens to disrupt severely the fair and efficient administration of the laws. I consequently dissent.

I

A

The legal question before us arises at the intersection of two general constitutional principles. On the one hand, Congress has broad power to enact statutes "necessary and proper" to the exercise of its specifically enumerated constitutional authority. [Congress] has drawn on that power over the past century to create numerous federal agencies in response to "various crises of human affairs" as they have arisen.

On the other hand, the opening sections of Articles I, II, and III of the Constitution separately and respectively vest "all legislative Powers" in Congress, the "executive Power" in the President, and the "judicial Power" in the Supreme Court (and such "inferior Courts as Congress may from time to time ordain and establish"). In doing so, these provisions imply a structural separation-of-powers principle. And that principle, along with the instruction in Article II, § 3 that the President "shall take Care that the Laws be faithfully executed," limits Congress' power to structure the Federal Government.

Indeed, this Court has held that the separation-of-powers principle guarantees the President the authority to dismiss certain Executive Branch officials at will. [*Myers*]).

But neither of these two principles is absolute in its application to removal cases. The Necessary and Proper Clause does not grant Congress power to free *all* Executive Branch officials from dismissal at the will of the President. Nor does the separation-of-powers principle grant the President an absolute authority to remove *any and all* Executive Branch officials at will. Rather, depending on, say, the nature of the office, its function, or its subject matter, Congress sometimes may, consistent with the Constitution, limit the President's authority to remove an officer from his post. See [*Humphrey's Executor; Morrison.*] And we must here decide whether the circumstances surrounding the statute at issue justify such a limitation. . . .

[The] question presented lies at the intersection of two sets of conflicting, broadly framed constitutional principles. And no text, no history, perhaps no precedent provides any clear answer.

B

When previously deciding this kind of nontextual question, the Court has emphasized the importance of examining how a particular provision, taken in context, is likely to function. . . .

[A] functional approach permits Congress and the President the flexibility needed to adapt statutory law to changing circumstances. That is why the "powers conferred upon the Federal Government by the Constitution were phrased in language broad enough to allow for the expansion of the Federal Government's role" over time. Indeed, the Federal Government at the time of the founding consisted of about 2,000 employees and served a population of about 4 million. Today, however, the Federal Government employs about *4.4 million workers* who serve a Nation of more than 310 million people living in a society characterized by rapid technological, economic, and social changes. . . .

The upshot is that today vast numbers of statutes governing vast numbers of subjects, concerned with vast numbers of different problems, provide for, or foresee, their execution or administration through the work of administrators organized within many different kinds of administrative structures, exercising different kinds of administrative authority, to achieve their legislatively mandated objectives. And, given the nature of the Government's work, it is not surprising that administrative units come in many different shapes and sizes.

The functional approach required by our precedents recognizes this administrative complexity and, more importantly, recognizes the various ways presidential power operates within this context — and the various ways in which a removal provision might affect that power. As human beings have known ever since Ulysses tied himself to the mast so as safely to hear the Sirens' song, sometimes it is necessary to disable oneself in order to achieve a broader objective. Thus, legally enforceable commitments — such as contracts, statutes that cannot instantly be changed, and, as in the case before us, the establishment of independent administrative institutions — hold the potential to empower precisely because of their ability to constrain. If the President seeks to regulate through impartial adjudication, then insulation of the adjudicator from removal at will can help him achieve that goal. And to free a technical decision maker from the fear of removal without cause can similarly help create legitimacy with respect to that official's regulatory actions by helping to insulate his technical decisions from nontechnical political pressure....

These practical reasons not only support our precedents' determination that cases such as this should examine the specific functions and context at issue; they also indicate that judges should hesitate before second-guessing a "for cause" decision made by the other branches....

There is no indication that the two comparatively more expert branches were divided in their support for the "for cause" provision at issue here....

II

A

To what extent then is the Act's "for cause" provision likely, as a practical matter, to limit the President's exercise of executive authority? In practical terms no "for cause" provision can, in isolation, define the full measure of executive power. This is because a legislative decision to place ultimate administrative authority in, say, the Secretary of Agriculture rather than the President, the way in which the statute defines the scope of the power the relevant administrator can exercise, the decision as to who controls the agency's budget requests and funding the relationships between one agency or department and another, as well as more purely political factors (including Congress' ability to assert influence) are more likely to affect the President's power to get something done....

Indeed, notwithstanding the majority's assertion that the removal authority is "*the* key" mechanism by which the President oversees inferior officers in the independent agencies, it appears that no President has ever actually sought to exercise that power by testing the scope of a "for cause" provision.

But even if we put all these other matters to the side, we should still conclude that the "for cause" restriction before us will not restrict presidential power significantly. For one thing, the restriction directly limits, not the President's power, but the power of an already independent agency. The Court seems to have forgotten that fact when it identifies its central constitutional problem: According to the Court, the President "is powerless to intervene" if he has determined that the Board members' "conduct merit[s] removal" because "[t]hat decision is vested instead in other tenured officers — the Commissioners — none of whom is subject to the President's direct control." But so long as the President is *legitimately* foreclosed from removing the *Commissioners* except for cause (as the majority assumes), nullifying the Commission's power to remove Board members only for cause will not resolve the problem the Court has identified: The President will *still* be "powerless to intervene" by removing the Board members if the Commission reasonably decides not to do so. . . .

B

At the same time, Congress and the President had good reason for enacting the challenged "for cause" provision. [The] Board adjudicates cases. This Court has long recognized the appropriateness of using "for cause" provisions to protect the personal independence of those who even only sometimes engage in adjudicatory functions.

Moreover, in addition to their adjudicative functions, the Accounting Board members supervise, and are themselves, technical professional experts. . . .

D

[Much] of the majority's opinion appears to avoid [a narrow holding] in favor of a broad, basically mechanical rule — a rule that, as I have said, is divorced from the context of the case at hand. And such a mechanical rule cannot be cabined simply by saying that, *perhaps,* the rule does not apply to instances that, at least at first blush, seem highly similar. . . .

The Court begins to reveal the practical problems inherent in its double for-cause rule when it suggests that its rule may not apply to "the civil service." The "civil service" is defined by statute to include "all appointive positions in . . . the Government of the United States," excluding the military, but including *all* civil "officer[s]" up to and including those who are subject to Senate confirmation. The civil service thus includes many officers indistinguishable from the members of both the Commission and the Accounting Board. . . .

But even if I assume that the majority categorically excludes the competitive service from the scope of its new rule, the exclusion would be insufficient. This is because the Court's "double for-cause" rule applies to appointees who are "inferior officer[s]." And who are they? Courts and scholars have struggled for more than a century to define the constitutional term "inferior officers," without much success. The Court does not clarify the concept. But without defining who is an inferior officer, to whom the majority's new rule applies, we cannot know the scope or the coherence of the legal rule that the Court creates....

Reading the criteria above as stringently as possible, I still see no way to avoid sweeping hundreds, perhaps thousands of high level government officials within the scope of the Court's holding, putting their job security and their administrative actions and decisions constitutionally at risk. To make even a conservative estimate, one would have to begin by listing federal departments, offices, bureaus and other agencies whose heads are by statute removable only "for cause." I have found 48 such [agencies.] Then it would be necessary to identify the senior officials in those agencies (just below the top) who themselves are removable only "for cause." I have identified 573 such high-ranking [officials]....

The potential list of those whom today's decision affects is yet larger. As JUSTICE SCALIA has observed, administrative law judges (ALJs) "are all executive officers." And ALJs are each removable "only for good cause established and determined by the Merit Systems Protection Board." But the members of the Merit Systems Protection Board are themselves protected from removal by the President absent good cause.

My research reflects that the Federal Government relies on 1,584 ALJs to adjudicate administrative matters in over 25 agencies....

And what about the military? Commissioned military officers "are 'inferior officers.'" There are over 210,000 active-duty commissioned officers currently serving in the armed forces. Numerous statutory provisions provide that such officers may not be removed from office except for cause (at least in peacetime). And such officers can generally be so removed only by *other* commissioned officers who themselves enjoy the same career protections.

The majority might simply say that the military is different. But it will have to explain *how* it is different. It is difficult to see why the Constitution would provide a President who is the military's "commander-in-chief," with *less* authority to remove "inferior" military "officers" than to remove comparable civil officials....

* * *

In my view the Court's decision is wrong — very wrong. [If] the Court were to look to the proper functional and contextual considerations, it would find the Accounting Board provision constitutional. [Its] rule of decision is both imprecise and overly broad. In light of the present imprecision, it must either narrow its rule arbitrarily, leaving it to apply virtually alone to the Accounting Board, or it will have to leave in place a broader rule of decision applicable to many other "inferior officers" as well. In doing the latter, it will undermine the President's authority. And it will create an obstacle, indeed pose a serious threat, to the proper functioning of that workable Government that the Constitution seeks to create — in provisions this Court is sworn to uphold. . . .

Note: The Meaning of Free Enterprise Fund

Does *Free Enterprise Fund* mark an important change in the Court's attitude toward the insulation of administrative officials from executive removal? Consider the following views:

1. Pildes, Free Enterprise Fund, Boundary Enforcing Decisions, and the Unitary Executive Branch Theory of Government Administration, 6 Duke J. Const. L. & Publ. Pol'y 1, 1-2 (2010):

[*Free Enterprise Fund*] presents the most expansive vision of presidential power over the structure of administrative agencies in perhaps ninety years. [The] Court found, for the first time, that the design of an administrative agency was unconstitutional even though Congress had not taken one of three steps: inserting itself directly into the removal process; inserting itself directly in the appointments process; or inserting itself in the substance of agency policymaking by retaining a congressional veto power over the agency's actions. . . .

Despite the extent to which the Court's rhetoric and outcome endorsed an exceptionally robust view of presidential power over administrative governance, the implications of *Free Enterprise Fund* for the more general struggle between Congress and the President [remain] obscure because the case presented such an idiosyncratic context.

2. Rao, A Modest Proposal: Abolishing Agency Independence in Free Enterprise Fund v. PCAOB, 79 Ford. L. Rev. 2541, 2544 (2011):

The Chief Justice's opinion in time may be viewed like *Marbury v. Madison*, reaching a narrow result on the immediate controversy at issue — the Board continues largely as before — while staking out ground for a judicial incursion against agency independence. As in *Marbury*, the Chief Justice could have gone a number of different directions, but the decision reaches a result that minimizes political opposition, while leaving open the possibility for more significant impact in future decisions. To see this case as inconsequential is to miss the forest for the trees.

3. Nourse & Figura, Toward a Representational Theory of the Executive, 91 B.U. L. Rev. 2733, 301 (2011):

The problem [in *Free Enterprise Fund*] was representational. Suppose that the President wanted to remove a [Board] member for failure to pursue his duty and the SEC tried to stop him. In that case, the SEC — an unelected, quasi-independent body with an attenuated representational relationship to the public — could trump the will of the President and the nation. In that respect, *Free Enterprise Fund* is like *Bowsher v. Synar*, where the risk was that the Comptroller General — who represents no one — would decide large budgetary questions contrary to the desire of the President or Congress....

[What] really matters in any inquiry of executive power is the power of the people — for it is only through the Constitution's connection of executive power to the power of the electorate that the President has any power at all.

5
EQUALITY AND THE CONSTITUTION

C. Equal Protection Methodology: Heightened Scrutiny and the Problem of Race

Page 619.   After section 3 of the Note, add the following:

3a. *A more radical challenge to existing doctrine?*   In Ricci v. DeStefano, 129 S. Ct. 2658 (2009), Justice Scalia raised the possibility that strict scrutiny for racial classifications might raise doubts about the constitutionality of much of the edifice of modern antidiscrimination law.   Recall that many federal antidiscrimination statutes — for example, Title VII of the Civil Rights Act of 1964, which deals with employment discrimination, and section 2 of the Voting Rights Act of 1965 — prohibit practices that have a disparate impact regardless of the defendant's intent.   In *Ricci*, the Court faced a Title VII and equal protection clause-based challenge to a city's decision not to certify the results of a promotional test for firefighters in light of the test's disparate impact on black and Latino applicants.   The Court disposed of the case on statutory grounds, not reaching the constitutional question.   In his concurrence, however, Justice Scalia observed that the Court's decision

> merely postpones the evil day on which the Court will have to confront the question: Whether, or to what extent, are the disparate-impact provisions of Title VII of the Civil Rights Act of 1964 consistent with the Constitution's guarantee of equal protection? The question is not an easy one. See generally Primus, Equal Protection and Disparate Impact: Round Three, 117 Harv. L. Rev. 493 (2003).

The difficulty is this: Whether or not Title VII's disparate-treatment pro-visions forbid "remedial" actions when a disparate-impact violation would *not* otherwise result — the question resolved by the Court today — it is clear that Title VII not only permits but affirmatively *requires* such actions when a disparate-impact violation *would* otherwise result. But if the Federal Government is prohibited from discriminating on the basis of race, *Bolling v. Sharpe*, 347 U.S. 497, 500 (1954), then surely it is also prohibited from enacting laws mandating that third parties — *e.g.*, employers, whether pri-vate, State, or municipal — discriminate on the basis of race. See *Buchanan v. Warley,* 245 U.S. 60, 78-82 (1917)....

To be sure, the disparate-impact laws do not mandate imposition of quotas, but it is not clear why that should provide a safe harbor. Would a private employer not be guilty of unlawful discrimination if he refrained from establishing a racial hiring quota but intentionally designed his hiring practices to achieve the same end? Surely he would. Intentional discrimina-tion is still occurring, just one step up the chain. Government compulsion of such design would therefore seemingly violate equal protection principles. Nor would it matter that Title VII requires consideration of race on a whole-sale, rather than retail, level....

[T]he war between disparate impact and equal protection will be waged sooner or later, and it behooves us to begin thinking about how — and on what terms — to make peace between them.

D. Equal Protection Methodology: Heightened Scrutiny and the Problem of Gender

Page 652. At the end of the first paragraph of section 1 of the Note, add the following.

Nguyen upheld differential treatment of parental transmission of citizenship predicated on women and men being differently situated at the moment of a child's birth. Can differential treatment in the transmission of citizenship be sustained absent such a difference? In this respect, consider Flores-Villar v. United States, ____ U.S. ____ (2011). At the time petitioner was born, the Immigration and Nationality Act provided that a child born outside the United States to unmarried parents could obtain citizenship at birth through his U.S.-citizen mother if she had been physically present in the United States for a minimum of one year before the child's birth. By contrast, if the child's father was a U.S. citizen, citizenship at birth was available only if the father had been physically present in the United States for at least ten years, five of them after the father's fourteenth birthday. Flores-Villar's father was only sixteen at the time of Flores-Villar's birth, thus making compliance with the INA's durational requirements impossible. Flores-Villar contended that the INA's physical-presence requirement violated the Fifth Amendment because it treated unwed fathers differently from unwed mothers. He argued that *Nguyen* did not control his case because the distinction there was "biologically based," while the age-based residency requirement at issue in his case had no basis in biology. In response, the government argued that the statute should be subjected to rationality review, but that it would survive intermediate scrutiny as well because extending citizenship based on maternal status was substantially related to the important government objective of reducing the number of children born stateless. With Justice Kagan recused, the Supreme Court affirmed by an equally divided Court the Ninth Circuit's decision upholding the statute.

E.   Equal Protection Methodology: The Problem of Sexual Orientation

Page 678.   At the end of section 2 of the Note, add the following:

In 2010, Congress set in motion a process to abandon the exclusion of gay people from military service. In the Don't Ask, Don't Tell Repeal Act of 2010, Pub. L. 111-321, 124 Stat. 3515, Congress provided for section 654 to be struck from the U.S. Code 60 days after the President transmits to Congress a certification signed by the President, the Secretary of Defense, and the Chairman of the Joint Chiefs of Staff, stating, among other things, that "the implementation of necessary policies and regulations" for including gay persons "is consistent with the standards of military readiness, military effectiveness, unit cohesion, and recruiting and retention of the Armed Forces." On July 22, 2011, President Obama transmitted the certification, under which repeal will automatically occur on September 20, 2011.

Page 678.   At the beginning of section 3 of the Note, after the citation to Baehr v. Lewin, add the following:

Varnum v. Brien, 763 N.W.2d 862, (Iowa 2009);

Page 682.   Before the final paragraph of section 3 of the Note, add the following.

In February 2011, Attorney General Eric Holder sent a letter to Speaker of the House John Boehner pursuant to 28 U.S.C. § 530D, which requires that the Attorney General notify Congress when he decides "to refrain (on the grounds that the provision is unconstitutional) from defending or asserting, in any judicial... proceeding, the constitutionality of any provision of any Federal statute." See http://www.justice.gov/opa/pr/2011/February/11-ag-223.html. In that letter, Attorney General Holder announced that the President had determined that 1 U.S.C. § 7, "as applied to same-sex couples who are legally married under state law, violates the equal protection component of the Fifth Amendment." Previously, in lawsuits filed in circuits that had applied rationality review to sexual-orientation classifications, the executive branch had defended DOMA. But once lawsuits were filed in circuits without binding precedent, the Department of Justice determined that "classifications based on sexual orientation warrant heightened scrutiny and that, as applied to same-sex couples legally married under state law," DOMA could not withstand such scrutiny.

Attorney General Holder's letter noted that the Supreme Court was "yet to rule on the appropriate level of scrutiny for classifications based on sexual orientation." But applying the Court's criteria for subjecting a classification to heightened scrutiny, including "(1) whether the group in question has suffered a history of discrimination; (2) whether individuals 'exhibit obvious, immutable, or distinguishing characteristics that define them as a discrete group'; (3) whether the group is a minority or is politically powerless; and (4) whether the characteristics distinguishing the group have little relation to legitimate policy objectives or to an individual's 'ability to perform or contribute to society.' See Bowen v. Gilliard, 483 U.S. 587, 602-603 (1987); City of Cleburne v. Cleburne Living Ctr., 473 U.S. 432, 441-442 (1985)," the Attorney General concluded that "[e]ach of these factors counsels in favor of being suspicious of classifications based on sexual orientation."

The letter then declared that "under heightened scrutiny, the United States cannot defend [DOMA's definition of marriage] by advancing hypothetical rationales, independent of the legislative record, as it has done in circuits where precedent mandates application of rational basis review. Instead, the United States can defend [DOMA] only by invoking Congress' actual justifications for the law." The Attorney General described Congress's actual reasons as "reflecting moral disapproval of gays and lesbians and their intimate and family relationships—precisely the kind of stereotype-based thinking and animus the Equal Protection Clause is designed to guard against."

Nonetheless, the Attorney General announced that DOMA would continue to be enforced by the executive branch "unless and until Congress repeals [it] or the judicial branch renders a definitive verdict against the law's constitutionality."

Page 682.   At the end of section 3 of the Note, add the following:

Following the California Supreme Court's decision in the Marriage Cases, the state's voters passed an initiative amending the state's constitution to provide that "Only marriage between a man and a woman is valid or recognized in California." In Strauss v. Horton, 46 Cal. 4th 364 (2009), the California Supreme Court upheld the initiative against a state constitutional challenge, but observed that strict scrutiny remained the appropriate standard for assessing discrimination on the basis of sexual orientation under the California constitution. And it concluded that "although [the initiative] eliminates the ability of same-sex couples to enter into an official relationship designated 'marriage,' in all other respects those couples continue to possess, under the state constitutional privacy and due process clauses, 'the core set of basic *substantive* legal rights and attributes traditionally associated with marriage,' including, 'most fundamentally, the opportunity of an individual to establish — with the person with whom the individual has chosen to share his or her life — an *officially recognized and protected family* possessing mutual rights and responsibilities and entitled to the same respect and dignity accorded a union traditionally designated as marriage.'"

6
IMPLIED FUNDAMENTAL RIGHTS

A. Introduction

Page 713.   After the first block quote in section 3 of the Note, add the following:

Compare Colby & Smith, Living Originalism, 59 Duke L.J. 239 (2009):

[Originalists] cannot agree amongst themselves on constitutional [interpretation]. What is sauce for the goose is sauce for the gander; if the substantial disagreement among nonoriginalists is persuasive evidence that nonoriginalist theory is incoherent, then the substantial disagreement among originalists must be equally powerful evidence that originalist theory lacks coherence, as well. The reality of originalism's internal discord should put an end to the ubiquitous argument that originalism is the only theoretically coherent approach to constitutional interpretation.

Page 713.   Before section 4 of the Note, add the following:

For an argument that "deciding issues based on original meanings makes sense in some kinds of cases but not others," see Primus, When Should Original Meaning Matter?, 107 Mich. L. Rev. 165 (2008). With respect to arguments for originalism grounded in the Constitution's democratic origins, the author asserts that "[paying] attention to original meanings makes sense in cases construing provisions that were adopted recently enough that the dead-hand problem does not arise. Original meaning [gradually] becomes less important until the provision's democratic authority expires completely." Id. at 169. With respect to arguments for originalism grounded in the rule of law, the author asserts that the arguments "[make] sense only in cases where the provision's original meaning is also its operative meaning, where 'operative meaning' is the meaning that a provision has to its contemporary audience. [If] a contrary meaning has taken hold, [then] displacing that operative meaning in favor of the original meaning might undermine the very rule-of-law values that originalist reasoning is supposed to support." Id. at 170.

Page 715.   Before section 5 of the Note, add the following:

For a skeptical analysis of public-meaning originalism in the context of *Heller*, see Tushnet, *Heller* and the New Originalism, 69 Ohio St. L.J. 609 (2008). The author concludes that "[unfortunately], the new originalism cannot deliver on its promises, as *Heller* shows. The reason is simple: The new originalism's search for *the*—that is, the single—conventional understanding of constitutional terms is doomed, at least in the most interesting cases. [History] is replete with ['contested] truths.' These contests are precisely contests over conventional meaning."

C. The Incorporation Controversy

Page 734.   At the end of section 1 of the Note, add the following:

The Court resolved the second amendment incorporation question in the case that follows.

McDONALD v. CITY OF CHICAGO

130 S. Ct. 3020 (2010)

JUSTICE ALITO announced the judgment of the Court and delivered the opinion of the Court with respect to Parts I, II–A, II–B, II–D, III–A, and III–B, in which [CHIEF JUSTICE ROBERTS], JUSTICE SCALIA, JUSTICE KENNEDY, and JUSTICE THOMAS join, and an opinion with respect to Parts II–C, IV, and V, in which the CHIEF JUSTICE, JUSTICE SCALIA, and JUSTICE KENNEDY join.

Two years ago, in District of Columbia v. Heller, 554 U.S. _____ (2008), we held that the Second Amendment protects the right to keep and bear arms for the purpose of self-defense, and we struck down a District of Columbia law that banned the possession of handguns in the home. [*Heller* is discussed in the main volume at pages 8 and 714]. The city of Chicago (City) and the village of Oak Park, a Chicago suburb, have laws that are similar to the District of Columbia's, but Chicago and Oak Park argue that their laws are constitutional because the Second Amendment has no application to the States. We have previously held that most of the provisions of the Bill of Rights apply with full force to both the Federal Government and the States. Applying the standard that is well established in our case law, we hold that the Second Amendment right is fully applicable to the States. . . .

II

A

Petitioners argue that the Chicago and Oak Park laws violate the right to keep and bear arms for two reasons. Petitioners' primary submission is that this right is among the "privileges or immunities of citizens of the United States" and that the narrow interpretation of the Privileges or Immunities Clause adopted in the *Slaughter-House Cases* should now be rejected. As a secondary argument, petitioners contend that the Fourteenth Amendment's Due Process Clause "incorporates" the Second Amendment right.

Chicago and Oak Park (municipal respondents) maintain that a right set out in the Bill of Rights applies to the States only if that right is an indispensable attribute of *any* "'civilized'" legal system. If it is possible to imagine a civilized country that does not recognize the right, the municipal respondents tell us, then that right is not protected by due process. And since there are civilized countries that ban or strictly regulate the private possession of handguns, the municipal respondents maintain that due process does not preclude such measures. . . .

C

[This portion of Justice Alito's opinion is joined only by Chief Justice Roberts and Justices Kennedy and Scalia].

[In] petitioners' view, the Privileges or Immunities Clause protects all of the rights set out in the Bill of Rights, as well as some others but petitioners are unable to identify the Clause's full scope. Nor is there any consensus on that question among the scholars who agree that the *Slaughter-House Cases'* interpretation is flawed. We see no need to reconsider that interpretation here. For many decades, the question of the rights protected by the Fourteenth Amendment against state infringement has been analyzed under the Due Process Clause of that Amendment and not under the Privileges or Immunities Clause. We therefore decline to disturb the *Slaughter-House* holding. At the same time, however, this Court's decisions in *Cruikshank*, *Presser*, and *Miller* [prior Supreme Court decisions holding that the second amendment was not incorporated] do not preclude us from considering whether the Due Process Clause of the Fourteenth Amendment makes the Second Amendment right binding on the States. See *Heller*, 554 U.S., at _____, n. 23 (slip op., at 48, n. 23). None of those cases "engage[d] in the sort of Fourteenth Amendment inquiry required by our later cases." *Ibid.* As explained more fully below, *Cruikshank*, *Presser*, and *Miller* all preceded the era in which the Court began the process of "selective incorporation" under the Due Process Clause, and we have never previously addressed the question whether the right to keep and bear arms applies to the States under that theory. . . .

D

1

In the late 19th century, the Court began to consider whether the Due Process Clause prohibits the States from infringing rights set out in the Bill of Rights. [The Court summarizes its early incorporation decisions and Justice Black's theory of total incorporation]. . . .

3

While Justice Black's theory was never adopted, the Court eventually moved in that direction by initiating what has been called a process of "selective incorporation," i.e., the Court began to hold that the Due Process Clause fully incorporates particular rights contained in the first eight Amendments. . . .

The Court made it clear that the governing standard is not whether any "civilized system [can] be imagined that would not accord the particular protection." Instead, the Court inquired whether a particular Bill of Rights guarantee is fundamental to our scheme of ordered liberty and system of justice.

The Court also shed any reluctance to hold that rights guaranteed by the Bill of Rights met the requirements for protection under the Due Process Clause. The Court eventually incorporated almost all of the provisions of the Bill of Rights. Only a handful of the Bill of Rights protections remain unincorporated.[13]

---

13. In addition to the right to keep and bear arms (and the Sixth Amendment right to a unanimous jury verdict) the only rights not fully incorporated are (1) the Third Amendment's protection against quartering of soldiers; (2) the Fifth Amendment's grand jury indictment requirement; (3) the Seventh Amendment right to a jury trial in civil cases; and (4) the Eighth Amendment's prohibition on excessive fines.

We never have decided whether the Third Amendment or the Eighth Amendment's prohibition of excessive fines applies to the States through the Due Process Clause. Our governing decisions regarding the Grand Jury Clause of the Fifth Amendment and the Seventh Amendment's civil jury requirement long predate the era of selective incorporation.

Finally, the Court abandoned "the notion that the Fourteenth Amendment applies to the States only a watered-down, subjective version of the individual guarantees of the Bill of Rights," stating that it would be "incongruous" to apply different standards "depending on whether the claim was asserted in a state or federal court."[14]

Employing this approach, the Court overruled earlier decisions in which it had held that particular Bill of Rights guarantees or remedies did not apply to the States.

III

With this framework in mind, we now turn directly to the question whether the Second Amendment right to keep and bear arms is incorporated in the concept of due process. In answering that question, as just explained, we must decide whether the right to keep and bear arms is fundamental to our scheme of ordered liberty, or as we have said in a related context, whether this right is "deeply rooted in this Nation's history and tradition," *Washington v. Glucksberg*, 521 U. S. 702, 721 (1997) (internal quotation marks omitted).

A

Our decision in *Heller* points unmistakably to the answer. Self-defense is a basic right, recognized by many legal systems from ancient times to the present day, and in *Heller*, we held that individual self-defense is "the central component" of the Second Amendment right.

Explaining that "the need for defense of self, family, and property is most acute" in the home, we found that this right applies to handguns because they are "the most preferred firearm in the nation to 'keep' and use for protection of

---

14. There is one exception to this general rule. The Court has held that although the Sixth Amendment right to trial by jury requires a unanimous jury verdict in federal criminal trials, it does not require a unanimous jury verdict in state criminal trials. See *Apodaca v. Oregon*, 406 U. S. 404 (1972). But that ruling was the result of an unusual division among the Justices, not an endorsement of the two-track approach to incorporation. In *Apodaca*, eight Justices agreed that the Sixth Amendment applies identically to both the Federal Government and the States. Nonetheless, among those eight, four Justices took the view that the Sixth Amendment does not require unanimous jury verdicts in either federal or state criminal trials, *Apodaca*, 406 U. S., at 406 (plurality opinion), and four other Justices took the view that the Sixth Amendment requires unanimous jury verdicts in federal and state criminal trials. Justice Powell's concurrence in the judgment broke the tie, and he concluded that the Sixth Amendment requires juror unanimity in federal, but not state, cases. *Apodaca,* therefore, does not undermine the well-established rule that incorporated Bill of Rights protections apply identically to the States and the Federal Government.

one's home and family." Thus, we concluded, citizens must be permitted "to use [handguns] for the core lawful purpose of self-defense. *Heller* makes it clear that this right is "deeply rooted in this Nation's history and tradition." ...

B

1

By the 1850's, the perceived threat that had prompted the inclusion of the Second Amendment in the Bill of Rights — the fear that the National Government would disarm the universal militia — had largely faded as a popular concern, but the right to keep and bear arms was highly valued for purposes of self-defense. ...

After the Civil War, many of the over 180,000 African Americans who served in the Union Army returned to the States of the old Confederacy, where systematic efforts were made to disarm them and other blacks. The laws of some States formally prohibited African Americans from possessing firearms. Throughout the South, armed parties, often consisting of ex-Confederate soldiers serving in the state militias, forcibly took firearms from newly freed slaves. ...

Union Army commanders took steps to secure the right of all citizens to keep and bear arms, but the 39th Congress concluded that legislative action was necessary. Its efforts to safeguard the right to keep and bear arms demonstrate that the right was still recognized to be fundamental.

The most explicit evidence of Congress' aim appears in § 14 of the Freedmen's Bureau Act of 1866, which provided that "the right ... to have full and equal benefit of all laws and proceedings concerning personal liberty, personal security, and the acquisition, enjoyment, and disposition of estate, real and personal, including the constitutional right to bear arms, shall be secured to and enjoyed by all the citizens ... without respect to race or color, or previous condition of slavery." Section 14 thus explicitly guaranteed that "all the citizens," black and white, would have "the constitutional right to bear arms."

The Civil Rights Act of 1866, which was considered at the same time as the Freedmen's Bureau Act, similarly sought to protect the right of all citizens to keep and bear arms. Section 1 of the Civil Rights Act guaranteed the "full and equal benefit of all laws and proceedings for the security of person and property, as is enjoyed by white citizens." This language was virtually identical to language in § 14 of the Freedmen's Bureau Act. And as noted, the latter provision went on to explain that one of the "laws and proceedings concerning personal liberty, personal security, and the acquisition, enjoyment, and disposition of estate, real and personal" was "the constitutional right to bear arms."

Congress, however, ultimately deemed these legislative remedies insufficient. Southern resistance, Presidential vetoes, and this Court's pre-Civil-War precedent persuaded Congress that a constitutional amendment was necessary to provide full protection for the rights of blacks. Today, it is generally accepted that the Fourteenth Amendment was understood to provide a constitutional basis for protecting the rights set out in the Civil Rights Act of 1866.

In debating the Fourteenth Amendment, the 39th Congress referred to the right to keep and bear arms as a fundamental right deserving of protection. ...

Evidence from the period immediately following the ratification of the Fourteenth Amendment only confirms that the right to keep and bear arms was considered fundamental. ...

The right to keep and bear arms was also widely protected by state constitutions at the time when the Fourteenth Amendment was ratified. ...

2

Despite all this evidence, municipal respondents contend that Congress, in the years immediately following the Civil War, merely sought to outlaw "discriminatory measures taken against freedmen, which it addressed by adopting a non-discrimination principle" and that even an outright ban on the possession of firearms was regarded as acceptable, "so long as it was not done in a discriminatory manner." [This] argument is implausible. [While] § 1 of the Fourteenth Amendment contains "an antidiscrimination rule," namely, the Equal Protection Clause, municipal respondents can hardly mean that § 1 does no more than prohibit discrimination. If that were so, then the First Amendment, as applied to the States, would not prohibit nondiscriminatory abridgments of the rights to freedom of speech or freedom of religion; the Fourth Amendment, as applied to the States, would not prohibit all unreasonable searches and seizures but only discriminatory searches and seizures — and so on. ...

IV

[This portion of Justice Alito's opinion is joined only by Chief Justice Roberts and Justices Kennedy and Scalia].

[Municipal] respondents' main argument is nothing less than a plea to disregard 50 years of incorporation precedent and return (presumably for this case only) to a by-gone era. Municipal respondents submit that the Due Process Clause protects only those rights "'recognized by all temperate and civilized governments, from a deep and universal sense of [their] justice.'" According to municipal respondents, if it is possible to imagine any civilized legal system that does not recognize a particular right, then the Due Process Clause does not make that right binding on the States. ...

This line of argument is, of course, inconsistent with the long-established standard we apply in incorporation cases. And the present-day implications of municipal respondents' argument are stunning. For example, many of the rights that our Bill of Rights provides for persons accused of criminal offenses are virtually unique to this country. . . .

We likewise reject municipal respondents' argument that we should depart from our established incorporation methodology on the ground that making the Second Amendment binding on the States and their subdivisions is inconsistent with principles of federalism and will stifle experimentation. Municipal respondents point out — quite correctly — that conditions and problems differ from locality to locality and that citizens in different jurisdictions have divergent views on the issue of gun control. . . .

There is nothing new in the argument that, in order to respect federalism and allow useful state experimentation a federal constitutional right should not be fully binding on the States. This argument was made repeatedly and eloquently by Members of this Court who rejected the concept of incorporation and urged retention of the two-track approach to incorporation. . . .

Time and again, however, those pleas failed. Unless we turn back the clock or adopt a special incorporation test applicable only to the Second Amendment, municipal respondents' argument must be rejected. Under our precedents, if a Bill of Rights guarantee is fundamental from an American perspective, then, unless stare decisis counsels otherwise,[30] that guarantee is fully binding on the States and thus limits (but by no means eliminates) their ability to devise solutions to social problems that suit local needs and values. . . .

We made it clear in *Heller* that our holding did not cast doubt on such longstanding regulatory measures as "prohibitions on the possession of firearms by felons and the mentally ill," "laws forbidding the carrying of firearms in sensitive places such as schools and government buildings, or laws imposing conditions and qualifications on the commercial sale of arms. We repeat those assurances here. Despite municipal respondents' doomsday proclamations, incorporation does not imperil every law regulating firearms. . . .

[Part V of the opinion, which responds to the arguments of Justices Stevens and Breyer, and which is joined only by Chief Justice Roberts and Justices Scalia and Kennedy, is omitted.]

---

30. As noted above, see n. 13, supra, cases that predate the era of selective incorporation held that the Grand Jury Clause of the Fifth Amendment and the Seventh Amendment's civil jury requirement do not apply to the States. See *Hurtado v. California*, 110 U. S. 516 (1884) (indictment); *Minneapolis & St. Louis R. Co. v. Bombolis*, 241 U. S. 211 (1916) (civil jury).

As a result of *Hurtado*, most States do not require a grand jury indictment in all felony cases, and many have no grand juries. As a result of *Bombolis*, cases that would otherwise fall within the Seventh Amendment are now tried without a jury in state small claims courts.

JUSTICE SCALIA, concurring.

I join the Court's opinion. Despite my misgivings about Substantive Due Process as an original matter, I have acquiesced in the Court's incorporation of certain guarantees in the Bill of Rights "because it is both long established and narrowly limited." This case does not require me to reconsider that view, since straightforward application of settled doctrine suffices to decide it. I write separately only to respond to some aspects of JUSTICE STEVENS' dissent. Not that aspect which disagrees with the majority's application of our precedents to this case, which is fully covered by the Court's opinion. But much of what JUSTICE STEVENS writes is a broad condemnation of the theory of interpretation which underlies the Court's opinion, a theory that makes the traditions of our people paramount. He proposes a different theory, which he claims is more "cautiou[s]" and respectful of proper limits on the judicial role. It is that claim I wish to address. . . .

The subjective nature of JUSTICE STEVENS' standard is [apparent] from his claim that it is the courts' prerogative — indeed their duty — to update the Due Process Clause so that it encompasses new freedoms the Framers were too narrow-minded to imagine. Courts, he proclaims, must "do justice to [the Clause's] urgent call and its open texture" by exercising the "interpretive discretion the latter embodies. (Why the people are not up to the task of deciding what new rights to protect, even though it is they who are authorized to make changes, see U. S. Const., Art. V, is never explained.) And it would be "judicial abdication" for a judge to "tur[n] his back" on his task of determining what Fourteenth Amendment covers by "outsourc[ing]" the job to "historical sentiment" — that is, by being guided by what the American people throughout our history have thought. It is only we judges, exercising our "own reasoned judgment," who can be entrusted with deciding the Due Process Clause's scope — which rights serve the Amendment's "central values" — which basically means picking the rights we want to protect and discarding those we do not. . . .

JUSTICE STEVENS moves on to the "most basic" constraint on subjectivity his theory offers: that he would "esche[w] attempts to provide any all-purpose, top-down, totalizing theory of 'liberty.'" The notion that the absence of a coherent theory of the Due Process Clause will somehow curtail judicial caprice is at war with reason. Indeterminacy means opportunity for courts to impose whatever rule they like; it is the problem, not the solution. The idea that interpretive pluralism would reduce courts' ability to impose their will on the ignorant masses is not merely naïve, but absurd. If there are no right answers, there are no wrong answers either. . . .

JUSTICE STEVENS also argues that requiring courts to show "respect for the democratic process" should serve as a constraint. That is true, but JUSTICE STEVENS would have them show respect in an extraordinary manner. In his view, if a right "is already being given careful consideration in, and subjected to ongoing calibration by, the States, judicial enforcement may not be appropriate." In other words, a right, such as the right to keep and bear arms, that has long been recognized but on which the States are considering restrictions, apparently deserves less protection, while a privilege the political branches (instruments of the democratic process) have withheld entirely and continue to withhold, deserves more. That topsy-turvy approach conveniently accomplishes the objective of ensuring that the rights this Court held protected in *Casey*, *Lawrence*, and other such cases fit the theory — but at the cost of insulting rather than respecting the democratic process.

The next constraint JUSTICE STEVENS suggests is harder to evaluate. He describes as "an important tool for guiding judicial discretion" "sensitivity to the interaction between the intrinsic aspects of liberty and the practical realities of contemporary society." I cannot say whether that sensitivity will really guide judges because I have no idea what it is. Is it some sixth sense instilled in judges when they ascend to the bench? Or does it mean judges are more constrained when they agonize about the cosmic conflict between liberty and its potentially harmful consequences? Attempting to give the concept more precision, JUSTICE STEVENS explains that "sensitivity is an aspect of a deeper principle: the need to approach our work with humility and caution." Both traits are undeniably admirable, though what relation they bear to sensitivity is a mystery. But it makes no difference, for the first case JUSTICE STEVENS cites in support, *Casey*, dispels any illusion that he has a meaningful form of judicial modesty in mind. . . .

III

JUSTICE STEVENS' response to this concurrence makes the usual rejoinder of "living Constitution" advocates to the criticism that it empowers judges to eliminate or expand what the people have prescribed: The traditional, historically focused method, he says, reposes discretion in judges as well. Historical analysis can be difficult; it sometimes requires resolving threshold questions, and making nuanced judgments about which evidence to consult and how to interpret it.

I will stipulate to that. But the question to be decided is not whether the historically focused method is a perfect means of restraining aristocratic judicial Constitution writing; but whether it is the best means available in an imperfect world. Or indeed, even more narrowly than that: whether it is demonstrably much better than what JUSTICE STEVENS proposes. I think it beyond all serious dispute that it is much less subjective, and intrudes much less upon the democratic process. It is less subjective because it depends upon a body of evidence susceptible of reasoned analysis rather than a variety of vague ethicopolitical

First Principles whose combined conclusion can be found to point in any direction the judges favor. [Moreover], the methodological differences that divide historians, and the varying interpretive assumptions they bring to their work, are nothing compared to the differences among the American people (though perhaps not among graduates of prestigious law schools) with regard to the moral judgments JUSTICE STEVENS would have courts pronounce. And whether or not special expertise is needed to answer historical questions, judges most certainly have no "comparative ... advantage" in resolving moral disputes. What is more, his approach would not eliminate, but multiply, the hard questions courts must confront, since he would not replace history with moral philosophy, but would have courts consider both. ...

JUSTICE THOMAS, concurring in part and concurring in the judgment.

I agree with the Court that the Fourteenth Amendment makes the right to keep and bear arms set forth in the Second Amendment "fully applicable to the States." I write separately because I believe there is a more straightforward path to this conclusion, one that is more faithful to the Fourteenth Amendment's text and history.

Applying what is now a well-settled test, the plurality opinion concludes that the right to keep and bear arms applies to the States through the Fourteenth Amendment's Due Process Clause because it is "fundamental" to the American "scheme of ordered liberty", and "deeply rooted in this Nation's history and tradition." I agree with that description of the right. But I cannot agree that it is enforceable against the States through a clause that speaks only to "process." Instead, the right to keep and bear arms is a privilege of American citizenship that applies to the States through the Fourteenth Amendment's Privileges or Immunities Clause. ...

As a consequence of this Court's marginalization of the [Privileges and Immunities] Clause [in *Slaughterhouse* and other cases], litigants seeking federal protection of fundamental rights turned to the remainder of §1 [of the fourteenth amendment] in search of an alternative fount of such rights. They found one in a most curious place — that section's command that every State guarantee "due process" to any person before depriving him of "life, liberty, or property." ...

All of this is a legal fiction. The notion that a constitutional provision that guarantees only "process" before a person is deprived of life, liberty, or property could define the substance of those rights strains credulity for even the most casual user of words. Moreover, this fiction is a particularly dangerous one. The one theme that links the Court's substantive due process precedents together is their lack of a guiding principle to distinguish "fundamental" rights that warrant protection from nonfundamental rights that do not. Today's decision illustrates the point. Replaying a debate that has endured from the inception of the Court's substantive due process jurisprudence, the dissents laud the "flexibility" in this Court's substantive due process doctrine while the plurality makes yet another effort to impose principled restraints on its exercise. But neither side argues that the meaning they attribute to the Due Process Clause was consistent with public understanding at the time of its ratification. ...

I cannot accept a theory of constitutional interpretation that rests on such tenuous footing. This Court's substantive due process framework fails to account for both the text of the Fourteenth Amendment and the history that led to its adoption, filling that gap with jurisprudence devoid of a guiding principle. I believe the original meaning of the Fourteenth Amendment offers a superior alternative, and that a return to that meaning would allow this Court to enforce the rights the Fourteenth Amendment is designed to protect with greater clarity and predictability than the substantive due process framework has so far managed. ...

The Privileges or Immunities Clause of the Fourteenth Amendment declares that "[n]o State ... shall abridge the privileges or immunities of citizens of the United States." In interpreting this language, it is important to recall that constitutional provisions are "'written to be understood by the voters.'" [*Heller*]. Thus, the objective of this inquiry is to discern what "ordinary citizens" at the time of ratification would have understood the Privileges or Immunities Clause to mean. ...

The group of rights-bearers to whom the Privileges or Immunities Clause applies is, of course, "citizens." By the time of Reconstruction, it had long been established that both the States and the Federal Government existed to preserve their citizens' inalienable rights, and that these rights were considered "privileges" or "immunities" of citizenship. ...

[Justice Thomas reviews the legislative history of the fourteenth amendment]. [For] purposes of discerning what the public most likely thought the Privileges or Immunities Clause to mean, it is significant that the most widely publicized statements by the legislators who voted on § 1 [point] unambiguously toward the conclusion that the Privileges or Immunities Clause enforces at least those fundamental rights enumerated in the Constitution against the States, including the Second Amendment right to keep and bear arms. ...

In the contentious years leading up to the Civil War, those who sought to retain the institution of slavery found that to do so, it was necessary to eliminate more and more of the basic liberties of slaves, free blacks, and white abolitionists. ...

The overarching goal of pro-slavery forces was to repress the spread of abolitionist thought and the concomitant risk of a slave rebellion. Indeed, it is difficult to overstate the extent to which fear of a slave uprising gripped slaveholders and dictated the acts of Southern legislatures. ...

The fear generated by [slave rebellions] led Southern legislatures to take particularly vicious aim at the rights of free blacks and slaves to speak or to keep and bear arms for their defense. . . .

After the Civil War, Southern anxiety about an uprising among the newly freed slaves peaked . . . .

As the Court explains, this fear led to "systematic efforts" in the "old Confederacy" to disarm the more than 180,000 freedmen who had served in the Union Army, as well as other free blacks. . . .

Section 1 guaranteed the rights of citizenship in the United States and in the several States without regard to race. But it was understood that liberty would be assured little protection if § 1 left each State to decide which privileges or immunities of United States citizenship it would protect. As Frederick Douglass explained before § 1's adoption, "the Legislatures of the South can take from him the right to keep and bear arms, as they can — they would not allow a negro to walk with a cane where I came from, they would not allow five of them to assemble together." "Notwithstanding the provision in the Constitution of the United States, that the right to keep and bear arms shall not be abridged," Douglass explained that "the black man has never had the right either to keep or bear arms." Absent a constitutional amendment to enforce that right against the States, he insisted that "the work of the Abolitionists [wa]s not finished."

This history confirms what the text of the Privileges or Immunities Clause most naturally suggests: Consistent with its command that "[n]o State shall . . . abridge" the rights of United States citizens, the Clause establishes a minimum baseline of federal rights, and the constitutional right to keep and bear arms plainly was among them. . . .

Three years after *Slaughter-House*, the Court in *Cruikshank* squarely held that the right to keep and bear arms was not a privilege of American citizenship, thereby overturning the convictions of militia members responsible for the brutal Colfax Massacre. [*Cruikshank* and the Colfax Massacre are discussed at page 454 of the main text.] *Cruikshank* is not a precedent entitled to any respect. The flaws in its interpretation of the Privileges or Immunities Clause are made evident by the preceding evidence of its original meaning, and I would reject the holding on that basis alone. But, the consequences of *Cruikshank* warrant mention as well.

Cruikshank's holding that blacks could look only to state governments for protection of their right to keep and bear arms enabled private forces, often with the assistance of local governments, to subjugate the newly freed slaves and their descendants through a wave of private violence designed to drive blacks from the voting booth and force them into peonage, an effective return to slavery. Without federal enforcement of the inalienable right to keep and bear arms, these militias and mobs were tragically successful in waging a campaign of terror against the very people the Fourteenth Amendment had just made citizens. . . .

Although Congress enacted legislation to suppress these activities, Klan tactics remained a constant presence in the lives of Southern blacks for decades. Between 1882 and 1968, there were at least 3,446 reported lynchings of blacks in the South. They were tortured and killed for a wide array of alleged crimes, without even the slightest hint of due process. Emmit Till, for example, was killed in 1955 for allegedly whistling at a white woman. The fates of other targets of mob violence were equally depraved.

The use of firearms for self-defense was often the only way black citizens could protect themselves from mob violence. . . .

In my view, the record makes plain that the Framers of the Privileges or Immunities Clause and the ratifying-era public understood — just as the Framers of the Second Amendment did — that the right to keep and bear arms was essential to the preservation of liberty. The record makes equally plain that they deemed this right necessary to include in the minimum baseline of federal rights that the Privileges or Immunities Clause established in the wake of the War over slavery. . . .

JUSTICE STEVENS, dissenting.

In *District of Columbia v. Heller*, the Court answered the question whether a federal enclave's "prohibition on the possession of usable handguns in the home violates the Second Amendment to the Constitution." The question we should be answering in this case is whether the Constitution "guarantees individuals a fundamental right," enforceable against the States, "to possess a functional, personal firearm, including a handgun, within the home." That is a different — and more difficult — inquiry than asking if the Fourteenth Amendment "incorporates" the Second Amendment. The so-called incorporation question was squarely and, in my view, correctly resolved in the late 19th century. Before the District Court, petitioners focused their pleadings on the special considerations raised by domestic possession, which they identified as the core of their asserted right. In support of their claim that the city of Chicago's handgun ban violates the Constitution, they now rely primarily on the Privileges or Immunities Clause of the Fourteenth Amendment. They rely secondarily on the Due Process Clause of that Amendment. Neither submission requires the Court to express an opinion on whether the Fourteenth Amendment places any limit on the power of States to regulate possession, use, or carriage of firearms outside the home.

I agree with the plurality's refusal to accept petitioners' primary submission. Their briefs marshal an impressive amount of historical evidence for their argument that the Court interpreted the Privileges or Immunities Clause too narrowly in the *Slaughter-House Cases*. But the original meaning of the Clause is not as clear as they suggest — and not nearly as clear as it would need to be to dislodge 137 years of precedent. ...

I further agree with the plurality that there are weighty arguments supporting petitioners' second submission, insofar as it concerns the possession of firearms for lawful self-defense in the home. But these arguments are less compelling than the plurality suggests; they are much less compelling when applied outside the home; and their validity does not depend on the Court's holding in *Heller*. For that holding sheds no light on the meaning of the Due Process Clause of the Fourteenth Amendment. Our decisions construing that Clause to render various procedural guarantees in the Bill of Rights enforceable against the States likewise tell us little about the meaning of the word "liberty" in the Clause or about the scope of its protection of nonprocedural rights.

This is a substantive due process case.

I. ...

The first, and most basic, principle established by our cases is that the rights protected by the Due Process Clause are not merely procedural in nature. At first glance, this proposition might seem surprising, given that the Clause refers to "process." But substance and procedure are often deeply entwined. Upon closer inspection, the text can be read to "impos[e] nothing less than an obligation to give substantive content to the words 'liberty' and 'due process of law,'" *Washington v. Glucksberg* (1997) (Souter, J., concurring in judgment), lest superficially fair procedures be permitted to "destroy the enjoyment" of life, liberty, and property, *Poe v. Ullman* (Harlan, J., dissenting), and the Clause's prepositional modifier be permitted to swallow its primary command. Procedural guarantees are hollow unless linked to substantive interests; and no amount of process can legitimize some deprivations. ...

The second principle woven through our cases is that substantive due process is fundamentally a matter of personal liberty. For it is the liberty clause of the Fourteenth Amendment that grounds our most important holdings in this field. It is the liberty clause that enacts the Constitution's "promise" that a measure of dignity and self-rule will be afforded to all persons. ...

It follows that the term "incorporation," like the term "unenumerated rights," is something of a misnomer. Whether an asserted substantive due process interest is explicitly named in one of the first eight Amendments to the Constitution or is not mentioned, the underlying inquiry is the same: We must ask whether the interest is "comprised within the term liberty." ...

The third precept to emerge from our case law flows from the second: The rights protected against state infringement by the Fourteenth Amendment's Due Process Clause need not be identical in shape or scope to the rights protected against Federal Government infringement by the various provisions of the Bill of Rights. ...

I do not mean to deny that there can be significant practical, as well as esthetic, benefits from treating rights symmetrically with regard to the State and Federal Governments. Jot-for-jot incorporation of a provision may entail greater protection of the right at issue and therefore greater freedom for those who hold it; jot-for-jot incorporation may also yield greater clarity about the contours of the legal rule. In a federalist system such as ours, however, this approach can carry substantial costs. When a federal court insists that state and local authorities follow its dictates on a matter not critical to personal liberty or procedural justice, the latter may be prevented from engaging in the kind of beneficent "experimentation in things social and economic" that ultimately redounds to the benefit of all Americans. *New State Ice Co. v. Liebmann* (Brandeis, J., dissenting). The costs of federal courts' imposing a uniform national standard may be especially high when the relevant regulatory interests vary significantly across localities, and when the ruling implicates the States' core police powers. . . .

II

So far, I have explained that substantive due process analysis generally requires us to consider the term "liberty" in the Fourteenth Amendment, and that this inquiry may be informed by but does not depend upon the content of the Bill of Rights. How should a court go about the analysis, then? Our precedents have established, not an exact methodology, but rather a framework for decisionmaking. In this respect, too, the Court's narrative fails to capture the continuity and flexibility in our doctrine. The basic inquiry was described by Justice Cardozo more than 70 years ago. When confronted with a substantive due process claim, we must ask whether the allegedly unlawful practice violates values "implicit in the concept of ordered liberty." If the practice in question lacks any "oppressive and arbitrary" character, if judicial enforcement of the asserted right would not materially contribute to "a fair and enlightened system of justice," then the claim is unsuitable for substantive due process protection. In Justice Cardozo's test is a recognition that the postulates of liberty have a universal character. Liberty claims that are inseparable from the customs that prevail in a certain region, the idiosyncratic expectations of a certain group, or the personal preferences of their champions, may be valid claims in some sense; but they are not of constitutional stature. Whether conceptualized as a "rational continuum" of legal precepts, *Poe* (Harlan, J., dissenting), or a seamless web of moral commitments, the rights embraced by the liberty clause transcend the local and the particular.

Justice Cardozo's test undeniably requires judges to apply their own reasoned judgment, but that does not mean it involves an exercise in abstract philosophy. [Historical] and empirical data of various kinds ground the analysis. Textual commitments laid down elsewhere in the Constitution, judicial precedents, English common law, legislative and social facts, scientific and professional developments, practices of other civilized societies, and, above all else, the "'traditions and conscience of our people,'" *Palko* (quoting *Snyder v. Massachusetts*, 291 U. S. 97, 105 (1934)), are critical variables. . . .

A rigid historical test is inappropriate in this case, most basically, because our substantive due process doctrine has never evaluated substantive rights in purely, or even predominantly, historical terms. . . .

The right to free speech, for instance, has been safeguarded from state infringement not because the States have always honored it, but because it is "essential to free government" and "to the maintenance of democratic institutions" — that is, because the right to free speech is implicit in the concept of ordered liberty. . . .

More fundamentally, a rigid historical methodology is unfaithful to the Constitution's command. For if it were really the case that the Fourteenth Amendment's guarantee of liberty embraces only those rights "so rooted in our history, tradition, and practice as to require special protection," *Glucksberg*, then the guarantee would serve little function, save to ratify those rights that state actors have already been according the most extensive protection. That approach is unfaithful to the expansive principle Americans laid down when they ratified the Fourteenth Amendment and to the level of generality they chose when they crafted its language; it promises an objectivity it cannot deliver and masks the value judgments that pervade any analysis of what customs, defined in what manner, are sufficiently "'rooted'"; it countenances the most revolting injustices in the name of continuity, for we must never forget that not only slavery but also the subjugation of women and other rank forms of discrimination are part of our history; and it effaces this Court's distinctive role in saying what the law is, leaving the development and safekeeping of liberty to majoritarian political processes. It is judicial abdication in the guise of judicial modesty. . . .

III

At this point a difficult question arises. In considering such a majestic term as "liberty" and applying it to present circumstances, how are we to do justice to its urgent call and its open texture — and to the grant of interpretive discretion the latter embodies — without injecting excessive subjectivity or unduly restricting the States' "broad latitude in experimenting with possible solutions to problems of vital local concern," *Whalen v. Roe*, 429 U. S. 589, 597 (1977)? One part of the answer, already discussed, is that we must ground the analysis in historical experience and reasoned judgment, and never on "merely personal and private notions." . . .

The most basic [guidepost] is that we have eschewed attempts to provide any all-purpose, top-down, totalizing theory of "liberty." That project is bound to end in failure or worse. The Framers did not express a clear understanding of the term to guide us, and the now-repudiated *Lochner* line of cases attests to the dangers of judicial overconfidence in using substantive due process to advance a broad theory of the right or the good. In its most durable precedents, the Court "has not attempted to define with exactness the liberty . . . guaranteed" by the Fourteenth Amendment. *Meyer*; see also, e.g., *Bolling*. By its very nature, the meaning of liberty cannot be "reduced to any formula; its content cannot be determined by reference to any code." *Poe* (Harlan, J., dissenting).

Yet while "the 'liberty' specially protected by the Fourteenth Amendment" is "perhaps not capable of being fully clarified," *Glucksberg*, it is capable of being refined and delimited. We have insisted that only certain types of especially significant personal interests may qualify for especially heightened protection.[24] . . .

Rather than seek a categorical understanding of the liberty clause, our precedents have thus elucidated a conceptual core. The clause safeguards, most basically, "the ability independently to define one's identity," *Roberts v. United States Jaycees*; "the individual's right to make certain unusually important decisions that will affect his own, or his family's, destiny," *Fitzgerald*, 523 F. 2d, at 719, and the right to be respected as a human being. Self-determination, bodily integrity, freedom of conscience, intimate relationships, political equality, dignity and respect—these are the central values we have found implicit in the concept of ordered liberty.

Another key constraint on substantive due process analysis is respect for the democratic process. If a particular liberty interest is already being given careful consideration in, and subjected to ongoing calibration by, the States, judicial enforcement may not be appropriate. When the Court declined to establish a general right to physician-assisted suicide, for example, it did so in part because "the States [were] currently engaged in serious, thoughtful examinations of physician-assisted suicide and other similar issues," rendering judicial intervention both less necessary and potentially more disruptive. Conversely, we have long appreciated that more "searching" judicial review may be justified when the rights of "discrete and insular minorities"—groups that may face systematic barriers in the political system—are at stake. Courts have a "comparative . . . advantage" over the elected branches on a limited, but significant, range of legal matters. . . .

---

24. That one eschews a comprehensive theory of liberty does not, pace JUSTICE SCALIA, mean that one lacks "a coherent theory of the Due Process Clause. It means that one lacks the hubris to adopt a rigid, context-independent definition of a constitutional guarantee that was deliberately framed in open-ended terms.

As this discussion reflects, to acknowledge that the task of construing the liberty clause requires judgment is not to say that it is a license for unbridled judicial lawmaking. To the contrary, only an honest reckoning with our discretion allows for honest argumentation and meaningful accountability.

IV. . . .

The question in this case, then, is not whether the Second Amendment right to keep and bear arms (whatever that right's precise contours) applies to the States because the Amendment has been incorporated into the Fourteenth Amendment. It has not been. The question, rather, is whether the particular right asserted by petitioners applies to the States because of the Fourteenth Amendment itself, standing on its own bottom. And to answer that question, we need to determine, first, the nature of the right that has been asserted and, second, whether that right is an aspect of Fourteenth Amendment "liberty." Even accepting the Court's holding in *Heller*, it remains entirely possible that the right to keep and bear arms identified in that opinion is not judicially enforceable against the States, or that only part of the right is so enforceable. . . .

As noted at the outset, the liberty interest petitioners have asserted is the "right to possess a functional, personal firearm, including a handgun, within the home." . . .

Understood as a plea to keep their preferred type of firearm in the home, petitioners' argument has real force. The decision to keep a loaded handgun in the house is often motivated by the desire to protect life, liberty, and property. It is comparable, in some ways, to decisions about the education and upbringing of one's children. For it is the kind of decision that may have profound consequences for every member of the family, and for the world beyond. In considering whether to keep a handgun, heads of households must ask themselves whether the desired safety benefits outweigh the risks of deliberate or accidental misuse that may result in death or serious injury, not only to residents of the home but to others as well. Millions of Americans have answered this question in the affirmative, not infrequently because they believe they have an inalienable right to do so—because they consider it an aspect of "the supreme human dignity of being master of one's fate rather than a ward of the State," *Indiana v. Edwards* (SCALIA, J., dissenting). Many such decisions have been based, in part, on family traditions and deeply held beliefs that are an aspect of individual autonomy the government may not control. Bolstering petitioners' claim, our law has long recognized that the home provides a kind of special sanctuary in modern life.

While the individual's interest in firearm possession is thus heightened in the home, the State's corresponding interest in regulation is somewhat weaker . . .

105

V

While I agree with the Court that our substantive due process cases offer a principled basis for holding that petitioners have a constitutional right to possess a usable fire arm in the home, I am ultimately persuaded that a better reading of our case law supports the city of Chicago. I would not foreclose the possibility that a particular plaintiff — say, an elderly widow who lives in a dangerous neighborhood and does not have the strength to operate a long gun — may have a cognizable liberty interest in possessing a handgun. But I cannot accept petitioners' broader submission. A number of factors, taken together, lead me to this conclusion.

First, firearms have a fundamentally ambivalent relationship to liberty. Just as they can help homeowners defend their families and property from intruders, they can help thugs and insurrectionists murder innocent victims. ...

Hence, in evaluating an asserted right to be free from particular gun-control regulations, liberty is on both sides of the equation. Guns may be useful for self-defense, as well as for hunting and sport, but they also have a unique potential to facilitate death and destruction and thereby to destabilize ordered liberty. ...

Second, the right to possess a firearm of one's choosing is different in kind from the liberty interests we have recognized under the Due Process Clause. Despite the plethora of substantive due process cases that have been decided in the post-*Lochner* century, I have found none that holds, states, or even suggests that the term "liberty" encompasses either the common-law right of self-defense or a right to keep and bear arms. I do not doubt for a moment that many Americans feel deeply passionate about firearms, and see them as critical to their way of life as well as to their security. Nevertheless, it does not appear to be the case that the ability to own a handgun, or any particular type of firearm, is critical to leading a life of autonomy, dignity, or political equality: The marketplace offers many tools for self-defense, even if they are imperfect substitutes, and neither petitioners nor their amici make such a contention. Petitioners' claim is not the kind of substantive interest, accordingly, on which a uniform, judicially enforced national standard is presumptively appropriate. ...

[The] experience of other advanced democracies, including those that share our British heritage, undercuts the notion that an expansive right to keep and bear arms is intrinsic to ordered liberty. Many of these countries place restrictions on the possession, use, and carriage of firearms far more onerous than the restrictions found in this Nation. ...

VI. ...

The preceding sections have already addressed many of the points made by JUSTICE SCALIA in his concurrence. But in light of that opinion's fixation on this one, it is appropriate to say a few words about JUSTICE SCALIA's broader claim: that his preferred method of substantive due process analysis, a method "that makes the traditions of our people paramount," is both more restrained and more facilitative of democracy than the method I have outlined. Colorful as it is, JUSTICE SCALIA's critique does not have nearly as much force as does his rhetoric. His theory of substantive due process, moreover, comes with its own profound difficulties. Although JUSTICE SCALIA aspires to an "objective," "neutral" method of substantive due process analysis, his actual method is nothing of the sort. Under the "historically focused" approach he advocates, numerous threshold questions arise before one ever gets to the history. At what level of generality should one frame the liberty interest in question? What does it mean for a right to be "'deeply rooted in this Nation's history and tradition'"? By what standard will that proposition be tested? Which types of sources will count, and how will those sources be weighed and aggregated? There is no objective, neutral answer to these questions. There is not even a theory — at least, JUSTICE SCALIA provides none — of how to go about answering them.

Nor is there any escaping *Palko*, it seems. To qualify for substantive due process protection, JUSTICE SCALIA has stated, an asserted liberty right must be not only deeply rooted in American tradition, "but it must also be implicit in the concept of ordered liberty." Applying the latter, *Palko*-derived half of that test requires precisely the sort of reasoned judgment — the same multifaceted evaluation of the right's contours and consequences — that JUSTICE SCALIA mocks in his concurrence today.

So does applying the first half. It is hardly a novel insight that history is not an objective science, and that its use can therefore "point in any direction the judges favor." Yet 21 years after the point was brought to his attention by Justice Brennan, JUSTICE SCALIA remains "oblivious to the fact that [the concept of 'tradition'] can be as malleable and elusive as 'liberty' itself." *Michael H.* (dissenting opinion). ...

JUSTICE SCALIA's method invites not only bad history, but also bad constitutional law. As I have already explained in evaluating a claimed liberty interest (or any constitutional claim for that matter), it makes perfect sense to give history significant weight: JUSTICE SCALIA's position is closer to my own than he apparently feels comfortable acknowledging. But it makes little sense to give history dispositive weight in every case. And it makes especially little sense to answer questions like whether the right to bear arms is "fundamental" by focusing only on the past, given that both the practical significance and the public understandings of such a right often change as society changes. What if the evidence had shown that, whereas at one time firearm possession contributed substantially to personal liberty and safety, nowadays it contributes nothing, or even tends to undermine them? Would it still have been reasonable to constitutionalize the right?

The concern runs still deeper. Not only can historical views be less than completely clear or informative, but they can also be wrong. Some notions that many Americans deeply believed to be true, at one time, turned out not to be true. Some practices that many Americans believed to be consistent with the Constitution's guarantees of liberty and equality, at one time, turned out to be inconsistent with them. The fact that we have a written Constitution does not consign this Nation to a static legal existence. Although we should always "pa[y] a decent regard to the opinions of former times," it "is not the glory of the people of America" to have "suffered a blind veneration for antiquity." The Federalist No. 14, (J. Madison). It is not the role of federal judges to be amateur historians. And it is not fidelity to the Constitution to ignore its use of deliberately capacious language, in an effort to transform foundational legal commitments into narrow rules of decision. . . .

JUSTICE BREYER, with whom JUSTICE GINSBURG and JUSTICE SOTOMAYOR join, dissenting.

In my view, JUSTICE STEVENS has demonstrated that the Fourteenth Amendment's guarantee of "substantive due process" does not include a general right to keep and bear firearms for purposes of private self-defense. As he argues, the Framers did not write the Second Amendment with this objective in view. Unlike other forms of substantive liberty, the carrying of arms for that purpose often puts others' lives at risk. And the use of arms for private self-defense does not warrant federal constitutional protection from state regulation.

The Court, however, does not expressly rest its opinion upon "substantive due process" concerns. Rather, it directs its attention to this Court's "incorporation" precedents and asks whether the Second Amendment right to private self-defense is "fundamental" so that it applies to the States through the Fourteenth Amendment.

I shall therefore separately consider the question of "incorporation." I can find nothing in the Second Amendment's text, history, or underlying rationale that could warrant characterizing it as "fundamental" insofar as it seeks to protect the keeping and bearing of arms for private self-defense purposes. Nor can I find any justification for interpreting the Constitution as transferring ultimate regulatory authority over the private uses of firearms from democratically elected legislatures to courts or from the States to the Federal Government. I therefore conclude that the Fourteenth Amendment does not "incorporate" the Second Amendment's right "to keep and bear Arms." And I consequently dissent. . . .

[Justice Breyer criticizes the *Heller* Court's historical analysis supporting an individual right to bear arms.]

My aim in referring to this history is to illustrate the reefs and shoals that lie in wait for those nonexpert judges who place virtually determinative weight upon historical considerations. In my own view, the Court should not look to history alone but to other factors as well — above all, in cases where the history is so unclear that the experts themselves strongly disagree. It should, for example, consider the basic values that underlie a constitutional provision and their contemporary significance. And it should examine as well the relevant consequences and practical justifications that might, or might not, warrant removing an important question from the democratic decisionmaking process. . . .

[There] is no popular consensus that the private self-defense right described in *Heller* is fundamental. The plurality suggests that two amici briefs filed in the case show such a consensus but, of course, numerous amici briefs have been filed opposing incorporation as well. Moreover, every State regulates fire arms extensively, and public opinion is sharply divided on the appropriate level of regulation. Much of this disagreement rests upon empirical considerations. One side believes the right essential to protect the lives of those attacked in the home; the other side believes it essential to regulate the right in order to protect the lives of others attacked with guns. It seems unlikely that definitive evidence will develop one way or the other. And the appropriate level of firearm regulation has thus long been, and continues to be, a hotly contested matter of political debate.

Moreover, there is no reason here to believe that incorporation of the private self-defense right will further any other or broader constitutional objective. We are aware of no argument that gun-control regulations target or are passed with the purpose of targeting "discrete and insular minorities." *Carolene Products.* Nor will incorporation help to assure equal respect for individuals. Unlike the First Amendment's rights of free speech, free press, assembly, and petition, the private self-defense right does not comprise a necessary part of the democratic process that the Constitution seeks to establish. Unlike the First Amendment's religious protections, the Fourth Amendment's protection against unreasonable searches and seizures, the Fifth and Sixth Amendments' insistence upon fair criminal procedure, and the Eighth Amendment's protection against cruel and unusual punishments, the private self-defense right does not significantly seek to protect individuals who might otherwise suffer unfair or inhumane treatment at the hands of a majority. Unlike the protections offered by many of these same Amendments, it does not involve matters as to which judges possess a comparative expertise, by virtue of their close familiarity with the justice system and its operation. And, unlike the Fifth Amendment's insistence on just compensation, it does not involve a matter where a majority might unfairly seize for itself property belonging to a minority.

Finally, incorporation of the right will work a significant disruption in the constitutional allocation of decisionmaking authority, thereby interfering with the Constitution's ability to further its objectives. . . .

[The] specific question before us is not whether there are references to the right to bear arms for self-defense throughout this Nation's history — of course there are — or even whether the Court should incorporate a simple constitutional requirement that firearms regulations not unreasonably burden the right to keep and bear arms, but rather whether there is a consensus that so substantial a private self-defense right as the one described in *Heller* applies to the States. In my view, [the historical] record is insufficient to say that the right to bear arms for private self-defense, as explicated by *Heller*, is fundamental in the sense relevant to the incorporation inquiry. [States] and localities have consistently enacted firearms regulations, including regulations similar to those at issue here, throughout our Nation's history. Courts have repeatedly upheld such regulations. And it is, at the very least, possible, and perhaps likely, that incorporation will impose on every, or nearly every, State a different right to bear arms than they currently recognize — a right that threatens to destabilize settled state legal principles. ...

D. Substantive Due Process: The Protection of Economic Interests and the Question of Redistribution

Page 759. Before section 2 of the Note, add the following:

Consider the following exchange in Stop the Beach Renourishment v. Florida Dept. of Environmental Protection, 130 S. Ct. 2592 (2010), between Justice Scalia, writing for a plurality of the Court and Justice Kennedy, writing for himself and Justice Sotomayor, on the modern applicability of economic substantive due process. The issue in the case was whether a state judicial decision about the property rights of beachfront property owners constituted a "taking" within the meaning of the fifth amendment as incorporated against the states by the fourteenth amendment. The Court was unanimous in holding that, on these facts, no taking had occurred, but the justices disagreed about what approach to adopt more generally regarding putative judicial takings. Justice Kennedy urged caution in applying takings doctrine in part because

[if] a judicial decision, as opposed to an act of the executive or the legislature, eliminates an established property right, the judgment could be set aside as a deprivation of property without due process of law. The Due Process Clause, in both its substantive and procedural aspects, is a

central limitation upon the exercise of judicial power. And this Court has long recognized that property regulations can be invalidated under the Due Process Clause.

In reply, Justice Scalia stated that

we have held for many years (logically or not) that the "liberties" protected by Substantive Due Process do not include economic liberties. Justice Kennedy's language propels us back to what is referred to (usually deprecatingly) as "the *Lochner* era." That is a step of much greater novelty, and much more unpredictable effect, than merely applying the Takings Clause to judicial action.

F. *Modern Substantive Due Process: Privacy, Personhood, and Family*

Page 842.   At the end of section 4 of the Note, add the following:

As you read the material that follows, consider the following assessment in Greene, The So-Called Right to Privacy, 43 U.C. Davis. L. Rev. 715, 717-718 (2010):

The doctrinal life of the constitutional right to privacy is over. [The] right to obtain an abortion is now conceptualized by its defenders either in terms of women's equality or, nonexclusively, as a specific application of a constitutional liberty right to make fundamental life decisions. The rights to use contraception and to participate in a consensual, noncommercial sexual relationship are also defended as aspects of the right to liberty, protected against state abridgement by the Due Process Clause. The projects and activities that the right to privacy was crafted to protect owe it a debt of gratitude, but the right to privacy as such has no clothes.

This should be a cause for celebration among progressives and libertarians. [It] is not impossible to construct a theoretical account that grounds the right to use contraception, to have an abortion, or to participate in intimate sexual relationships in a right to privacy, but doing so invites the troublesome corollary that the justice underlying these rights has anything at all to do with publicity, information-sharing, or discretion more generally. As importantly, the rights to equality and liberty can boast the textual hook that the right to privacy has always coveted. [To] the extent the conservative textualist movement that Justice Scalia has pushed has won tactical turf battles over constitutional methodology, locating a textual basis for rights previously described under the privacy rubric beats back the infantry attack, even if it doesn't quite win the war.

Page 898.   Before section 2 of the Note, add the following:

Compare Suk, The Trajectory of Trauma: Bodies and Minds of Abortion Discourse, 110 Colum. L. Rev. 1193, 1197 (2010):

[A] significant context for the newly prominent legal discourses of abortion regret is the legal reception of psychological trauma that has continually gained momentum through feminist legal thought and reform since the 1970s. [The] reasoning continues [a] feminist discourse of trauma around women's bodies and sexuality. This intellectual context, which has been all but ignored, gives important meaning to the present discourse of women's psychological pain in our legal system. The ideas informing abortion regret are utterly familiar once contextualized in modern legal understandings of women in the period since *Roe*....

A major contribution of feminist critique since the 1970s has been to show how concepts of coercion and consent are not clear-cut. Hence, today, we have a range of legal policies in which protecting women sometimes entails treating choices that seem to harm them as not meaningfully voluntary. This kind of questioning of whether women are truly choosing for themselves appears to inform antiabortion concerns about abortion trauma.

Page 910.   Before the Note, add the following:

For an argument that "the system's support of family privacy hinges critically on social inequalities," see Roberts, The Dialectic of Privacy and Punishment in the Gendered Regulation of Parenting, 5 Stan. J. Civ. Rts. & Civ. Lib. 191, 200 (2009). The author argues that "[the welfare] system's race and class geography means that most parents, especially middle-class and affluent white parents, justifiably sense little risk of ever being involved in it." She suggests that "these parents are encouraged to accept the private childrearing norm by the miniscule risk of social workers knocking on their door."

G. Procedural Due Process

Page 951.   At the end of section 1c of the Note, add the following:

d. *DNA testing.* In District Attorney's Office for the Third Judicial District v. Osborne, 129 S. Ct. 2308 (2009), the Court, in a five-to-four decision written by Chief Justice Roberts, held that there was no liberty interest in access to DNA evidence. Osborne had been convicted sixteen years earlier of kidnapping, assault, and sexual assault. The evidence against him included a statement by Jackson, who admitted to participating in the rape and assault, that Osborne had been a passenger in his car during the incident; an uncertain photo identification by the victim; statements by other witnesses that shortly before the incident, Jackson had driven off with Osborne; and an axe handle, similar to the one at the scene of the crime, found in Osborne's room.

The state performed DQ Alpha DNA testing on sperm found in a condom left at the scene. This is a relatively inexact form of DNA testing. The semen had a genotype that matched a blood sample taken from Osborne. Osborne is black, and approximately 16 percent of black individuals have this genotype.

Osborne's trial lawyer later testified that she did not request RFLP testing, a more precise DNA procedure, because she believed her client guilty and thought that the more precise test would harm his defense. However, Osborne claimed that he had specifically asked his lawyer to request the more precise test. The lawyer stated that she had no memory of Osborne making this request, but said that she was "willing to accept" that he had.

After his conviction, Osborne admitted his guilt in the course of parole hearings — a requirement in order to be eligible for parole.

In this federal lawsuit, Osborne claimed the right to access to the DNA evidence so that he could perform at his own expense STR testing — a much more accurate DNA procedure that was not available at the time of his trial.

Writing for the Court, Chief Justice Roberts observed that "the availability of technologies not available at trial cannot mean that every criminal conviction or even every criminal conviction involving biological evidence, is suddenly in doubt. The dilemma is how to harness DNA's power to prove innocence without unnecessarily overthrowing the established system of criminal justice. [That] task belongs primarily to the legislature."

Chief Justice Roberts observed that forty-six states, although not Alaska, where this case arose, had enacted statutes dealing with access to DNA. These laws, while allowing some access, also imposed conditions like a requirement of demonstrating materiality or a sworn statement that the applicant is innocent.

The Court acknowledged that Osborne had a liberty interest in demonstrating his innocence with new evidence under state law. It did not follow, however that "the Due Process Clause requires that certain familiar preconviction trial rights be extended to protect Osborne's postconviction liberty interest. [A] criminal defendant proved guilty after a fair trial does not have the same liberty interests as a free man."

According to the Court, the standard was "whether consideration of Osborne's claim within the framework of the State's procedures for postconviction relief 'offends some principle of justice so rooted in the traditions and conscience of our people as to be ranked as fundamental,' or 'transgresses any recognized principle of fundamental fairness in operation.'" (Quoting Medina v. California, 505 U.S. 437, 446, 448 (1992)).

The Court found Alaska's procedures adequate under this standard.

> Alaska provides a substantive right to be released on a sufficiently compelling showing of new evidence that establishes innocence. [The] State provides for discovery in postconviction proceedings, and has [specified] that this discovery procedure is available to those seeking access to DNA evidence. These procedures are not without limits. The evidence must indeed be newly available, [must] have been diligently pursued, and must also be sufficiently material. These procedures [are] not inconsistent with the "traditions and conscience of our people" or with "any recognized principle of fundamental fairness."

The Court also rejected Osborne's claim that he had been denied substantive due process, a claim that it characterized as "a freestanding right to DNA evidence untethered from the liberty interests he hopes to vindicate with it."

> The elected governments of the States are actively confronting the challenges DNA technology poses to our criminal justice systems and our traditional notions of finality, as well as the opportunities it affords. To suddenly constitutionalize this area would short-circuit what looks to be a prompt and considered legislative response.

In a concurring opinion, Justice Alito, joined by Justice Kennedy and joined in this part by Justice Thomas, pointed out that the state had valid interests in denying DNA testing. DNA testing "often fails to provide 'absolute proof' of anything." Moreover, "the State has important interests in maintaining the integrity of its evidence, and the risks associated with evidence contamination increase every time someone attempts to extract new DNA from a sample."

Finally, Justice Alito noted that "[the] resources required to process and analyze [hundreds] of thousands of samples have created severe backlogs in state crime labs across the country."

Justice Stevens, joined by Justices Ginsburg and Breyer and joined in part by Justice Souter, dissented:

> The State of Alaska possesses physical evidence that, if tested, will conclusively establish whether [Osborne] committed rape and attempted murder. If he did, justice has been served by his conviction and sentence. If not, Osborne has needlessly spent decades behind bars while the true culprit has not been brought to justice. The DNA test Osborne seeks is a simple one, its cost modest, and its results uniquely precise. Yet for reasons the State has been unable or unwilling to articulate, it refuses to allow Osborne to test the evidence at his own expense and to thereby ascertain the truth once and for all.

Contrary to the majority's position, Justice Stevens argued that state procedures were inadequate to provide Osborne with access to the evidence and that "[t]he fact that nearly all the States have now recognized some post-conviction right to DNA evidence makes it more, not less, appropriate to recognize a limited federal right to such evidence in cases where litigants are unfairly barred from obtaining relief in state court."

Justice Souter also filed a dissenting opinion.

Page 957. Before section 2 of the Note, add the following:

In Turner v. Rodgers, 131 S. Ct. 2507 (2011), the Court, in an opinion by Justice Breyer, held that the due process clause did not automatically require the state to provide counsel to an indigent person confronting civil contempt for failure to pay child support, even if the individual faces incarceration. The Court nonetheless held that Turner's incarceration violated the due process clause because the state had failed to provide him with "alternative safeguards."

Using the *Mathews* balancing test, the Court conceded that the importance of private interest at stake — loss of personal liberty through imprisonment — "argues strongly for the right to counsel." The Court nonetheless thought that three other considerations made counsel unnecessary. First, the critical issue in cases of nonsupport is ability to pay, but this issue would have to be resolved without counsel in any event to determine whether the defendant was indigent and therefore eligible for state-provided counsel. Second, the private individual opposing the nonpaying parent is often without counsel. Finally, alternative safeguards could reduce the risk of error without providing counsel. These safeguards included notice to the defendant that ability to pay was a critical issue, the use of a form to elicit relevant financial information, opportunity for the defendant to respond to statements and questions about his financial status at the hearing, and an express finding by the court that the defendant had the ability to pay. Because Turner had not been afforded these alternative safeguards, the Court held that his incarceration violated the due process clause.

In a dissenting opinion joined by Justice Scalia and joined in part by Chief Justice Roberts and Justice Alito, Justice Thomas agreed that the due process clause did not guarantee a right to counsel. However, because the issue was not raised by the parties, the dissenters would not have decided whether alternative procedural safeguards were required.

Page 960.   After section 4 of the Note, add the following:

5. *Bias.* Does the Due Process Clause guarantee an unbiased decisionmaker? What does "bias" mean in this context?

Consider Caperton v. A. T. Massey Coal Co., 129 S. Ct. 2252 (2009). A West Virginia jury found that defendant Massey was guilty of fraudulent misrepresentation, concealment, and tortuous interference with existing contractual relations and awarded plaintiff Caperton $50 million in damages. Knowing that the Supreme Court of Appeals of West Virginia would consider an appeal in the case, Blankenship, Massey's chairman and chief executive officer, spent over $3 million directly and indirectly supporting the election of Benjamin to a seat on the Court. This was more than the total amount spent by all other Benjamin supporters, three times the amount spent by Benjamin's own committee, and, apparently, $1 million more than the total amount spent by the campaign committees of both candidates combined. Benjamin won the election. Despite repeated requests that he recuse himself, Benjamin sat on the appeal in the Massey case and cast the deciding vote in a three-to-two decision to reverse the result below.

In a five-to-four decision, the Court, in an opinion by Justice Kennedy, held that the due process clause required Benjamin's recusal. The Court noted that "[n]ot every campaign contribution by a litigant or attorney creates a probability of bias that requires a judge's recusal, but this is an exceptional case."

[There] is a serious risk of actual bias — based on objective and reasonable perceptions — when a person with a personal stake in a particular case had a significant and disproportionate influence in placing the judge on the case by raising funds or directing the judge's election campaign when the case was pending or imminent. The inquiry centers on the contribution's relative size in comparison to the total amount of money contributed to the campaign, the total amount spent in the election, and the apparent effect such contribution had on the outcome of the election. . . .

Just as no man is allowed to be a judge in his own cause, similar fears of bias can arise when — without the consent of the other parties — a man chooses the judge in his own cause. And applying this principle to the judicial election process, there was here a serious, objective risk of actual bias that required Justice Benjamin's recusal.

Chief Justice Roberts, joined by Justices Scalia, Thomas, and Alito, dissented:

I, of course, share the majority's sincere concerns about the need to maintain a fair, independent, and impartial judiciary — and one that appears to be such. But I fear that the Court's decision will undermine rather than promote these values. . . .

Unlike the established grounds for disqualification, a "probability of bias" cannot be defined in any limited way. The Court's new "rule" provides no guidance to judges and litigants about when recusal will be constitutionally required. This will inevitably lead to an increase in allegations that judges are biased, however groundless those charges may be. The end result will do far more to erode public confidence in judicial impartiality than an isolated failure to recuse in a particular case.

Justice Scalia also wrote a dissenting opinion.

H.   The Contracts and Takings Clauses

Page 1009.   At the end of the Note, add the following:

6. *Judicial takings.*   Can a judicial shift in common law property rules constitute an unconstitutional taking? The Court sharply divided on this question in Stop the Beach Renourishment v. Florida Dept. of Environmental Protection, 130 S. Ct. 2592 (2010). At issue was a Florida program to repair beach erosion by depositing sand on eroded beaches. The program had the effect of turning previously submerged land into beachfront. The Florida Supreme Court held that under Florida common law property principles, this land

belonged to the government rather than the private property owners, whose land had previously extended to the shore line. A unanimous Court, in an opinion written by Justice Scalia, held that the Florida court's holding did not constitute a change in the common law and, therefore, was not an uncompensated taking. Writing for only four of the eight Justices participating, Justice Scalia, joined by Chief Justice Roberts and Justices Thomas and Alito, went on to state that

> The Takings Clause [is] not addressed to the action of a specific branch or branches. It is concerned simply with the act, and not with the governmental actor. [There] is no textual justification for saying that the existence or the scope of a State's power to expropriate private property without just compensation varies according to the branch of government effecting the expropriation. Nor does common sense recommend such a principle. It would be absurd to allow a State to do by judicial decree what the Takings Clause forbids it to do by legislative fiat. ...
>
> If a legislature *or a court* declares that what was once an established right of private property no longer exists, it has taken that property, no less than if the State had physically appropriated it or destroyed its value by regulation.

Justice Scalia conceded that the Framers did not envision that the takings clause would apply to judicial action:

> They doubtless did not, since the Constitution was adopted in an era when courts had no power to "change" the common law. [Where] the text they adopted is clear, however, [what] counts is not what they envisioned but what they wrote.

Writing for himself and Justice Sotomayor, Justice Kennedy argued that the case did not require the Court to determine when or whether a judicial decision determining the rights of property owners violated the takings clause and pointed to "certain difficulties that should be considered before accepting [such a] theory." Justice Kennedy suggested that the due process clause might better serve the function of protecting settled property expectations in this situation.

Justice Breyer, joined by Justice Ginsburg, agreed that "[there] is no need now to decide more than [that] the Florida Supreme Court's decision in this case did not amount to a 'judicial taking.'" He argued that Justice Scalia's approach "would invite a host of federal takings claims without the mature consideration of potential procedural or substantive legal principles that might limit federal interference in matters that are primarily the subject of state law" and that the Court therefore should not resolve the issue in this case.

Justice Stevens did not participate.

Under Justice Scalia's approach, suppose that a state court overrules a prior decision, holding that the prior decision had misinterpreted the common law and that the new decision returned to common law principles. If the new decision diminishes property rights protected by the prior decision, is it a taking?

7
FREEDOM OF
EXPRESSION

A. *Introduction*

Page 1023.   After subsection 1c of the Note, add the following:

d. Lidsky, Nobody's Fools: The Rational Audience as First Amendment Ideal, 2010 U. Ill. L. Rev. 299:

[The Supreme] Court defaults to a set of normative assumptions which, taken together, reflects an idealized vision of the audience [for] speech. The first of these assumptions is that audiences are capable of rationally assessing the truth, quality, and credibility [of] speech. The second is that more speech is generally preferable to less.

[Empirical] work in the fields of cognitive psychology and behavioral economics suggests that both the rational audience and the more-is-better assumptions may be demonstrably false. [Behavioral] economics [recognizes] that "markets are not perfectly efficient, people are not always good guardians of their own self-interest and there might be limited circumstances when government could usefully slant the decision-making architecture" to encourage better policy decisions. [This] suggests that the marketplace of ideas is flawed because humans are flawed: they are not rational information processors, and more information often leads to worse decisions instead of better ones. . . .

Yet the implications of this evidence for First Amendment doctrine are unclear. Government actors are not immune from the constraints on rationality affecting their fellow citizens. And even if individuals are only rational in fits and starts, the evidence is not at all clear that this irrationality infects aggregate decision making. [Moreover, the rationality assumption] is also important as an aspirational norm. First Amendment doctrine encourages us to develop our capacities to engage in the level of public discourse democratic theory demands. [Perhaps] more significantly, both the rationality assumption and the more-is-better assumption serve as a check on government's increasingly powerful attempts to use its agenda-setting power to manipulate public discourse. Finally, a State that indulges an irrationality assumption [fails] to respect the autonomy of its citizens, an autonomy upon which a self-governing democracy depends.

Even if the assumptions underlying marketplace theory are false, it does not necessarily follow that citizens would be better served by increased filtering of information flowing into the marketplace of ideas. Experts are often subject to the same cognitive biases as the rest of us, and self-interest is just as likely to taint their decisions. [Filtering] is unlikely to be performed by completely disinterested parties, and less than perfect decision making may be a reasonable price to pay to preserve First Amendment, and indeed democratic, values.

e. For a feminist critique of the search for truth rationale, see Williams, Feminist Theory and Freedom of Speech, 84 Ind. L.J. 999 (2009).

Page 1027.   After subsection c of the Note, add the following:

d. *Free speech in ancient Greece.* For an interesting comparison of American and Athenian free speech principles, see Werhan, The Classical Athenian Ancestry of American Freedom of Speech, 2008 Sup. Ct. Rev. 293.

B. *Content-Based Restrictions: Dangerous Ideas and Information*

Page 1042.   After section 5 of the Note, add the following:

5A. *Why should it matter whether the harm is imminent?* Consider Healy, Brandenburg in a Time of Terror, 84 Notre Dame L. Rev. 655, 705-709 (2009):

When a speaker urges listeners to commit a crime right now or very soon and those listeners are likely to comply, there is almost nothing the government or anyone else can do to prevent the crime from occurring. [The] government's only alternative is to criminalize the advocacy in the hope of deterring speakers from engaging in it to begin with. But when a speaker urges listeners to violate law in the future, the government has several alternatives. First, [the] police have at least some ability to prevent the crime from occurring. [Second], when a speaker advocates future crime, other speakers have an opportunity to rebut his arguments and discourage his listeners from breaking the law. [The] third alternative to government regulation is not so much an alternative as a reason to think that prohibiting advocacy of future crime is not necessary to prevent the crime from occurring. When a speaker urges listeners to break the law, they may initially be persuaded by the force of his arguments and the intensity of his convictions. But as time passes and listeners reflect on the speaker's message, the persuasive force of his words may diminish. This seems especially likely when listeners are urged to violate the [law, because most] people are socially conditioned to follow the law and do not commit crimes lightly. [Finally], determining whether criminal advocacy is likely to lead to crime is not easy. The success of speech depends on a range of factors that cannot easily be assessed by the speaker at the time he speaks, by the police at the time of arrest, or by courts at the time of trial. In addition, because those who advocate crime are usually not sympathetic, the likelihood of success is almost certain to be overestimated.

Page 1046.   Before section 1 of the Note, add the following:

1a. *Benjamin Gitlow.* Gitlow was represented at trial by Clarence Darrow. "Gitlow informed Darrow that if put on the witness stand, he 'would not deny, but affirm and defend every communist principle in the *Left Wing Manifesto.*' That was not welcome news to Darrow, but he realized Gitlow was beyond argument: 'Well, I suppose a revolutionist must have his say in court even if it kills him.'" When Gitlow addressed the court, he made his position clear: "'I am a revolutionist. [I]n order to bring about socialism, capitalist governments must be overthrown. My whole life has been dedicated to the movement which I am in. No jail will change my opinion.' [Darrow] tried to soften the message [by presenting] Gitlow as one in a long line of eccentric 'dreamers,'" but to no avail. Defendants in similar prosecutions were pardoned by New York Governor Al Smith, who explained that "The public assertion of an erroneous doctrine is perhaps the surest way to disclose the error," but Gitlow declined a pardon so he could enable the ACLU to take his case to the Supreme Court. Shortly after the Court upheld his conviction, Gitlow was pardoned by Governor Smith. Years later, after being disillusioned by developments in the Soviet Union, Gitlow publicly repudiated his former views. In 1939, he testified before the Dies

Committee (the forerunner of the House Un-American Activities Committee) and by the 1950s he was testifying regularly against alleged Communists in prosecutions under the Smith Act and condemned the ACLU for being too-willing to defend Communists. Lendler, The Time to Kill a Snake: *Gitlow v. New York* and the Bad-Tendency Doctrine, 36 J. Sup. Ct. Hist. 11 (No. 1) (2011).

Page 1051.   At the end of section 4 of the Note, add the following:

Is the "right to associate" protected at all by the First Amendment? If so, does it give First Amendment protection to shopping clubs, the Red Cross, and Metropolitan Museum of Art? Consider Bhagwat, Associational Speech, 120 Yale L. J. 978, 994, 1000-1001 (2011):

> [S]elf-governance has been advanced as a theory of *free speech*. [But] it is better understood as a theory of the First Amendment generally. [F]ree speech and a free press are undoubtedly essential components of democratic self-governance. But so are the freedoms of assembly, association, and petition. All of these protected activities are distinct, though interrelated, forms of citizen participation in government that work in tandem to make that participation meaningful. . . .
>
> Protected associations are those whose primary goals are relevant to the democratic process. These include not only expression but also political organization, value formation, and the cultivation of skills relevant to participation in the democratic process. [An] environment organization, such as the Sierra Club, for example, might run publicity campaigns, lobby and litigate, but it might also organize local clean-up days, tree planting, and hikes. The latter activities are not themselves protected by the First Amendment, but the existence and autonomy of an association directed at such goals should be protected because of the value-forming function of such activities, regardless of whether that association also engages in expression or in the political process. . . .
>
> In contrast to the wide range of broadly democratic associations that deserve First Amendment protection, certain associations whose primary goals are immaterial to democracy do not. The most obvious are commercial associations, including for-profit corporations and other commercial [entities], whose primary goal is to make money.

Do you agree that an environmental group that does nothing but plant trees and plan hikes is entitled to First Amendment protection? What about a gun club that exists to plan hunting expeditions? Do you agree that "commercial associations," like Joe's Garage, aren't protected by the First Amendment? What if Joe's Garage makes contributions to political candidates who support laws that benefit garages?

Page 1066.   After section 4d of the Note, add the following:

e. *Solicitation v. incitement.* Suppose X meets Y in a bar and tries to persuade Y to kill Z, X's husband. Assuming the government can prove that X intended to persuade Y to kill Z, can X be convicted of soliciting the commission of a murder? Is this situation governed by *Brandenburg*? If not, why not? Suppose X posts on a website that she hates her husband, that he has made her life miserable, and that she wants someone to "kill the bastard." To that end, she includes his photograph and detailed information about his daily routine. Is this situation governed by *Brandenburg*?

In United States v. White, 610 F.3d 956 (7th Cir. 2010), the Court of Appeals upheld an indictment for soliciting a crime of violence based on an internet posting in which White identified an individual who had served on the jury that convicted a well-known white supremacist, stating that "everyone associated" with the trial "deserved assassination." Consider the court's reasoning: "Speech related to the express and advocacy of unpopular, and even violent ideas, receives *Brandenburg* protection. [But] speech integral to criminal conduct [remains] outside [First Amendment] protection. This type of speech "brigaded with action" becomes an overt act [that] can be regulated. [In the case of criminal solicitation, the speech — asking another to commit a crime — is the punishable act. [The] crime is complete once the words are spoken with the requisite intent. [Also], a specific person-to-person request is not required. [So], whether or not the First Amendment protects White's right to post personal information about Juror A [turns] on his intent in posting that information. If White's intent [was] to request that one of his readers harm Juror A, then the crime of solicitation would be complete. [If], on the other hand, White intent was to make a political point about [the trial] or to facilitate opportunities for other people to make [their] views known to Juror A, then he would not be guilty of solicitation." Is *White* distinguishable from *Claiborne Hardware*?

Page 1066.   After Section 4 of the Note, add the following:

4A. *Material Support.* A federal statute declares it unlawful for any person knowingly to provide "material support" to a designated foreign terrorist

125

organization. "Material support" includes, among other things, "training, expert advice or assistance." Plaintiffs want to train two designated foreign terrorist organizations, which engage in political and humanitarian as well as violent terrorist activities, how to use international law to resolve disputes peacefully, and to engage in political advocacy on behalf of these organizations and their causes.

Plaintiffs assert that the statute violates the First Amendment because it does not require the government to prove that, in assisting these organizations, they specifically intend to further the organizations' unlawful activities. Plaintiffs rely on *Scales*, in which the Court held that an individual could not constitutionally be punished for being a "knowing" member of the Communist Party, which had "both legal and illegal aims," unless the government proved that he specifically intended to promote the Party's illegal aims (that is, in the context of *Scales*, "to bring about the overthrow of government as speedily as circumstances would permit").

In Holder v. Humanitarian Law Project, 130 S. Ct. 2705 (2010), the Court, in a six-to-three decision, distinguished *Scales* and upheld the material support provision. Writing for the Court, Chief Justice Roberts distinguished *Scales* on the ground that it dealt with mere membership, rather than with the provision of "material support."

What, then, is "material support"? Suppose a supporter of a foreign terrorist organization gives a speech claiming that the organization's activities are morally justified? Can she be punished under the material support statute because she has "knowingly" provided support to a designated organization? This would seem to take First Amendment jurisprudence all the way back to *Shaffer* and *Schenck*. To avoid this difficulty, Chief Justice Roberts reasoned that the statute does not forbid independent advocacy, but only "speech to, under the direction of, or in coordination with" a designated terrorist organization. Is this a persuasive distinction? Is the notion akin to conspiracy — but without any requirement of specific intent to further the unlawful conduct?

In addressing the First Amendment issue, Roberts observed that "[e]veryone agrees that the Government's interest in combating terrorism is an urgent objective of the highest order." The plaintiffs maintained, however, that their speech is intended to "advance only the legitimate activities of the designated terrorist organizations, not their terrorism." Roberts responded that Congress had made specific findings that "any form of material support furnished 'to' a foreign terrorist organization" will have "harmful effects," regardless of the intent of the speaker. For example, such "support frees up other resources within the organization that may be put to violent ends" and "helps lend legitimacy to foreign terrorist groups — legitimacy that makes it easier for those groups to persist, to recruit members, and to raise funds — all of which facilitate more terrorist attacks." Moreover, allowing such support "furthers terrorism by straining the United States' relationships with its allies," who "would react sharply to Americans furnishing material support to" terrorist organizations that threaten their interests, "and would hardly be mollified by the explanation that the support was meant only to further those groups' 'legitimate' activities."

Roberts insisted that the conclusions of Congress and the Executive about the dangers of such support are "entitled to deference" because the statute "implicates sensitive and weighty interests of national security and foreign affairs." Although "we do not defer to the Government's reading of the First Amendment, even when such interests are at stake," it is also the case that in these circumstances "conclusions must often be based on informed judgment rather than concrete evidence, and that reality affects what we may reasonably insist on from the Government" in terms of proof of danger. "Given the sensitive interests in national security and foreign affairs at stake, the political branches have adequately substantiated their determination that, to serve the Government's interest in preventing terrorism, it was necessary to prohibit providing material support in the form of training [and] expert advice [to] foreign terrorist groups, even if the supporters meant to promote only the groups' nonviolent ends."

Roberts added that "the dissent fails to address the real dangers at stake. It [seems] unwilling to entertain the prospect that training and advising a designated foreign terrorist organization on how to take advantage of international entities might benefit that organization in a way that facilitates its terrorist activities. In the dissent's world, such training is all to the good. Congress and the Executive, however, have concluded that we live in a different world: one in which the designated foreign terrorist organizations 'are so tainted by their criminal conduct that any contribution to such an organization facilitates that conduct.'"

Finally, Roberts made clear that "we in no way suggest that a regulation of independent speech would pass constitutional muster, even if the Government were to show that such speech benefits foreign terrorist organizations," and we "do not suggest that Congress could extend the same prohibition on material support [to] domestic organizations." Is there a principled basis for these distinctions?

Justice Breyer, joined by Justices Ginsburg and Sotomayor, dissented: "In my view, the Government has not make the strong showing necessary to justify under the First Amendment the criminal prosecution of those who engage [in] the communication and advocacy of political ideas and lawful means of achieving political ends. ["Coordination"] with a group that engages in unlawful activity [does] not deprive the plaintiffs of the First Amendment's [protection]. [The] First Amendment protects advocacy of even *unlawful* action so long as that advocacy is not 'directed to inciting or producing *imminent lawless action* and . . . *likely to incite or produce* such action.' [Quoting *Brandenburg*.] Here the plaintiffs seek to advocate peaceful, *lawful* action to secure *political* ends; and they seek to teach others how to do the same. . . .

"[W]here, as here, a statute applies criminal penalties [for such speech], I should think we would scrutinize the statute and justifications 'strictly' — to determine whether the prohibition is justified by a 'compelling' need that cannot be 'less restrictively' accommodated. [I] doubt that the statute [can] survive any reasonably applicable First Amendment standard. [To] put the matter more specifically, precisely how does application of the statute to the protected activities before us *help achieve* [the government's important interest in protecting the security of the United States]? [The] Government makes two efforts to answer this question. *First*, [it] says that the plaintiffs' support for these organizations is 'fungible' in the same sense as other forms as banned support. [But there] is no *obvious* way in which undertaking advocacy for political changes through peaceful means [is] fungible with other resources that might be put to more sinister ends in the way that donations of money, food, or computer training are fungible. [The] Government has provided us with no empirical information that might convincingly support this claim. . . .

"*Second*, the Government says that the plaintiffs' proposed activities will 'bolste[r] a terrorist organization's efficacy and strength' and 'undermin[e] this nation's efforts to *delegitimize and weaken* those groups.' [Yet] the Government does not claim that the statute forbids *any* speech 'legitimating' a terrorist group. Rather, it reads the statute as [permitting] membership in terrorist organizations [and] 'independent advocacy' on behalf of these organizations. The Court, too, emphasizes that activities 'not *coordinated with*' the terrorist groups are not banned. [But any speech that defends a group or its cause can help] to legitimate that group. Thus, were the law to accept a 'legitimating' effect [as] providing sufficient grounds for imposing [a] ban, the First Amendment battle would be lost in untold instances where it should be won. Once one accepts this argument, there is no natural stopping place. The argument applies as strongly to 'independent' as to 'coordinated' advocacy. [Moreover], the 'legitimacy' justification is itself inconsistent with critically important First Amendment case law. Consider the cases involving the protection the First Amendment offered those who joined the Communist Party intending only to further its peaceful activities. . . .

"[The] risk that those who are taught will put otherwise innocent speech or knowledge to bad use is omnipresent. [To] accept this argument without more and to apply it to the teaching of a subject such as international human rights law is to adopt a rule of law that [would] forbid the teaching of any subject in a case where national security interests conflict with the First Amendment. The Constitution does not allow all such conflicts to be decided in the Government's favor. [The] majority emphasizes that it [must] defer strongly to Congress' 'informed judgment.' [But] 'whenever the fundamental rights of free speech and assembly are alleged to be invaded, it must remain open [for judicial] determination whether there actually did exist at the time a clear danger; whether the danger, if any, was imminent; and whether the evil apprehended was one so substantial as to justify the stringent restriction interposed by the legislature.' [Quoting Brandeis in *Whitney*.] [And] the fact that other nations may like us less for granting [First Amendment] protection cannot in and of itself carry the day. . . .

"I would read the statute as criminalizing First-Amendment protected pure speech [only] when the defendant knows or intends that those activities will assist the organization's unlawful terrorist actions. Under this reading, the Government would have to show, at a minimum, that such defendants provided support that they knew was significantly likely to help the organization pursue its unlawful terrorist aims. [This] reading does not require the Government to undertake the difficult task of proving which, as between peaceful and non-peaceful purposes, a defendant specifically preferred; knowledge is enough."

Under the Court's approach, could a lawyer be convicted for filing a brief on behalf of an alleged terrorist asserting that his constitutional rights had been violated? Is attorney advice protected by the First Amendment? See Knake, Attorney Advice and the First Amendment, 68 Wash. & Lee L. Rev. 639 (2011). Why does Justice Breyer refer to "pure" speech? Is giving money to a terrorist organization to enable it to defend its legal rights "speech" within the meaning of the First Amendment? Is it "pure" speech? Does Breyer's opinion go far enough? Should he have required a showing of specific intent, as the Court did in *Scales*? Does it matter to the constitutionality of the statute that it prohibits not just speech, but *any* material support, including not only speech but also money, lodging, false documentation, communications equipment, facilities, weapons, and transportation?

4B. *A Comparative Perspective.* Mehdi Zana is the former mayor of Diyarbakur, the largest city in southeast Turkey. In 1985, serious disturbances erupted in this area of Turkey between the government's security forces and members of the PKK (Workers' Party of Kurdistan). The PKK's aim was to bring about the secession of part of Turkey's territory, and to achieve that end it committed widespread acts of violence, including murder, kidnapping, and armed robbery. By 1996, the confrontation had claimed the lives of 4,036 civilians and 3,884 members of the security forces. During this time, ten of the eleven provinces in southeast Turkey had been subjected to emergency rule. In this context, Zana made the following remarks in an interview with journalists: "I support the PKK, [but] I am not in favour of massacres. Anyone can make mistakes, and the PKK kill women and children by mistake." This statement was widely circulated in the media. Zana was prosecuted under Turkish law for having "defended an act punishable by law as a serious crime" and "endangering public safety." What result under *Brandenburg*? Is that the "right" result?

Zana was convicted by the Turkish National Security Court and he appealed to the European Court of Human Rights, arguing that his conviction violated Article 10 of the Convention for the Protection of Human Rights and Fundamental Freedoms, which provides:

> Everyone has the right to freedom of expression. This right shall include freedom to hold opinions and to receive and impart information and ideas without interference by public authority. [The] exercise of these freedoms, since it carries with it duties and responsibilities, may be subject to such formalities, conditions, restrictions or penalties as are prescribed by law and are necessary in a democratic society, in the interests of national security, territorial integrity or public safety, for the prevention of disorder or crime, for the protection of health or morals, for the protection of the reputation or rights of others, for preventing the disclosure of information received in confidence, or for maintaining the authority and impartiality of the judiciary.

In Zana v. Turkey, 27 Eur. H.R. Rep. 667 (1997), excerpted in Gey, Free Speech and the Incitement of Violence or Unlawful Behavior: Statutes Directed at Speech, in V. Amar & M. Tushnet, Global Perspectives on Constitutional Law 146 (2009), the court stated:

> [Zana's] words could be interpreted in several ways but, at all events, they are both contradictory and ambiguous. [The] statement cannot, however, be looked at in isolation. It had a specific significance in the circumstances of the cases, as [Zana] must have realized. [In] those circumstances the support given to the PKK [by] the former mayor of [the] most important city in south-east Turkey, in an interview published in a major national daily newspaper, had to be regarded as likely to exacerbate an already explosive situation. [Having regard to all these factors, [the] Court considers that the interference [with freedom of speech] was proportionate to the legitimate aims pursued. There has consequently been no breach of Article 10 of the Convention.

For a similar analysis, consider President Lincoln's approach to free speech in a strikingly similar situation during the Civil War. See G. Stone, Perilous Times: Free Speech in Wartime 94-120 (2004).

Page 1067. At the end of section 1 of the Note, add the following:

Can the government investigate an organization because its advocacy raises concerns about possible future violence without satisfying *Brandenburg*? If so, why? See Rosenthal, First Amendment Investigations and the Inescapable Pragmatism of the Common Law of Free Speech, 86 Ind. L. J. 1 (2011).

More broadly, to what extent does the First Amendment protect a right of "intellectual privacy"—that is, a right that limits the authority of the government to gather information about our phone calls, email communications, reading habits, and Internet usage? Consider Richards, Intellectual Privacy, 87 Tex. L. Rev. 387, 394, 399, 403-404 (2008):

> [T]he processes protected by intellectual privacy occur before we are ready to speak. These protections are not so much right to speak as they are the ways in which our minds develop something novel or interesting to say. [The] threat to intellectual privacy has [become particularly] significant in recent years with the growth of new technologies and the creation of massive quantities of intellectual records. [Imagine] a system of free speech that is deeply protective of the act of speaking, but which has little protection for the act of thinking. Under a system like this, people could speak freely on a whole host of controversial issues [but] the government would be free to secretly monitor phone calls, Internet usage, and the movements and associations of individuals. [If] we value [the] cognitive processes that produce new ideas, then some measure of intellectual privacy, some respite from cognitive surveillance, is essential.

Page 1071. At the end of section 8 of the Note, add the following:

If a school allows students to wear t-shirts with the message "gay: fine by me" or "it's O.K. to be gay," must it also allow students to wear t-shirts with the message "homosexuality is shameful" or "homosexuality is a sin"? If it bans the latter, must it also ban the former? See Curtis, Be Careful What You Wish For: Gays, Dueling High School T-Shirts, and the Perils of Suppression, 44 Wake For. L. Rev. 431 (2009).

Page 1091. At the end of the Note, add the following:

SNYDER v. PHELPS, 131 S. Ct. 1207 (2011). Suppose the Nazis had just marched in Skokie. Could individual residents who were shocked and outraged

131

by their conduct have sued them for damages for the intentional infliction of emotional distress? Consider *Snyder*.

For at least 20 years, the congregation of the Westboro Baptist Church in Topeka, Kansas, picketed hundreds of military funerals to communicate its belief that God hates the United States for its tolerance of homosexuality, particularly in America's military. As part of this campaign, Fred Phelps, who founded the church, and six Westboro Baptist parishioners traveled to Maryland to picket the funeral of Marine Lance Corporal Matthew Snyder, who was killed in Iraq in the line of duty. The picketing took place on public land approximately 1,000 feet from the church where the funeral was held. The picketers peacefully displayed their signs — stating, *e.g.,* "Thank God for Dead Soldiers," "Fags Doom Nations," "America is Doomed," and "You're Going to Hell" — for about 30 minutes before the funeral began.

Matthew Snyder's father (Snyder) saw the tops of the picketers' signs when driving to the funeral, but did not learn what was written on them until watching a news broadcast later that night. Snyder filed a civil action against Phelps and Westboro asserting a state tort claim for intentional infliction of emotional distress. A jury held Westboro liable for millions of dollars in compensatory and punitive damages. The trial judge reduced the punitive damages award, but left the verdict otherwise intact. The court of appeals reversed, concluding that Westboro's statements were entitled to First Amendment protection. The Supreme Court affirmed.

Chief Justice Roberts delivered the opinion of the Court: "Whether the First Amendment prohibits holding Westboro liable for its speech in this case turns largely on whether that speech is of public or private concern, as determined by all the circumstances of the case. [The] First Amendment reflects 'a profound national commitment to the principle that debate on public issues should be uninhibited, robust, and wide-open.' That is because 'speech concerning public affairs is more than self-expression; it is the essence of self-government.' [Accordingly], 'speech on public issues occupies the highest rung of the hierarchy of First Amendment values, and is entitled to special protection.' ...

"Speech deals with matters of public concern when it can 'be fairly considered as relating to any matter of political, social, or other concern to the community' or when it 'is a subject of legitimate news interest; that is, a subject of general interest and of value and concern to the public.' [Deciding] whether speech is of public or private concern requires us to examine the 'content, form, and context' of that speech, as revealed by the whole record.' [The] 'content' of Westboro's signs plainly relates to broad issues of interest to society at large, rather than matters of 'purely private concern.' [While] these messages may fall short of refined social or political commentary, the issues they highlight — the political and moral conduct of the United States and its citizens, the fate of our Nation, [and] homosexuality in the military [are] matters of public import. The signs certainly convey Westboro's position on those issues, in a manner designed [to] reach as broad a public audience as possible. . . .

"Snyder goes on to argue that Westboro's speech should be afforded less than full First Amendment protection [because] the church members exploited the funeral 'as a platform to bring their message to a broader audience.' There is no doubt that Westboro chose to stage its picketing at the Naval Academy, the Maryland State House, and Matthew Snyder's funeral to increase publicity for its views and because of the relation between those sites and its views — in the case of the military funeral, because Westboro believes that God is killing American soldiers as punishment for the Nation's sinful policies. [Westboro's] choice of where and when to conduct its picketing is not beyond the Government's regulatory reach — it is 'subject to reasonable time, place, or manner restrictions.' [But the] record confirms that any distress occasioned by Westboro's picketing turned on the content and viewpoint of the message conveyed, rather than any interference with the funeral itself. A group of parishioners standing at the very spot where Westboro stood, holding signs that said 'God Bless America' and 'God Loves You,' would not have been subjected to liability. It was what Westboro said that exposed it to tort damages. [Given] that Westboro's speech was at a public place on a matter of public concern, [it] cannot be restricted simply because it is upsetting or arouses contempt. 'If there is a bedrock principle underlying the First Amendment, it is that the government may not prohibit the expression of an idea simply because society finds the idea itself offensive or disagreeable.'

"The jury here was instructed that it could hold Westboro liable for intentional infliction of emotional distress based on a finding that Westboro's picketing was 'outrageous.' 'Outrageousness,' however, is a highly malleable standard with 'an inherent subjectiveness about it which would allow a jury to impose liability on the basis of the jurors' tastes or views, or perhaps on the basis of their dislike of a particular expression.' In a case such as this, a jury is 'unlikely to be neutral with respect to the content of [the] speech,' posing 'a real danger of becoming an instrument for the suppression of . . . vehement, caustic, and sometimes unpleasan[t]' expression. Such a risk is unacceptable; 'in public debate [we] must tolerate insulting, and even outrageous, speech in order to provide adequate 'breathing space' to the freedoms protected by the First Amendment.' [For] all these reasons, the jury verdict imposing tort liability on Westboro for intentional infliction of emotional distress must be set aside."

Justice Alito dissented: "Our profound national commitment to free and open debate is not a license for the vicious verbal assault that occurred in this case. [Phelps and Westboro] have strong opinions on certain moral, religious, and political issues, and the First Amendment ensures that they have almost limitless opportunities to express their views. They may write and distribute books, articles, and other texts; they may create and disseminate video and audio recordings; they may circulate petitions; they may speak to individuals and groups in public forums and in any private venue that wishes to accommodate them; they may picket peacefully in countless locations; they may appear on television and speak on the radio; they may post messages on the Internet and send out e-mails. And they may express their views in terms that are "uninhibited," "vehement," and "caustic." It does not follow, however, that they may intentionally inflict severe emotional injury on private persons at a time of intense emotional sensitivity by launching vicious verbal attacks that make no contribution to public debate. [I] think it is clear that the First Amendment does not entirely preclude liability for the intentional infliction of emotional distress by means of speech.

"'[P]ersonal abuse is not in any proper sense communication of information or opinion safeguarded by the Constitution'. When grave injury is intentionally inflicted by means of an attack like the one at issue here, the First Amendment should not interfere with recovery. . . .

"This attack, which was almost certain to inflict injury, was central to [Westboro's] well-practiced strategy for attracting public attention. On the morning of Matthew Snyder's funeral, respondents could have chosen to stage their protest at countless locations. But of course, a small group picketing at any [other location] would have probably gone unnoticed. The Westboro Baptist Church, however, has devised a strategy that remedies this problem. The more outrageous the funeral protest, the more publicity the Westboro Baptist Church is able to obtain. [Allowing] family members to have a few hours of peace without harassment does not undermine public debate. I would therefore hold that, in this setting, the First Amendment permits a private figure to recover for the intentional infliction of emotional distress caused by speech on a matter of private concern."

D. Content-Based Restrictions: "Low" Value Speech

Page 1106. After section 8 of the Note, add the following:

8a. What happened to Daniel Ellsberg? Consider Collins & Chaltain, We Must Not Be Afraid to Be Free 84-85 (2011):

Before the oral arguments were made in New York Times v. United States, Daniel Ellsberg was arrested and charged with espionage. [He] faced twelve felony charges and a possible total of 115 years in prison. The criminal trial began on January 3, 1973, [and] dragged on for several months. Then, in its final weeks, series of shocking disclosures unfolded. [First,] federal district judge Matthew Byrne learned that the office of Ellsberg's psychiatrist had been broken into in an attempt to acquire damning information about him. Shortly thereafter, Nixon was directly linked to the break-in. Members of his cabinet began resigning in quick succession in an attempt to deflect unwanted attention away from the president. But it was too late. Then, in the midst of the unraveling of the Nixon presidency, the FBI informed Judge Byrne that, despite many previous denials, it had in [fact] electronically surveiled Ellsberg. [On May 12, 1973, Byrne] dismissed the case. . . . "I am of the opinion," he wrote, "that the only remedy available that would assure the due process and the fair administration of justice is that this trial be terminated."

Page 1107. Before the final paragraph on the page, add the following:

How should we think about Julian Assange and WikiLeaks? Floyd Abrams was one of the lawyers who argued the Pentagon Papers case for the New York Times. Consider his views, expressed in a 2011 speech, about WikiLeaks:

"In making public 77,000 U.S. confidential military reports from Afghanistan, [WikiLeaks] included over 100 names of confidential Afghan sources of information to our nation, putting them at risk of retaliation by the Taliban. [There] are simply too many examples of WikiLeaks having released materials of significant harm with only the slightest potential public benefit. There was the release, for example, of a classified cable that listed facilities around the world whose disruption, not to say destruction, would threaten American security. There was, as well, the release of a classified report describing the radio frequency [American jammers in Iraq] used to cut off signals to remotely detonated explosives. The report gives information, quite specific in nature, of how the jammers functions and which frequencies they stop. When criticized for releasing the classified document which related to some jammers then still in use, Mr. Assange responded by saying 'WikiLeaks represents whisteblowers in the same way that lawyers represent their clients — fairly and impartially. Our "job" is to safely and impartially conduct the whistleblower's message to the public, not to inject our own nationality or beliefs.' [If WikiLeaks] is nothing more or less than a conduit for the transmission of secrets from sources to the public [then] it is not engaged in journalism. . . . Consider [that] Mr. Assange has acknowledged that [before releasing 77,000 classified documents,] he and his colleagues had *read* only

2,000 of them. [My] point is not the WikiLeaks has not played some useful role. It has. But it has too often behaved recklessly. ... "

In such circumstances, can Assange and WikiLeaks be criminally punished for their actions?

Page 1135. At the beginning of the Note, add the following:

1a. *Historical context.* At the time of this decision, the South was in the throes of the civil rights movement. The South was deeply concerned about public opinion in the rest of country. The more the national media covered civil rights protests in the South, the more public opinion turned against those who were seeking to preserve segregation. Strategic lawsuits for libel brought by public officials against the national media for technical misstatements in news reports about civil rights protests were intended to deter the national media from covering the civil rights movement. This strategy was made especially effective because Southern juries were inclined to grant excessive damage awards against those who were embarrassing the South. In 1964, a $500,000 award for libel in a case like the one brought by Sullivan was quite extraordinary. Such awards could cripple an institution like the *New York Times*, especially in light of the fact that there were many similar actions pending against the *New York Times* in the South. The Court was acutely aware of this state of affairs, and that awareness no doubt led the justices to take the libel issue seriously as a First Amendment matter and to see the case as analogous to the traditional notion of seditious libel.

In effect, such lawsuits suggested that "the nation could no longer tolerate a system of local censorship, because in many cases local censorship would effectively constitute national censorship. In a world in which information needed to flow at a national scale, restrictions at the local level could significantly disrupt the flow of information everywhere. [The] several hundred copies of the *Times* that found their way into Alabama forced the Court to reconsider the historical prerogative of every local jurisdiction to strike its own balance between an interest in an individual's reputation and a free press." L. Bollinger, Uninhibited, Robust, and Wide-Open: A Free Press for a New Century 66 (2010).

Page 1145. At the end of the Note, add the following:

d. Consider Schauer, Facts and the First Amendment, 57 UCLA. L. Rev. 897 (2010):

President Obama was not born in Kenya. President Bush did not have advance notice of the September 11 attacks. [The] Holocaust is not a myth fabricated by Zionists and their supporters. [That] large numbers of people believe things that are false despite being told the truth [is] hardly a revelation. [The] phenomenon of persistent factual falsity should be an occasion for pause or embarrassment to the free speech tradition. [The] embarrassment [comes most] importantly from the fact that the widespread existence of public falsity is a topic about which the tradition has essentially nothing to say. . . .

[P]ublic noncommercial factual falsity will likely remain constitutionally protected for the foreseeable future. [In] a culture of pervasive distrust of government, and with a First Amendment tradition in which distrust of government looms large as a free speech justification, the likelihood of any change in the doctrine is remote. The Supreme Court's statement in *Gertz* that "[u]nder the First Amendment there is no such thing as a false idea" is a statement [about] the American free speech tradition. This is a tradition in which distrust of government to decide which ideas are true and which are false has been extended not only to the kinds of social, political, moral, religious, and cultural ideas that we actually do label as "ideas," but also to propositions of fact. [The] willingness to sanction Holocaust denial in numerous liberal and open democratic societies is in stark contrast to American practice. . . .

Page 1152.   At the end of the Note, add the following:

6. *Confidentiality and privacy*. Consider three situations: (a) X sees plaintiff enter an HIV clinic and publishes (accurately) on the Internet that plaintiff has HIV. (b) Plaintiff sees Dr. Y about his HIV, but before consulting him plaintiff insists that Dr. Y sign a confidentiality agreement. Y signs the agreement but later publishes on the Internet that plaintiff has HIV. (c) Plaintiff visits Hospital Z to seek treatment for HIV. There is no discussion between plaintiff and Z about confidentiality, but a state law provides that health care providers may not publicly disclose whether any particular patient has HIV. Nonetheless, Z publishes on the Internet the fact that X has HIV. X sues X, Y, and Z. How would you analyze each of the three cases under the First Amendment?

Note that case (a) is predicated on the common law tort of invasion of privacy, case (b) is an action for breach of contract, and case (c) is an action to enforce a statutorily created right. Consider the proposition that case (b) is the easiest of three for finding liability, because "when government power is used to dictate the terms of civil duties not to speak [the] special dangers of this power warrant application of the First Amendment, [but] when private parties create the content of speech-restrictive rule, the First Amendment should not apply." Solove & Richards, Rethinking Free Speech and Civil Liability, 109 Colum. L. Rev. 1650, 1686 (2009). Consider Cohen v. Cowles Media Co., 501 U.S. 663 (1991), holding that where X reveals information to Y on condition that Y will not disseminate the information further, X can sue Y for breach of contract or promissory estoppel because "generally applicable laws do not offend the First Amendment simply because" they have an incidental effect on speech.

7. *Privacy and the internet.* Consider the following views:

a. Solove, Speech, Privacy, and Reputation on the Internet, in Levmore & Nussbaum, eds., The Offensive Internet 15, 16, 18, 21, 28 (2010):

> Before the Internet, gossip would spread by word of mouth and remain within the boundaries of a social circle. [In] the village of yesteryear, people had to live under the ever-present judgmental eye of their fellow villagers. [One] of the benefits of the modern world was that people could escape from the oppressiveness of the small village fishbowl. But no longer. We now live in a "global village," [but] with a pernicious twist. In the small village, people knew each other well, and disreputable information would be judged within the context of a person's entire life. Now, people are judged out of context based on information fragments found online. . . .
>
> Broad-based exposure of personal information diminishes the ability to protect reputation by shaping the image that is presented to others. Reputation plays an important role in society, and preserving private details of one's life is essential to it. We look to people's reputations to decide whether to make friends, go on a date, hire a new employee, or undertake a prospective business deal. [People] want to have the option of "starting over," or reinventing themselves throughout their lives. [In] the past, episodes of youthful experimentation and foolishness were eventually forgotten, giving us an opportunity to start anew, to change, and to grow. But with so much information online, it is harder to make these moments forgettable. People must now live with the digital baggage of their pasts. . . .
>
> It is still possible to protect privacy, but doing so requires that we rethink outdated understandings of the concept. [The modern understanding of privacy should recognize] that a person should retain some control over personal information that becomes publicly available. [For example, suppose] a person discloses information on a Facebook page that is set up so that only the person's friends can view it. Suppose the person has fifty friends. Is the information still private? I believe [that] it is. [If] one of the person's friends were to disseminate the information beyond the

group of friends, such a disclosure could be understood to be a breach of confidentiality.

b. Chander, Youthful Indiscretion in an Internet Age, in Levmore & Nussbaum, eds., The Offensive Internet 124, 125, 135-136 (2010):

[N]ew technologies make the public disclosure tort more necessary than ever before. In particular, [the] disclosure tort is especially appropriate to regulate the display of nude photographs and videos not authorized for public dissemination. The power of the image, particularly sexual images, requires the special attention of the law. [It] might be argued that publicizing [such images] will, over time, lead society to accept [them] as [not] embarrassing. [A] related argument [is] that such [images] will soon be no longer worthy of reprobation. [One's] own indiscretion will perhaps be lost amidst a sea of similar [images]. [But] the disclosure tort itself covers only disclosures that are highly offensive to a reasonable person, and thus allows for changes in social standards. If society does indeed believe a particular disclosure to be unobjectionable, [then] no tort claim will lie. ...

While it is possible that society will become blasé to such [images], it is easy to underestimate the dangers. After all, within the community of youth, these behaviors may well be common, so much so that anyone not engaging in them may even be ridiculed as prudish. [What] if the individual has children — might she be concerned about what comes to their attention? [What] of the snickers of opposing counsel [when] they email photos while a lawyer takes the stand?

c. Stone, Privacy, the First Amendment, and the Internet, in Levmore & Nussbaum, eds., The Offensive Internet 174, 175-176 (2010):

It is sometimes said that the harm from speech on the Internet is potentially greater than the harm from speech in other media, because the potential audience is much larger, the speech remains indefinitely discoverable, and information can be easily located through search engines like Google. All of this is true. [But] none of this is relevant to whether the speech should be protected in the first place.

If speech is sufficiently valuable to merit First Amendment protection when it is spoken over a backyard fence or published in a local newspaper, then (at least presumptively) it is also sufficiently valuable to be protected when it is disseminated on the Internet. This is so because just as the harm caused by the speech may be magnified by the power of the Internet, so too is the value of the speech. As a general proposition, as speech reaches a larger audience, its cumulative value will increase in the same proportion as its cumulative harm. [The] balance between value and harm remains more or less constant.

d. Stone, supra this Note, at 192, 194:

[L]egal enforcement of the concept of non-newsworthiness [is now] stagger-ingly problematic. Consider [a] student who posts accurately on a blog deal-ing with her school that a teacher [was] seen in a gay bar. Within the confines of the school community, it would be difficult to argue that this is non-newsworthy information or that the student could be punished for revealing it to others. But with modern technology, this information will be available not only to those in the particular school community, at that time and place, but to all Internet users and forever. [In] the world of the Internet it is no longer possible to segregate audiences based on immediate relevance of information to the community. [This] may be liberating or it may be unner-ving and unwelcome, but in no event is it a state of affairs that can mean-ingfully be addressed by the invasion of privacy tort. [As a practical matter, the disclosure tort is a relic] of an earlier and vastly simpler era. . . .

The most realistic way to protect privacy today is at its source. By pro-hibiting highly intrusive methods of gaining information that people want to keep confidential it is still possible to enable individuals who truly care about their privacy to preserve it, if they act carefully and with discretion. But once information is out of the bottle, once we share it with others, once others know it, we can longer hope to put it back. If that era ever existed, it is now the past.

Page 1169.   After *Thompson v. Western States Medical Center*, add the following:

SORRELL v. IMS HEALTH, INC., 131 S. Ct. 2653 (2011). Pharmaceutical manufacturers market their drugs to doctors through a process known as "detailing." This typically involves a salesman's (or "detailer's") visit to a doctor's office to persuade the doctor to prescribe a particular brand-name drug. Knowledge of the doctor's prescription practices — called "prescriber-identifying information" — enables the detailer to determine which doctors are likely to be interested in particular drugs and how best to present the sales pitch. Pharmacies receive prescriber-identifying information whenever they fill pre-scriptions. Many pharmacies sell this information to data miners, who then analyze the information and sell it to pharmaceutical manufacturers, who then give it to their detailers to enable them to refine their marketing approach and increase sales. In 2007, Vermont enacted legislation prohibiting pharmacies from selling prescriber-identifying information for the purpose of marketing prescription drugs. In *Sorrell*, the Court, in a six-to-three decision, held that this law violated the First Amendment.

Justice Kennedy wrote the opinion of the Court: "Vermont's law enacts content- and speaker-based restrictions on the sale [and] use of prescriber-identifying information. The provision [prohibits] sale [of the information based] on the content of the purchaser's speech. For example, those who wish to engage in 'educational communications' may purchase the information. The statute [therefore disfavors] marketing, that is, speech with a particular content. [More] than that, the statute disfavors specific speakers, namely pharmaceutical manufacturers. [The] law [thus] burdens disfavored speech by disfavored speakers. [It] follows that heightened judicial scrutiny is warranted. . . .

"The State argues that a different analysis applies here because [the law] burdens only commercial speech. [But even under] a commercial speech inquiry, [the] State must show at least that the statute directly advances a substantial government interest and that the measure is drawn to achieve that interest. [The] State contends that its law is necessary to protect medical privacy, including physician confidentiality. [But] under Vermont's law, pharmacies may share prescriber-identifying information with anyone for any reason save one: They must not allow the information to be used for marketing. [Given] the information's [many] permissible uses, the State's asserted interest in physician confidentiality does not justify the burden [the law] places on protected expression.

"[The State also] claims that detailing makes people 'anxious' about whether doctors have their patients' best interests at heart. [But] this asserted interest is contrary to basic First Amendment principles. Speech remains protected even when it may 'stir people to action,' 'move them to tears,' or 'inflict great pain.' [Quoting *Snyder v. Phelps*.] If pharmaceutical marketing affects treatment decisions, it does so because doctors find it persuasive. Absent circumstances far from those presented here, the fear that speech might persuade provides no law basis for quieting it. [Citing *Brandenburg*.]

"[The State further] contends that [its law] advances important public policy goals by lowering the costs of medical services and promoting public health. If prescriber-identifying information were available for use by detailers, the State contends, then detailing would be effective in promoting brand-name drugs that are more expensive and less safe than generic alternatives. [While these] goals may be proper, [the law] does not advance them in a permissible way. [The] State seeks to achieve its policy objectives through the indirect means of restraining certain speech by certain speakers. . . . Those who seek to censor [expression] often assert that disfavored speech has adverse effects. But the 'fear that people would make bad decisions if given truthful information' cannot justify content-based burdens on speech. [Citing *Thompson, Virginia Board of Pharmacy,* and *44 Liquormart*]."

Justice Breyer, joined by Justices Ginsburg and Kagan, dissented: "[O]ur cases make clear that the First Amendment offers considerably less protection to the maintenance of a free marketplace for goods and services [than for] a marketplace that provides access to 'social, political, esthetic, moral, and other ideas and experiences.' [To] apply a 'heightened' standard of review [in a case like this] would risk what then-Justice Rehnquist [once described] as a 'retur[n] to the bygone era of *Lochner*.' [There] are several reasons why the Court should review Vermont's law 'under the standard appropriate for the review of economic legislation,' not 'under a heightened standard appropriate for the review of First Amendment issues.' . . . .

"[T]he Court [emphasizes] that this is a case involving both 'content-based' and 'speaker-based' restrictions. But neither of those categories [has] ever before justified greater scrutiny when regulatory activity affects commercial speech. [The] absence of any such precedent is understandable. Regulatory programs necessarily draw distinctions on the basis of content. Electricity regulators, for example, oversee company statements, pronouncements, and proposals, but only about electricity. [And] the FDA oversees the form and content of labeling, advertising, and sales proposals or drugs, but not of furniture. [Nor], in the context of a regulatory program, is it unusual for particular rules to be 'speaker-based,' affecting only a class of entities, namely, the regulated firms. [If] the Court means to create constitutional barriers to regulatory rules that might affect the *content* of a commercial message, it has embarked upon an unprecedented task — a task that threatens significant judicial interference with widely accepted regulatory activity. [By] inviting courts to scrutinize whether a State's legitimate regulatory interests can be achieved in less restrictive ways whenever they touch (even indirectly) upon commercial speech, today's majority risks repeated the mistakes of the past."

Page 1175.   At the end of section 1 of the Note, add the following:

Bezanson, Art and the Constitution 93 Iowa L. Rev. 1593 (2008).

Page 1189.   After section 1 of the Note, add the following:

1a. *Why must speech be "patently offensive" in its depiction of sex to be obscene?* Consider Nussbaum, From Disgust to Humanity 11-21 (2010):

[One view about disgust is that human nature was] purposively designed (perhaps by God) in such a way that its visceral responses give us important information about what is good for us. Disgust thus contains a "wisdom" that lies beneath all rational argument. It "revolts against the excesses of human willfulness, warning us not to transgress. ... " [People] do feel deep disgust with certain practices [and] believe that these practices threaten the social fabric. [The] primary objects of disgust are reminders of human animality and mortality: feces, other bodily fluids, corpses, and animals or insects who have related properties (slimy, smelly, oozy). ...

It is not surprising that sexuality is an area of life in which disgust often plays a role. Sex involves the exchanges of bodily fluids, and it marks us as bodily beings rather than angelic transcendent beings. So sex is a site of anxiety for anyone who is ambivalent about having an animal and mortal nature. [But] disgust provides no good reason for limiting liberties. ...

Page 1198. At the end of the Note, add the following:

5. *Sexting.* Consider Humbach, "Sexting" and the First Amendment, 37 Hastings Const. L.Q. 433 (2010):

Two Florida teenagers took over one hundred photographs of themselves naked and engaging [in] lawful "sexual behavior." The two were subsequently charged under Florida law [with] "producing [a] photograph [they] knew to include the sexual conduct of a child." [In] Ohio, a fifteen-year-old girl used her cell phone to send nude photos of herself and was charged with "illegal use of a minor in nudity-oriented material." [A] recent study shows that about twenty percent of U.S. teenagers (including eleven percent of teen girls ages thirteen to sixteen) admit to producing and distributing nude or semi-nude pictures of themselves.

Can these teenagers constitutionally be convicted of producing and disseminating child pornography? Suppose the photos include "lewd exhibition of the genitals" or same-sex sexual conduct?

Page 1201. Before section 5, insert the following:

UNITED STATES v. STEVENS, 130 S. Ct. 1577 (2010). 18 U.S.C. § 48 establishes a criminal penalty of up to five years in prison for anyone who knowingly "creates, sells, or possesses a depiction of animal cruelty," if done "for commercial gain" in interstate or foreign commerce. A depiction of "animal cruelty" is defined as one "in which a living animal is intentionally maimed, mutilated, tortured, wounded, or killed," if that conduct violates federal or state law where "the creation, sale, or possession takes place." The law exempts from prohibition any depiction "that has serious religious, political, scientific, educational, journalistic, historical, or artistic value."

The legislative background of § 48 focused primarily on the interstate market for "crush videos," which depict women crushing small animals like mice and hamster to death with their bare feet or while wearing high heeled shoes, sometimes while talking to the animals in a kind of dominatrix patter. Apparently these depictions appeal to persons with a very specific sexual fetish who find them sexually arousing. The acts depicted in crush videos are typically prohibited by the animal cruelty laws enacted by all 50 States and the District of Columbia. But crush videos rarely disclose the participants' identities, inhibiting prosecution of the underlying conduct.

This case, however, involved an application of § 48 to depictions of dogfighting. Dogfighting is unlawful in all 50 States and the District of Columbia, and has been restricted by federal law since 1976. Robert Stevens ran a business, "Dogs of Velvet and Steel," and an associated Web site, through which he sold videos of pit bulls engaging in dogfights and attacking other animals. His videos included contemporary footage of dogfights in Japan (where such conduct is legal) as well as footage of American dogfights from the 1960's and 1970's. On the basis of these videos, Stevens was convicted of violating § 48. The en banc Third Circuit declared § 48 facially unconstitutional and vacated Stevens's conviction.

In an eight-to-one decision, the Supreme Court affirmed. Chief Justice Roberts delivered the opinion of the Court: "The Government's primary submission is that § 48 necessarily complies with the Constitution because the banned depictions of animal cruelty, as a class, are categorically unprotected by the First Amendment. We disagree. . . .

"From 1791 to the present, [the] First Amendment has 'permitted restrictions upon the content of speech in a few limited areas,' [including, for example, obscenity, defamation, and incitement]. [Citing *Chaplinsky*.] The Government argues that 'depictions of animal cruelty' should be added to the list. It contends that depictions of 'illegal acts of animal cruelty' that are 'made, sold, or possessed for commercial gain' necessarily 'lack expressive value,' and may accordingly 'be regulated as *unprotected* speech.' [The] prohibition of animal cruelty [has] a long history in American law, [but] we are unaware of any similar tradition excluding *depictions* of animal cruelty from 'the freedom of speech' codified in the First Amendment. . . .

"The Government contends that 'historical evidence' about the reach of the First Amendment is not 'a necessary prerequisite for regulation today,' and that categories of speech may be exempted from the First Amendment's protection without any long-settled tradition of subjecting that speech to regulation. Instead, the Government points to Congress's 'legislative judgment that ... depictions of animals being intentionally tortured and killed [are] of such minimal redeeming value as to render [them] unworthy of First Amendment protection,' and asks the Court to uphold the ban on the same basis. The Government thus proposes that a claim of categorical exclusion should be considered under a simple balancing test: 'Whether a given category of speech enjoys First Amendment protection depends upon a categorical balancing of the value of the speech against its societal costs.' [Quoting Brief for United States].

"As a free-floating test for First Amendment coverage, that sentence is startling and dangerous. The First Amendment's guarantee of free speech does not extend only to categories of speech that survive an ad hoc balancing of relative social costs and benefits. The First Amendment itself reflects a judgment by the American people that the benefits of its restrictions on the Government outweigh the costs. Our Constitution forecloses any attempt to revise that judgment simply on the basis that some speech is not worth it. ...

"To be fair to the Government, its view did not emerge from a vacuum. As the Government correctly notes, this Court has often *described* historically unprotected categories of speech as being 'of such slight social value as a step to truth that any benefit that may be derived from them is clearly outweighed by the social interest in order and morality.' [*Chaplinsky.*] But such descriptions are just that — descriptive. They do not set forth a test that may be applied as a general matter to permit the Government to imprison any speaker so long as his speech is deemed valueless or unnecessary, or so long as an ad hoc calculus of costs and benefits tilts in a statute's favor.

"When we have identified categories of speech as fully outside the protection of the First Amendment, it has not been on the basis of a simple cost-benefit analysis. [Our decisions] cannot be taken as establishing a freewheeling authority to declare new categories of speech outside the scope of the First Amendment. Maybe there are some categories of speech that have been historically unprotected, but have not yet been specifically identified or discussed as such in our case law. But if so, there is no evidence that 'depictions of animal cruelty' is among them. We need not foreclose the future recognition of such additional categories to reject the Government's highly manipulable balancing test as a means of identifying them. ...

"Because we decline to carve out from the First Amendment any novel exception for § 48, we review Stevens's First Amendment challenge under our existing doctrine. [Stevens] argues that § 48 applies to common depictions of ordinary and lawful activities, and that these depictions constitute the vast majority of materials subject to the statute. The Government makes no effort to defend such a broad ban as constitutional. Instead, the Government's entire defense of § 48 rests on interpreting the statute as narrowly limited to specific types of 'extreme' material. . . .

"We read § 48 to create a criminal prohibition of alarming breadth. To begin with, the text of the statute's ban on a 'depiction of animal cruelty' nowhere requires that the depicted conduct be cruel. [Moreover, although § 48 does require that the depicted conduct be 'illegal,' the] application of § 48 to depictions of illegal conduct extends to conduct that is illegal in only a single jurisdiction. Under [the statute, a] depiction of entirely lawful conduct runs afoul of the ban if that depiction later finds its way into another State where the same conduct is unlawful. This provision greatly expands the scope of § 48, because although there may be 'a broad societal consensus' against cruelty to animals, there is substantial disagreement on what types of conduct are properly regarded as cruel.

"[In] the District of Columbia, for example, all hunting is unlawful. Other jurisdictions permit or encourage hunting, and there is an enormous national market for hunting-related depictions in which a living animal is intentionally killed. Hunting periodicals have circulations in the hundreds of thousands or millions, and hunting television programs, videos, and Web sites are equally popular. [Nonetheless,] because the statute allows each jurisdiction to export its laws to the rest of the country, § 48(a) extends to *any* magazine or video depicting lawful hunting, so long as that depiction is sold within the Nation's Capital. Those seeking to comply with the law thus face a bewildering maze of regulations. [The] sharp-tailed grouse may be hunted in Idaho, but not in Washington. [Moreover, the] disagreements among the States [extend] well beyond hunting. State agricultural regulations permit different methods of live-stock slaughter in different places or as applied to different animals. [Even] cockfighting, long considered immoral in much of America, is legal in Puerto Rico. An otherwise-lawful image of any of these practices, if sold or possessed for commercial gain within a State that happens to forbid the practice, falls within the prohibition of § 48(a).

"The only thing standing between defendants who sell such depictions and five years in federal prison — other than the mercy of a prosecutor — is the statute's exceptions clause. Subsection (b) exempts from prohibition 'any depiction that has serious religious, political, scientific, educational, journalistic, historical, or artistic value.' The Government argues that this clause substantially narrows the statute's reach: News reports about animal cruelty have 'journalistic' value; pictures of bullfights in Spain have 'historical' value; and instructional hunting videos have 'educational' value. [But much valuable speech under the First Amendment does not] fall within one of the enumerated categories. [Most] hunting videos, for example, are not obviously instructional in nature, [but] 'have primarily entertainment value.' [The] Government offers no principled explanation why these depictions of hunting or depictions of

Spanish bullfights would be *inherently* valuable while those of Japanese dog-fights are not. . . .

"The Government explains that the language of § 48(b) was largely drawn from our opinion in *Miller* v. *California*, which excepted from its definition of obscenity any material with 'serious literary, artistic, political, or scientific value.' According to the Government, this incorporation of the *Miller* standard into § 48 is therefore surely enough to answer any First Amendment objection. In *Miller* we held that 'serious' value shields depictions of sex from regulation as obscenity. We did not, however, determine that serious value could be used as a general precondition to protecting *other* types of speech in the first place. *Most* of what we say to one another lacks 'religious, political, scientific, educational, journalistic, historical, or artistic value' (let alone serious value), but it is still sheltered from government regulation. [Thus,] the protection of the First Amendment presumptively extends to many forms of speech that do not qualify for the serious-value exception of § 48(b), but nonetheless fall within the broad reach of § 48(c). . . .

"Our construction of § 48 decides the constitutional question; the Government makes no effort to defend the constitutionality of § 48 as applied beyond crush videos and depictions of animal fighting. It argues that those particular depictions are intrinsically related to criminal conduct or are analogous to obscenity (if not themselves obscene), and that the ban on such speech is narrowly tailored to reinforce restrictions on the underlying conduct, prevent additional crime arising from the depictions, or safeguard public mores. But the Government nowhere attempts to extend these arguments to depictions of any other activities — depictions that are presumptively protected by the First Amendment but that remain subject to the criminal sanctions of § 48. [We] therefore need not and do not decide whether a statute limited to crush videos or other depictions of extreme animal cruelty would be constitutional. We hold only that § 48 [is] substantially overbroad, and therefore invalid under the First Amendment."

Why are depictions of animal cruelty different from depictions of child sexual abuse? Consider Chief Justice Roberts's explanation: "In *Ferber*, [we] classified child pornography as [unprotected speech]. We noted that the State [had] a compelling interest in protecting children from abuse, and that the value of using children in these works (as opposed to simulated conduct or adult actors) was *de minimis*. But our decision did not rest on this 'balance of the competing interests' alone. We made clear that *Ferber* presented a special case: The market for child pornography was 'intrinsically related' to the underlying abuse, and was 'an integral part of the production of such materials, an activity illegal throughout the Nation.' As we noted, '[i]t rarely has been suggested that the constitutional freedom for speech and press extends its immunity to speech or writing used as an integral part of conduct in violation of a valid criminal statute.' *Ferber* thus grounded its analysis in a previously recognized, long-established category of unprotected speech." Is this persuasive?

The Court held in *Ferber* and *Ashcroft* that the government can constitutionally prohibit the sale or exhibition of child pornography only because the government has a "compelling" interest in "safeguarding the physical and psychological well-being of a minor." The Court explained that the prohibition of child pornography serves this "compelling" interest in two ways: (1) by drying up the market for such materials and thereby eliminating the incentive to create them, and (2) by protecting the victims from the emotional and psychological harm caused by the continued circulation of the images.

Does the government have a similarly "compelling" argument in the animal cruelty context?

Consider the following arguments: (1) As evidenced by the many circumstances (including hunting and slaughtering food animals) in which we permit cruelty to animals, we clearly do not take the interest in preventing animal cruelty as seriously as we take the interest in preventing child sexual abuse, which is never permitted. (2) Unlike people, animals have no consciousness of the continuing exhibition of the depiction of their abuse and therefore suffer no comparable emotional or psychological injury.

Is it possible, after *Stevens*, to draft a statute prohibiting the depiction of animal cruelty that would survive First Amendment scrutiny?

Justice Alito was the lone dissenter: "The Court strikes down in its entirety a valuable statute [that] was enacted not to suppress speech, but to prevent horrific acts of animal cruelty — in particular, the creation and commercial exploitation of 'crush videos,' a form of depraved entertainment that has no social value. The Court's approach [is] unwarranted. [Today's] decision [strikes] down § 48 using what has been aptly termed the 'strong medicine' of the overbreadth doctrine. [I] do not think the present record supports the Court's conclusion that § 48 bans a substantial quantity of protected speech.

"[In arguing that § 48 is substantially overbroad, the] Court relies primarily on depictions of hunters killing or wounding games and depictions of animals being slaughtered for food. [But] hunting is legal in all 50 States, and § 48 applies only to a depiction of conduct that is illegal in the jurisdiction in which the depiction is created, sold, or possessed. Therefore, in all 50 States, the creation, sale, or possession for sale of the vast majority of hunting depictions indisputably falls outside § 48's reach. [I] would hold that § 48 does not apply to depictions of hunting. [Moreover], even if the hunting of wild animals were otherwise covered by § 48(a), I would hold that hunting depictions fall within the exception in § 48(b) for depictions that have 'serious' (*i.e.,* not 'trifling') 'scientific,' 'educational,' or 'historical' value.

"[Similarly, the Court's reliance on depictions of animal slaughter does] not show that the statute is substantially overbroad. [As with hunting], § 48 can reasonably be construed to apply only to depictions involving acts of animal cruelty as defined by applicable state or federal law, and anti-cruelty laws do not ban the [slaughter of animals for food. Moreover,] nothing in the record suggests that any one has ever created, sold, or possessed for sale a depiction of the slaughter of food animals [that] would not easily qualify under the exception set out in § 48(b). . . .

"In sum, we have a duty to interpret § 48 so as to avoid serious constitutional concerns, and § 48 may reasonably be construed not to reach almost all, if not all, of the depictions that the Court finds constitutionally protected. Thus, § 48 does not appear to have a large number of unconstitutional applications. Invalidation for overbreadth is appropriate only if the challenged statute suffers from *substantial* overbreadth — judged not just in absolute terms, but in relation to the statute's 'plainly legitimate sweep.' As I explain in the following Part, § 48 has a substantial core of constitutionally permissible applications.

"[T]he primary conduct that Congress sought to address through its passage of § 48] was the creation, sale, or possession of 'crush' videos. But before the enactment of § 48, the underlying conduct depicted in crush videos was nearly impossible to prosecute. These videos [were] made in secret, generally without a live audience, and 'the faces of the women inflicting the torture in the material often were not shown, nor could the location of the place where the cruelty was being inflicted or the date of the activity be ascertained from the depiction.' Thus, law enforcement authorities often were not able to identify the parties responsible for the torture. [In] light of the practical problems thwarting the prosecution of the creators of crush videos under state animal cruelty laws, Congress concluded that the only effective way of stopping the underlying criminal conduct was to prohibit the commercial exploitation of the videos of that conduct. . . .

"Crush videos present a highly unusual free speech issue because they are so closely linked with violent criminal conduct. The videos record the commission of violent criminal acts, and it appears that these crimes are committed for the sole purpose of creating the videos. In addition, [Congress] was presented with compelling evidence that the only way of preventing these crimes was to target the sale of the videos. Under these circumstances, I cannot believe that the First Amendment commands Congress to step aside and allow the underlying crimes to continue.

"The most relevant of our prior decisions is *Ferber*. [In] *Ferber,* an important factor — I would say the most important factor — was that child pornography involves the commission of a crime that inflicts severe personal injury to the 'children who are made to engage in sexual conduct for commercial purposes.' [As] later noted in *Ashcroft* v. *Free Speech Coalition*, in *Ferber* '[t]he production of the work, not its content, was the target of the statute.' [*Ferber* also] emphasized [that] these underlying crimes could not be effectively combated without targeting the distribution of child pornography. [And, finally,] the

Ferber Court noted that the value of child pornography 'is exceedingly modest, if not *de minimis,*' and that any such value was 'overwhelmingly outweigh[ed]' by 'the evil to be restricted.'

"All three of these characteristics are shared by § 48, as applied to crush videos. [It] must be acknowledged that § 48 differs from a child pornography law in an important respect: preventing the abuse of children is certainly much more important than preventing the torture of the animals used in crush videos. But while protecting children is unquestionably *more* important than protecting animals, the Government also has a compelling interest in preventing the torture depicted in crush videos. [The] animals used in crush videos are living creatures that experience excruciating pain. [Applying] the principles set forth in *Ferber*, I would hold that crush videos are not protected by the First Amendment. . . .

"Application of the *Ferber* framework also supports the constitutionality of § 48 as applied to depictions of brutal animal fights. [First,] such depictions, like crush videos, record the actual commission of a crime involving deadly violence. Dogfights are illegal in every State and the District of Columbia. [Second], Congress had an ample basis for concluding that the crimes depicted in these videos cannot be effectively controlled without targeting the videos. [Third], depictions of dogfights that fall within § 48's reach have by definition no appreciable social value. [Finally], the harm caused by the underlying criminal acts greatly outweighs any trifling value that the depictions might be thought to possess. . . .

"In sum, § 48 may validly be applied to at least two broad real-world categories of expression covered by the statute: crush videos and dogfighting videos. Thus, the statute has a substantial core of constitutionally permissible applications. [Accordingly, I would] reject respondent's claim that § 48 is facially unconstitutional under the overbreadth doctrine."

BROWN v. ENTERTAINMENT MERCHANTS ASS'N, 131 U.S. 2729 (2011). In *Brown*, the Court invalidated a California law imposing restrictions on violent video games. Justice Scalia delivered the opinion of the Court: "California Assembly Bill 1179 prohibits the sale or rental of 'violent video games' to [minors]. The Act covers games 'in which the range of options available to a player includes killing, maiming, dismembering, or sexually assaulting an image of a human being, if those acts are depicted' in a manner that 'a reasonable person, considering the game as a whole, would find appeals to a deviant or morbid interest of minors,' that is 'patently offensive to prevailing standards in the community as to what is suitable for minors,' and that 'causes the game, as a whole, to lack serious literary, artistic, political, or scientific value for minors.' . . .

"[V]ideo games qualify for First Amendment protection. The Free Speech Clause exists principally to protect discourse on public matters, but we have long recognized that it is difficult to distinguish politics from entertainment, and dangerous to try. [Like] the protected books, plays, and movies that preceded them, video games communicate ideas — and even social messages — through many familiar literary devices (such as characters, dialogue, plot, and music) and through features distinctive to the medium (such as the player's interaction with the virtual world). That suffices to confer First Amendment protection. [W]hatever the challenges of applying the Constitution to ever-advancing technology, 'the basic principles of freedom of speech and the press, like the First Amendment's command, do not vary' when a new and different medium for communication appears.

"The most basic of those principles is this: '[A]s a general matter, ... government has no power to restrict expression because of its message, its ideas, its subject matter, or its content.' There are of course exceptions. '"From 1791 to the present," ... the First Amendment has "permitted restrictions upon the content of speech in a few limited areas].'" These limited areas — such as obscenity [*Roth*, incitement [*Brandenburg*], and fighting words [*Chaplinsky*] — represent 'well-defined and narrowly limited classes of speech, the prevention and punishment of which have never been thought to raise any Constitutional problem.' Last Term, in *Stevens*, we held that new categories of unprotected speech may not be added to the list by a legislature that concludes certain speech is too harmful to be tolerated. [There] was no American tradition of forbidding the *depiction of* animal cruelty—though States have long had laws against *committing* it. [As] in *Stevens*, California has tried to make violent-speech regulation look like obscenity regulation, [but] the obscenity exception to the First Amendment does not cover whatever a legislature finds shocking, but only depictions of 'sexual conduct.'

"[B]ecause speech about violence is not obscene, it is of no consequence that California's statute mimics the New York statute regulating obscenity for minors that we upheld in *Ginsberg*. [The] California Act [does] not adjust the boundaries of an existing category of unprotected speech to ensure that a definition designed for adults is not uncritically applied to children. California does not argue that it is empowered to prohibit selling offensively violent works *to adults*. ... Instead, it wishes to create a wholly new category of content-based regulation that is permissible only for speech directed at children. That is unprecedented and mistaken. [No] doubt a State possesses legitimate power to protect children from harm, but that does not include a free-floating power to restrict the ideas to which children may be exposed. [California's] argument would fare better if there were a long standing tradition in this country of specially restricting children's access to depictions of violence, but there is none. Certainly the *books* we give children to read — or read to them when they are younger — contain no shortage of gore. [As] her just deserts for trying to poison Snow White, the wicked queen is made to dance in red hot slippers 'till she fell dead on the [floor].' Hansel and Gretel (children!) kill their captor by baking her in an oven. High-school reading lists are full of similar fare. Homer's Odysseus blinds Polyphemus the Cyclops by grinding out his eye with a heated stake. [And] Golding's Lord of the Flies recounts how a schoolboy called Piggy is savagely murdered *by other children* while marooned on an island. . . .

"California claims that video games present special problems because they are "interactive," [but as] Judge Posner has observed, all literature is interactive. '[T]he better it is, the more interactive. . . . ' *American Amusement Machine Assn.* v. *Kendrick,* 244 F. 3d 572, 577 (CA7 2001). [Justice] Alito has done considerable independent research to identify, video games in which 'the violence is astounding.' 'Victims are dismembered, decapitated, disemboweled, set on fire, and chopped into little pieces. . . . Blood gushes, splatters, and pools.' Justice Alito recounts all these disgusting video games in order to disgust us — but disgust is not a valid basis for restricting expression. . . .

"Because the Act imposes a restriction on the content of protected speech, it is invalid unless California can demonstrate that it passes strict scrutiny — that is, unless it is justified by a compelling government interest and is narrowly drawn to serve that interest. [California] cannot meet that standard. At the outset, it acknowledges that it cannot show a direct causal link between violent video games and harm to minors. [Indeed,] the State's evidence is not compelling. California relies primarily [on a few] research psychologists whose studies purport to show a connection between exposure to violent video games and harmful effects on children. These studies have been rejected by every court to consider them, and with good reason: They do not prove that violent video games *cause* minors to *act* aggressively (which would at least be a beginning). Instead, '[n]early all of the research is based on correlation, not evidence of causation, and most of the studies suffer from [significant] flaws in methodology.' [Even] taking for granted [the conclusion] that violent video games produce some effect on children's feelings of aggression, those effects are both small and indistinguishable from effects produced by other media. [It appears that] the 'effect sizes' of children's exposure to violent video games are 'about the same' as that produced by their exposure to [cartoons] starring Bugs Bunny or the Road Runner, [or] video games like Sonic the Hedgehog that are rated "E" (appropriate for all ages), or even when they 'vie[w] a picture of a gun.'

"Of course, California has (wisely) declined to restrict Saturday morning cartoons, the sale of games rated for young children, or the distribution of pictures of guns. The consequence is that its regulation is wildly underinclusive when judged against its asserted justification, which in our view is alone enough to defeat it. Underinclusiveness raises serious doubts about whether the government is in fact pursuing the interest it invokes, rather than disfavoring a particular speaker or viewpoint. Here, California has singled out the purveyors of video games for disfavored treatment — at least when compared to booksellers, cartoonists, and movie producers — and has given no persuasive reason why.

152

"The Act is also seriously underinclusive in another respect. The California Legislature is perfectly willing to leave this dangerous, mind-altering material in the hands of children so long as one parent (or even an aunt or uncle) says it's OK. [That] is not how one addresses a serious social problem.

"California claims that the Act is justified in aid of parental authority: By requiring that the purchase of violent video games can be made only by adults, the Act ensures that parents can decide what games are appropriate. [But] California cannot show that the Act's restrictions meet a substantial need of parents who wish to restrict their children's access to violent video games but cannot do so. The video-game industry has in place a voluntary rating system designed to inform consumers about the content of games. [Moreover,] the Act's purported aid to parental authority is vastly overinclusive. Not all of the children who are forbidden to purchase violent video games on their own have parents who *care* whether they purchase violent video games. While some of the legislation's effect may indeed be in support of what some parents of the restricted children actually want, its entire effect is only in support of what the State thinks parents *ought* to want. This is not the narrow tailoring to 'assisting parents' that restriction of First Amendment rights requires."

Justice Alito, joined by Chief Justice Roberts, concurred in the result because "the law's definition of 'violent video game' is impermissibly vague." Justice Alito argued that it was unnecessary to go beyond that conclusion to resolve the case, but he nonetheless suggested that he disagreed "with the approach taken in the Court's opinion." He reasoned that in "considering the application of unchanging constitutional principles to new and rapidly evolving technology, [we] should not jump to the conclusion that new technology is fundamentally the same as some older thing with which we are familiar. And we should not hastily dismiss the judgment of legislators, who may be in a better position than we are to assess the implications of new technology."

Justice Thomas dissented: "The Court's decision [does] not comport with the original public understanding of the First Amendment. [The] practices and beliefs of the founding generation establish that 'the freedom of speech,' as originally understood, does not include a right to speak to minors (or a right of minors to access speech) without going through the minors' parents or guardians. [Because] the Constitution is a written instrument, 'its meaning does not alter.' 'That which it meant when adopted, it means now.' [The] founding generation would not have considered it an abridgment of 'the freedom of speech' to support parental authority by restricting speech that bypasses minors' parents."

Justice Breyer also dissented: "In my view, California's statute provides 'fair notice' of what is prohibited,' and consequently is not impermissibly vague. [I] can find no vagueness-related differences between California's law and the New York law upheld in *Ginsberg*. ..."

"Like the majority, I believe that the California law must be 'narrowly tailored' to further a 'compelling interest,' without there being a 'less restrictive' alternative that would be 'at least as effective.' [But I would not apply this strict standard mechanically. Rather, in applying it, I would evaluate the degree to which the statute injures speech-related interests, the nature of the potentially-justifying 'compelling interests,' the degree to which the statute furthers that interest, the nature and effectiveness of possible alternatives, and, in light of this evaluation, whether, overall, 'the statute works speech-related harms . . . out of proportion to the benefits that the statute seeks to provide.' First Amendment standards applied in this way are difficult but not impossible to satisfy. [Citing his dissenting opinion in *Holder v. Humanitarian Law Project*.] . . .

"California's law imposes no more than a modest restriction on expression. [All] it prevents is a child or adolescent from buying, without a parent's assistance, a gruesomely violent video [game]. The interest that California advances in support of the statute is compelling. As the Court has previously described that interest, it consists of both (1) the 'basic' parental claim 'to authority in their own household to direct the rearing of their children,' which makes it proper to enact 'laws designed to aid discharge of [parental] responsibility, and (2) the State's 'independent interest in the well-being of its youth.' [Quoting *Ginsberg*.] Both interests are present here. . . .

"[Moreover,] there is considerable evidence that California's statute significantly furthers this compelling interest. [There] are many scientific studies that support California's views. [Some] of these studies [explain] that the closer a child's behavior comes, not to watching, but to *acting* out horrific violence, the greater the potential psychological harm. [Of course, experts] debate the conclusions of all these studies [and] critics have produced studies [that] reach different conclusions. [I], like most judges, lack the social science expertise to say definitively who is right. [But unlike] the majority, I would find sufficient grounds in these studies [for] this Court to defer to an elected legislature's conclusion that the video games in question are particularly likely to harm children. . . .

"I add that the majority's [conclusion] creates a serious anomaly in First Amendment law. [What] sense does it make to forbid selling to a 13-year-old boy a magazine with an image of a nude woman, while protecting a sale to that 13-year-old of an interactive video game in which he actively, but virtually, binds and gags the woman, then tortures and kills her?"

Page 1206. Before section 3 of the Note, add the following:

3a. *Why does "fuck" offend?* Consider C. Fairman, *FUCK*: Word Taboo and Protecting Our First Amendment Liberties 27-29, 44-45, 55, 60 (2009):

Taboo is a proscription on behavior for a specific community in a specific context. In every culture, there are both taboo acts [and] taboo words. [There] are typical categories of taboo. [Body] effluvia — feces, urine, menstrual fluid, snot, and semen — are often subject to taboo. Sex organs and sex acts are also frequently taboo targets. [Collectively], they all deal with situations in which one is at risk of serious harm. [Our] bodily fluids not only harbor disease but can contaminate others. . . .

But I'm concerned with taboo words, not acts. I can wrap my mind around cleanliness taboos such as avoiding contact with bodily fluids, don't play with your feces, etc. But how does this transform into a taboo against saying *shit*? It's as if Prohibition in the 1920s forbade not just the sale of alcohol but saying the word *whiskey* as well. . . .

The transmutation has a scientific explanation. Let me use effluvia taboos as an illustration. Researchers in public health hygiene [contend] and our hygiene instincts are the product of disgust. [Seeing] a disgust trigger (like vomit or pus) automatically produces a subconscious hygienic reaction. Disgust helps us avoid those things that were associated with the risk of disease in our evolutionary past. [Even] thinking about our excretions (and the body parts associated with them) generates disgust. Because the disgust reaction is involuntary, hearing the words triggers the response. . . .

[There are two forms of the word *fuck*. They] can be labeled as *Fuck*[1] and *Fuck*.[2] *Fuck*[1] means literally "to copulate." . . . *Fuck*[2] doesn't have any intrinsic meaning at all. Rather, it's merely a word that has offensive force. It can be substituted for other swear words. It [can] express all kinds of emotions. [As in "Fuck the draft."] The critical relationship between *Fuck*[1] and *Fuck*[2] is the migration of usage. *Fuck* starts out [as a] as sexual reference [with] taboo attached. Over time, the referential meaning of *Fuck*[1] gave way to the emotional meanings of *Fuck*.[2] The taboo that first attached to *Fuck*[1] migrates to emotional *Fuck*[2] despite its nonsexual meaning. The sexual reference is gone, but the taboo remains. . . .

When you hear fuck, your brain automatically produces an emotional reaction to the word's taboo — all those unhealthy feelings and fears about sex. You can't stop this reflexive processing of the taboo, but you do have choices on how to react. [Some people] don't merely refrain from using the word; they're crusaders designed to stomp out its use, [including] nonsexual *Fuck*[2].

155

Page 1214.   Before section 1 of the Note, add the following:

1A. *Fleeting expletives and the continuing viability of* Pacifica. In 2004, the Federal Communications Commission amended the approach that was upheld in *Pacifica* and held for the first time that any use of the words "fuck" and "shit" could be actionably indecent, even if the word was not used in a sexual manner and even if it was used only once. The 2004 order dealt with an NBC broadcast of the Golden Globe Awards, in which the singer Bono commented, "This is really, really fucking brilliant." The Commission explained that the broadcast was "patently offensive" because the word "fuck" "is one of the most vulgar, graphic and explicit descriptions of sexual activity in the English language." The Commission argued that its action was necessary to "safeguard the well-being of the nation's children from the most objectionable, most offensive language."

FCC v. Fox Television Stations, 129 S. Ct. 1800 (2009), dealt with decisions by the FCC involving the singer Cher's use of the word "fuck" during the Billboard Music Awards ("I've also had critics for the last forty years saying that I was on my way out every year. Right. So fuck 'em.") and the actress Nicole Richie's use of the words "shit" and "fucking" in another award ceremony ("Have you ever tried to get cow shit out of a Prada purse? It's not so fucking simple."). In both instances, the FCC held that the fleeting use of these expletives violated its new 2004 order. The Court of Appeals held that the 2004 order was invalid under the Administrative Procedure Act because it was arbitrary and capricious. The Supreme Court reversed, but did not reach the First Amendment question.

In his opinion for the Court, Justice Scalia offered the following observation that is relevant to the continuing vitality of *Pacifica*: "[The Court of Appeals] believed that children today 'likely hear this language far more often from other sources than they did in the 1970's when the Commission first began sanctioning indecent speech,' and that cuts against more stringent regulation of broadcasts. Assuming the premise is true, [the] conclusion does not necessarily follow. The Commission could reasonably conclude that the pervasiveness of foul language, and the coarsening of public entertainment in other media such as cable, justify more stringent regulation of broadcast programs so as to give conscientious parents a relatively safe haven for their children."

In a concurring opinion, Justice Thomas called *Pacifica* into question. Noting that *Pacifica* was premised in part on the doctrine that the government could regulate broadcasting more than other means of communication because of the "scarcity of broadcast frequencies," Thomas argued that that doctrine was incoherent in 1978 and, in any event, had completely been outstripped by technological advances in the years since.

Justice Breyer, joined by Justices Stevens, Souter, and Ginsburg, dissented on the ground that the 2004 order violated the Administrative Procedure Act.

Page 1226.   Before section 3 of the Note, add the following:

2a. *Hate speech and violence.* Consider Bell, Restraining the Heartless: Racist Speech and Minority Rights, 84 Ind. L. J. 963, 979 (2009):

> The structure of First Amendment doctrine [has] led to a regime that is ill prepared to deal with important negative consequences of racist speech, [as] demonstrated by the following example. In 1996, Matthew Hale assumed leadership of the World Church of the Creator (WTC), an organization dedicated to the supremacy of the White race. Among other things, Hale preached that racial and ethnic minorities are inferior to Whites. In 1999, one of his followers, Benjamin Smith, took his gospel dehumanizing minorities seriously. Smith embarked on a shooting spree targeting Jews, Blacks, and Asian Americans that left two people dead and twelve people injured. Because Hale had not explicitly preached violence, his speech was protected. The U.S. approach, which protects racist speech that does not threaten or incite violence, fails to acknowledge that White supremacists' racist ideology blames racial and ethnic minorities for all of society's ills. When demagogues and leaders of hate groups use racist and hate propaganda, they are seeking followers whose attachment to the organization is premised on seeing members of out groups as less than human. Once minorities are assumed to be subhuman, there is no longer any reason not to eliminate them by attacking them physically. [Contrary] to the views of critics of hate speech legislation who dismiss arguments suggesting a connection between racist rhetoric and violence, the actions of Smith and others like him suggest that racist speech urging listeners to disregard the humanity of particular citizens may have violent and not unforeseeable consequences.

Page 1228.   At the end of section d of the Note, add the following:

Consider also Heyman, The Dark Side of the Force: The Legacy of Justice Holmes for First Amendment Jurisprudence, 19 Wm. & Mary Bill Rts. J. 661, 717 (2011): "[T]he American position on political hate speech [is largely] the legacy of Justice Holmes. [From] a Holmesian perspective [there] is no principled distinction between hate speech and any other form of political expression. [He] would say that, under our political system, advocates of group hatred should be just as free as anyone else to 'fight to make the kind of a world that [they] should like,' and that if their views 'are destined to be accepted by the dominant forces of the community, the only meaning of free speech is that they should be given their chance and have their way.' [Holmes'] view does not provide an adequate rationale for free speech [because] it undermines the liberal humanist principles that should be regarded as central to the First Amendment."

Page 1229.   At the end of subsection f of the Note, add the following:

ff. Waldron, Dignity and Defamation: The Visibility of Hate, 123 Harv. L. Rev. 1597, 1599-1600, 1627 (2010):

[H]ate speech regulation can be understood as the protection of a certain sort of precious public good: a visible assurance offered by society to all of its members that they will not be subject to abuse, defamation, humiliation, discrimination, and violence on grounds of race, ethnicity, religion, gender, and in some cases sexual orientation. [The] most important aim of these laws [is] simply to diminish the presence of visible hatred in society by protecting the public commitment to their equal standing in society against public denigration. . . .

In a well-ordered society, [people] know that when they leave home in the morning they can reasonably count on not being discriminated against, humiliated, or terrorized. [When] a society is defaced with anti-Semitic signage, burning crosses, or defamatory racial leaflets, that sort of assurance evaporates. [In a society that tolerates hate speech], people no longer have the benefit of a general public assurance [of] human dignity. President Lyndon Johnson once gave this reason for the moral necessity of the Civil Rights Act: "A man has a right not to be insulted in front of his children." The security that people look for is security against the soul-shriveling humiliation that accompanies the manifestation of injustice in society.

Page 1249.   At the end of *Note: R.A.V. and Black*, add the following:

4. *Express incitement and express threats.* In the incitement situation, the Court, following the leading of Judge Learned Hand in *Masses*, seems to require that for incitement of unlawful conduct to come within the low value category of express incitement the incitement must be *express*. Is *Black*'s treatment of threats consistent with that requirement? Is a burning cross an *express* threat?

Does it make any sense to require express incitement but not express threats? See Taylor, Free Expression and Expressness, 33 N.Y.U. Rev. L & Soc. Ch. 375 (2009). Is a noose equivalent to a burning cross? See Bell, The Hangman's Noose and the Lynch Mob: Hate Speech and the Jena Six, 44 Har. Civ. Rts.-Civ. Lib. L. Rev. 329 (2009).

Page 1253. After section 3 of the Note, add the following:

4. *Cyber gender harassment.* Consider Citron, Law's Expressive Value in Combating Cyber Gender Harassment, 108 Mich. L. Rev. 373, 378-382 (2009):

Although cyber gender harassment encompasses various behaviors, it has a set of core features: (1) its victims are female, (2) the harassment is aimed at particular women, and (3) the abuse invokes the targeted individual's gender in sexually threatening and degrading ways. [Examples] of cyber gender harassment show that it routinely involves threats of rape and other forms of sexual violence. It often reduces targeted women to sexual objects and includes humiliating comments that reinforce gender-constructed stereotypes, such as "[w]ho let this woman out of the kitchen?" and "why don't you make yourself useful and go have a baby."

... For instance, anonymous posters targeted NYU law student Jill Filipovic on the social networking site AutoAdmit. Under a thread entitled "can someone post a pic of Jill H. [sic] from NYU?," posters uploaded Ms. Filipovic's Facebook profile and picture. Posters made clear that they attended school with Ms. Filipovic by noting "I sat next to Jill F for an hour." [Anonymous] posters threatened Ms. Filipovic with rape: "I want to brutally rape that Jill slut" [and] "maybe you'd have to kill her afterward." They created menacing message threads, such as "Official Jill Filipovic RAPE thread" and "I have it on good authority that Jill F has rape fantasies." Posters discussed photo-shopping a picture of Ms. Filipovic's head onto a porn star's body and claimed that she had a number of abortions.

The harassment negatively affected Ms. Filipovic's law school studies. After seeing the threatening threads, Ms. Filipovic skipped class, fearing that students in her community would write about her whereabouts. When she attended class, she avoided participating in discussions as she did not want to say something stupid and have it appear online. Because she could not determine who might be the anonymous AutoAdmit posters, she avoided making friends in law school. [In] the wake of the attacks, she felt depressed and helpless.

To what extent, if any, can these sorts of attacks be the subject of legal redress on the ground that they consist of incitement, libel, threats, intentional infliction of emotional distress, or invasions of privacy? Is some broader basis of liability necessary and constitutionally permissible? See Citron, Cyber Civil Rights, 80 B.U. L. Rev. 61 (2009).

E. Content-Neutral Restrictions

Page 1273. At the end of section 9 of the Note, add the following:

Wells, Privacy and Funeral Protests, 87 N.C. L. Rev. 151 (2008).

Page 1274. At the end of section 10 of the Note, add the following:

See also Krotoszynski, The Return of Seditious Libel, 55 UCLA L. Rev. 1239 (2008) (criticizing federal courts for upholding such restrictions by crediting inflated claims of security needs when the real motive for the restrictions is the desire of political leaders not to be embarrassed by speech that criticizes them).

Page 1291. At the end of section 2 of the Note, add the following:

Suppose a town has an ordinance prohibiting any use of a loudspeaker in a residential neighborhood between the hours of 8:00 P.M. and 8:00 A.M. Presumably, this ordinance is a constitutional, content-neutral regulation of speech. Now suppose the town amends the ordinance to allow the use of loudspeakers in residential neighborhoods until 10:00 P.M. for political campaign speech within two weeks of an election. Is the amended ordinance unconstitutional after *Mosley*? Consider Ammori, Beyond Content-Neutrality: Understanding Content-Based Promotion of Democratic Speech, 61 Fed. Comm. L. J. 273, 277, 283, 324 (2009):

Government need not be "neutral" regarding speech [that] is traditionally believed necessary for an informed citizenry. [Free] speech doctrine [should] explicitly distinguish between laws meant to promote [content] necessary for an informed citizenry and those meant to suppress disfavored content. [Content-promoting] laws do not necessarily reflect a censorial purpose. [Laws] promoting democratic content pose different risks from content-based laws meant to suppress disfavored content, and the constitutional test applied to content-promoting laws should focus on the main risk: viewpoint discrimination.

Page 1299.   After section 1 of the Note, add the following:

1A. *Payroll deductions for political activities.* Until 2003, public employees in Idaho could authorize both a payroll deduction for general union dues and a separate payroll deduction for union political activities. In 2003, the Idaho legislature prohibited payroll deductions for political purposes. A group of Idaho public employee unions challenged the 2003 legislation on the ground that it violated the First Amendment. In Ysursa v. Pocatello Education Association, 129 S. Ct. 1093 (2009), the Court rejected this claim.

Chief Justice Roberts wrote the opinion of the Court: "Restrictions on speech based on its content are 'presumptively invalid' and subject to strict scrutiny. [But 'a] legislature's decision not to subsidize the exercise of a fundamental right does not infringe the right, and thus is not subject to strict scrutiny.' [The] State is not constitutionally obligated to provide payroll deductions at all. [While] publicly administered payroll deductions for political purposes can enhance the unions' exercise of First Amendment rights, Idaho is under no obligation to aid the unions in their political activities. And the State's decision not to do so is not an abridgment of the unions' speech. [Given] that the State has not infringed the unions' First Amendment rights, the State need only demonstrate a rational basis to justify the ban on political payroll deductions. [The] prohibition is [justified] by the State's interest in avoiding the reality or appearance of government favoritism or entanglement with partisan politics."

Justice Ginsburg filed a concurring opinion. Justices Stevens, Breyer, and Souter filed dissenting opinions. Would the outcome be different if the State prohibited payroll deductions to support the Democratic Party? Would the outcome be different if the State prohibited private employers from allowing payroll deductions for political purposes? In fact, the 2003 legislation prohibited private employers from allowing such deductions. The State conceded that that part of the 2003 statute violated the First Amendment. Why should it matter whether the law restricts private employers rather than public employers?

Page 1305.   After the Note, add the following:

CHRISTIAN LEGAL SOCIETY CHAPTER v. MARTINEZ, 130 S. Ct. 2971 (2010). Hastings College of the Law, a public law school within the University of California system, extends official recognition to student groups through its "Registered Student Organization" (RSO) program. RSOs receive certain benefits, including the use of school funds, facilities, and channels of communication, as well as the use of Hastings' name and logo. In exchange for such recognition, RSOs must abide by certain conditions. All RSOs must comply with the school's Nondiscrimination Policy, which forbids discrimination on the basis of race, religion, gender, national origin, age, disability, ancestry, and sexual orientation. Hastings interprets this policy to mandate acceptance of *all* students.

In 2004, students at Hastings created the Christian Legal Society by affiliating with a national Christian association that charters student chapters at law schools throughout the country. These chapters must adopt bylaws that, *inter alia*, require members and officers to sign a "Statement of Faith" and to conduct their lives in accord with prescribed principles. CLS excludes from affiliation anyone who engages in "unrepentant homosexual conduct" or holds religious convictions different from those in the Statement of Faith. Hastings rejected CLS's application for RSO status on the ground that the group excluded students based on religion and sexual orientation. CLS filed this action asserting that Hastings' "accept all-comers" policy violates its First Amendment rights of expression and association.

The Court, in a five-to-four decision, rejected CLS's claim. Justice Ginsburg delivered the opinion of the Court: "[Hastings], through its RSO program, established a limited public forum. [See *Rosenberger*]. [The] Court has permitted restrictions on access to a limited public forum, like the RSO program here, [if they are] reasonable and viewpoint neutral. [We first] consider whether the Hastings' policy is reasonable. [With] appropriate regard for school administrators' judgment, we review the justifications Hastings offers in defense of its all-comers requirement. First, the open-access policy 'ensures that the leadership, educational, and social opportunities afforded by [RSOs] are available to all students. [Second], the all-comers requirement helps Hastings police the written terms of its Nondiscrimination Policy without inquiring into an RSOs motivation for membership restrictions. [Third], the Law School reasonably adheres to the view that an all-comers [policy] 'encourages tolerance, cooperation, and learning among students.' [Fourth], Hastings' policy [conveys] the Law School's decision 'to decline to subsidize with public monies and benefits [discriminatory conduct].'...

"The Law School's policy is all the more creditworthy in view of the 'substantial alternative channels that remain open for [CLS-student] communication to take place. [Student groups] commonly maintain a presence at universities without official school affiliation. Based on the record before us, CLS [hosted] a variety of activities the year after Hastings denied it recognition, and the number of students attending those meetings and events doubled. [It bears emphasizing] that nonrecognition of a student organization is [not] equivalent to prohibiting its members from speaking....

"CLS [assails] the reasonableness of the all-comers policy [by forecasting] that the policy will facilitate hostile takeovers; if organizations must open their arms to all, CLS contends, saboteurs will infiltrate groups to subvert their mission and message. This supposition strikes us as more hypothetical than real, [but if] students begin to exploit an all-comers policy by hijacking organizations to distort or destroy their missions, Hastings presumably would revisit and revise its policy....

"We next consider whether Hastings' all-comers policy is viewpoint neutral. [It is] hard to imagine a more viewpoint-neutral policy than one requiring *all* student groups to accept *all* comers. [CLS] attacks the regulation by pointing to its effect: The policy is vulnerable to constitutional assault, CLS contends, because 'it systematically and predictably burdens most heavily those groups whose viewpoints are out of favor with the campus mainstream.' [This] argument stumbles from its first step because '[a] regulation that serves purposes unrelated to the content of expression is deemed neutral, even if it has an incidental effect on some speakers or messages but not others. [Moreover,] Hastings' requirement that student groups accept all [comers] 'is justified without reference to the content [or viewpoint] of the regulated speech. The Law School's policy aims at the *act* of rejecting would-be group members without reference to the reasons motivating that [behavior]. CLS' conduct — not its Christian perspective — is [what] stands between the group and RSO status. [Finding] Hastings' open-access condition on RSO status reasonable and viewpoint neutral, we reject CLS' free-speech and expressive-association claims."

Note that the Court decided the case on the basis of a stipulation by the parties that Hastings had interpreted and applied the Nondiscrimination Policy as an "accept all-comers" policy. Would it change the analysis if the Court had considered the constitutionality of the Nondiscrimination Policy itself — that is, as a policy denying RSO status to organizations discriminating on the basis of certain *particular* characteristics (that is, race, religion, gender, sexual orientation, etc.)?

Does it matter that this case involves a subsidy rather than a prohibition? Suppose, for example, the state made it unlawful for any group or organization to deny membership to any person. Would such a law be constitutional as applied to the Democratic Party, if it wants to exclude Republicans from voting in its upcoming primary? Would it be constitutional as applied to a synagogue that restricts membership only to Jews? Suppose that, instead of prohibiting such selective membership, the state merely denied tax-exempt status to any group or organization that isn't open to all comers?

Consider the Court's response to this question: "CLS, in seeking what is effectively a state subsidy, faces only indirect pressure to modify its membership policies; CLS may exclude any person for any reason if it forgoes the benefits of official recognition. [Our] decisions have distinguished between policies that require action and those that withhold benefits. [CLS] seeks not parity with other organizations, but a preferential exemption from Hastings' policy. The First Amendment shields CLS against state prohibition of the organization's expressive activity, [but] CLS enjoys no constitutional right to state subvention of its selectivity." Suppose Hastings denied RSO status only to student organizations that promote religion? On compelled association, see Section V-E-2, in the main volume.

Justice Alito, joined by Chief Justice Roberts and Justices Scalia and Thomas, dissented: "The proudest boast of our free speech jurisprudence is that we protect the freedom to express 'the thought that we hate.' Today's decision rests on a very different principle: no freedom for expression that offends prevailing standards of political correctness in our country's institutions of higher learning. [Hastings] currently has more than 60 registered groups and, in all its history, has denied registration to exactly one: the Christian Legal Society."

Justice Alito maintained that, for procedural reasons, the Nondiscrimination Policy rather than the accept-all-comers policy was properly at issue in the case, and he therefore proceeded to consider the constitutionality of that policy: "[Many RSOs at Hastings] are dedicated to expressing a message. For example, Silenced Right, a pro-life group, [teaches] that 'all human life [is] sacred and has inherent dignity,' while [the] American Constitution Society [seeks] 'to counter [a] narrow conservative vision' of American law.' [Under the Nondiscrimination Policy, such groups may exclude members who do not share the organization's views, without losing their RSO status, because discrimination of the basis of political, philosophical, cultural or social viewpoints is not prohibited. The Nondiscrimination Policy] singled out one category of expressive associations for disfavored treatment: groups formed to express a religious message. Only religious groups were required to admit students who did not share their views. An environmentalist group was not required to admit students who rejected global warming. [But] CLS was required to admit avowed atheists. This was patent viewpoint discrimination. It is no wonder that the Court makes no attempt to defend the constitutionality of the Nondiscrimination Policy."

164

Although the Court found it unnecessary to consider the constitutionality of the Nondiscrimination Policy because of the parties' stipulation, Justice Stevens filed a separate concurring opinion responding to Justice Alito: "In the dissent's view, by refusing to grant CLS an exemption from the Nondiscrimination Policy, Hastings violated CLS's rights, for by proscribing unlawful discrimination on the basis of religion, the policy discriminated unlawfully on the basis of religion. [But] the Nondiscrimination Policy is content and viewpoint neutral. It does not reflect a judgment by school officials about any student group's speech. [Indeed], it does not regulate expression or belief at all. [What] the policy does reflect is a judgment that discrimination [on] the basis of certain factors, such as race and religion, is less tolerable than discrimination on the basis of other factors."

Justice Alito responded to this argument: "Justice Stevens [argues] that the Nondiscrimination Policy is viewpoint neutral because it 'does not regulate expression or belief at all' but instead regulates conduct. This Court has held, however, that the particular conduct at issue here constitutes a form of expression that is protected by the First Amendment. It is [well] established that the First Amendment shields the right of a group to engage in expressive association by limiting membership to persons whose admission does not significantly interfere with the group's ability to convey its views. [Citing *Boy Scouts v. Dale*, at page 434 of the main volume.] [Moreover, the Nondiscrimination Policy] also discriminates on the basis of viewpoint regarding sexual morality. CLS has a particular viewpoint on this subject, namely, that sexual conduct outside marriage [is] wrongful. Hastings would not allow CLS to express this viewpoint by limiting membership to persons willing to express a sincere agreement with CLS's views. By contrast, [a] Free Love Club could require members to affirm that they reject the traditional view of sexual morality to which CLS adheres. It is hard to see how this can be viewed as anything other than viewpoint discrimination."

Justice Alito then turned to the "accept-all-comers" version of the Hastings policy: "There can be no dispute that [the First Amendment] would not permit a generally applicable law mandating that private religious groups admit members who do not share the group's beliefs. Religious groups like CLS obviously engage in expressive association, and no legitimate state interest could override the powerful effect that an accept-all-comers law would have on the ability of religious groups to express their views. The State of California surely could not demand that all Christian groups admit members who believe that Jesus was merely human. [Muslim] groups could not be forced to admit person who are viewed as slandering Islam. [But] the Court now holds that Hastings [may] impose these very same requirements on students who wish to [gain the benefits of RSO status]. The Court lists four justifications offered by Hastings in defense of the accept-all-comers policy, [but these justifications] are insufficient. [Moreover], statements in the majority opinion make it seem as if the denial of registration did not hurt CLS at all. [Beyond that, though, the] majority's emphasis on CLS's ability to endure [by] using private facilities and means of communication [is] quite amazing. This Court does not customarily brush aside a claim of unlawful discrimination with the observation that the effects of the discrimination were really not so bad. . . .

"The Court is also wrong in holding that the accept-all-comers policy is viewpoint neutral. The Court proclaims that it would be 'hard to imagine a more viewpoint-neutral policy, but I would not be so quick to jump to this conclusion. Even if it is assumed that the policy is viewpoint neutral on its face, there is strong evidence in the record that the policy was announced as a pretext. The adoption of a facially neutral policy for the purpose of suppressing the expression of a particular viewpoint is viewpoint discrimination. Here, CLS has made a strong showing that Hastings's sudden adoption [of] its accept-all-comers policy was a pretext for the law school's unlawful denial of CLS's registration application under the Nondiscrimination Policy. . . .

"I do not think it is an exaggeration to say that today's decision is a serious setback for freedom of expression in this country. [I] can only hope this decision will turn out to be an aberration."

Page 1313.   At the end of section 3 of the Note, add the following:

Consider also Norton, The Measure of Government Speech: Identifying Expression's Source, 88 B.U. L. Rev. 587, 589, 595-597, 629-630 (2008):

[T]he Supreme Court has shielded the government's expression from Free Speech Clause scrutiny. [Government] speech merits this insulation because it is both inevitable and valuable. In particular, government speech facilitates significant First Amendment interests in sharing knowledge and discovering truth by informing the public on a wide range of topics. [A] message's source can have positive or negative effects on its persuasiveness, depending on observers' assessments of the source's credibility [and] because public attitudes towards government vary widely [assessments] of government credibility differ too. [One danger of government speech is] that the government may manipulate the public's attitudes towards its views by deliberately obscuring its identity as a message's source. Government speech is thus most valuable and least dangerous when its government source is apparent, enabling the public to more accurately assess the message's credibility. . . .

In *Rust*, [doctors and nurses] delivered the contested counseling [without] any requirement that its governmental origins be disclosed. Under these circumstances, patients might well misunderstand clinic employees to be offering their own independent counsel, rather than speaking as agents required to espouse the government's view. [Because] health professionals may be seen as more credible than the government in this setting based on public perception of their expertise and objectivity, patients may have been misled into evaluating the counseling differently than they would have if the speakers had made clear its governmental source. [*Rust*] thus illustrates the danger of treating expression that fails to satisfy the demands of functional transparency as government speech free from First Amendment scrutiny.

Page 1314.   At the end of the Note, insert the following:

5. *Mandatory Abortion Counseling.* Is there a constitutional right not be subjected to government speech? Consider Corbin, The First Amendment Right Against Compelled Listening, 89 B.U. L. Rev. 939, 1001-1007 (2009):

In South Dakota, doctors must tell women who have decided not to continue their pregnancy that [the] abortion will "terminate the life of a whole, separate, unique, living human being." [In] Oklahoma, the legislature passed a law stating that women must have an ultrasound at least an hour before her abortion, and that her doctor must show her the image and provide a simultaneous description of the ultrasound. . . .

[Can these women be constitutionally compelled] to hear the government's message? [The] goal of these mandatory abortion counseling regulations is to convince women to change their minds about terminating their unwanted pregnancy. [Besides] being one-sided, the compelled counseling is often inaccurate. Several assertions about the potential consequences of abortion are false, such as increased risks of suicide, infertility and breast cancer. . . .

South Dakota's and Oklahoma's ideological and viewpoint-based "informed consent" laws violate the right against compelled listening. [The] state's paternalistic efforts to persuade women to think in one particular way should fail. [The] government should not be able to foist information onto listeners in order to convince them to make beneficial decisions any more than it can censor information to prevent listeners from making poor decisions.

Page 1317. Before *National Endowment for the Arts v. Finley*, add the following:

PLEASANT GROVE CITY, UTAH V. SUMMUM, 129 S. Ct. 1129 (2009).
Pioneer Park, a public park in Pleasant Grove City, contains fifteen permanent displays, eleven of which were donated to the city by private groups. These include an historic granary, a wishing well, a September 11 monument, and a Ten Commandments monument donated by the Fraternal Order of Eagles in 1971. Summum is a religious organization founded in 1975 and headquartered in Salt Lake City. In 2003, Summum's president requested permission to erect a stone monument in Pioneer Park. The monument would contain the Seven Aphorisms of Summum, which according to Summum doctrine were inscribed on the original tablet handed down by God to Moses on Mount Sinai. The city denied the request, explaining that it permitted monuments to be displayed in the park only if they "directly related to the history of Pleasant Grove" or they "were donated by groups with longstanding ties to the Pleasant Grove community." The Court of Appeals for the Tenth Circuit held that because public parks have traditionally been regarded as public forums, the city could not constitutionally reject the Seven Aphorisms monument absent a compelling justification for doing so. In a unanimous decision, the Supreme Court reversed.

Justice Alito delivered the opinion of the Court: "The [fundamental] disagreement [centers] on the nature of [the city's] conduct when [it] permitted privately donated monuments to be erected in Pioneer Park. [Was the city] engaging in [its] own expressive conduct? Or [was it] providing a forum for private speech? [If the city was] engaging in [its] own expressive conduct, then the Free Speech Clause has no application. The Free Speech Clause restricts government regulation of private speech; it does not regulate government speech. [Citing *Rust*.] [Indeed,] it is not easy to imagine how government could function if it lacked this freedom. . . .

"While government speech is not restricted by the Free Speech Clause, the government does not have a free hand to regulate private speech on government property. [There] may be situations in which it is difficult to tell whether a government entity is speaking on its own behalf or is providing a forum for private speech, but this case does not present such a situation. Permanent monuments displayed on public property typically represent government speech. [When] a government entity arranges for the construction of a monument, it does so because it wishes to convey some thought or instill some feeling in those who see the structure. [Just] as government-commissioned and government-financed monuments speak for the government, so do privately financed and donated monuments that the government accepts and displays to the public on government land. [Throughout] our Nation's history, the general government practice with respect to donated monuments has been one of selective receptivity. [Government] decisionmakers select the monuments that portray what they view as appropriate for the place in question, taking into account such content-based factors as esthetics, history, and local culture. The monuments that are accepted, therefore, are meant to convey and have the effect of conveying a government message, and they thus constitute government speech. ...

"[Summum] voices the legitimate concern that the government speech doctrine not be used as a subterfuge for favoring certain private speakers over others based on viewpoint. [Summum] and the Court of Appeals analogize the installation of permanent monuments in a public park to the delivery of speeches and the holding of marches and demonstrations, and they thus invoke the rule that a public park is a traditional public forum for these activities. But 'public forum principles ... are out of place in the context of this case.' The forum doctrine has been applied in situations in which government-owned property or a government program was capable of accommodating a large number of public speakers without defeating the essential function of the land or the program. For example, a park can accommodate many speakers and, over time, many parades and demonstrations. [A] public university's student activity fund can provide money for many campus activities. [Citing *Rosenberger*.] A public university's buildings may offer meeting space for hundreds of student groups. [Citing *Widmar*.] [By] contrast, public parks can accommodate only a limited number of permanent monuments. [It] is hard to imagine how a public park could be opened up for the installation of permanent monuments by every person or group wishing to engage in that form of expression. [Indeed,] if public parks were considered to be traditional public forums for the purpose of erecting privately donated monuments, most parks would have little choice but to refuse all such donations. And where the application of forum analysis would lead almost inexorably to closing of the forum, it is obvious that forum analysis is out of place. [Therefore,] forum analysis simply does not apply to the installation of permanent monuments on public property.

"[We] hold that the City's decision to accept certain privately donated monuments while rejecting [Summum's] is best viewed as a form of government speech. As a result, the City's decision is not subject to the Free Speech Clause. ... "

Justice Stevens, joined by Justice Ginsburg, filed a concurring opinion, noting that the Court's "recently minted government speech doctrine" is "of doubtful merit." Justice Scalia, joined by Justice Thomas, filed concurring opinion, emphasizing that the city's display of the Ten Commandments monument does not violate the Establishment Clause. Justice Breyer filed a concurring opinion, arguing that the government speech doctrine must be understood as "a rule of thumb, not a rigid category." Justice Souter filed a concurring opinion, expressing "qualms" about the argument that "public monuments are government speech categorically."

How does one square this decision with the establishment clause? Can the city, invoking the government speech doctrine, legitimately allow a twenty-foot-high cross to be displayed in a public park as an exercise of government speech? See the discussion of the *McCreary County* and *Van Orden* cases at page 1487 of the main text.

Page 1325. At the end of the page, add the following:

For the view that the Framers understood the First Amendment to protect symbolic expression, see Volokh, Symbolic Expression and the Original Meaning of the First Amendment, 97 Geo. L.J. 1057 (2009).

Page 1334. At the end of section 6 of the Note, add the following:

6A. *When is an incidental restriction not "incidental"?* A paradigm example of an incidental restriction might be a law prohibiting any person to speed, as applied to an individual who speeds in order to express his opposition to speed limits. Note that two factors are present in this situation: (1) the law is not directed at speech and (2) it is not the expressive element of the act that causes the harm the state seeks to prevent. Both factors must be present for the incidental effect doctrine to apply. Consider, for example, a prosecution for breach of the peace based on an inflammatory speech given by an individual on a street corner that causes a fight. The breach of the peace statute is not directed at speech, as such. It applies to all sorts of non-speech conduct, such as making loud noises late at night in a residential neighborhood or parking one's car on a sidewalk. In that sense, the statute has only an incidental effect on speakers. But because the speaker has breached the peace because of the response of others to the message he has conveyed, the Court does not treat this as a mere incidental effect. Indeed, this is implicit in the World War I cases in which defendants were prosecuted for "obstructing the draft" and in the hostile audience cases in which they were prosecuted for breach of the peace. Put simply, where the relevant harm is caused by the message, the incidental effects doctrine is inapplicable.

Along these lines, consider Holder v. Humanitarian Law Project, 130 S. Ct. 2705 (2010), which involved the constitutionality of a federal statute declaring it unlawful for any person knowingly to provide "material support" to a foreign terrorist organization, where the statute defined "material support" as including, among other things, property, money, lodging, safehouses, facilities, weapons, and expert advice. Plaintiffs, who wanted to advise foreign terrorist organizations how to further their ends through legal channels, challenged the constitutionality of the statute as applied to them. The government argued that the statute had only an incidental effect on speech and that O'Brien should govern. Although the Court upheld the statute on other grounds, it unanimously rejected the government's argument:

> O'Brien does not provide the applicable standard for reviewing a content-based regulation of speech, and [this statute] regulates speech on the basis of its content. [The government] argues that [the statute falls under O'Brien] because it *generally* functions as a regulation of conduct. That argument runs headlong into a number of our precedents, most prominently Cohen v. California, [which] involved a generally applicable regulation of conduct, barring breaches of the peace. But when Cohen was convicted for wearing a jacked bearing an epithet, we did not apply O'Brien. Instead, we recognized that the generally applicable law was directed at Cohen because of what his speech communicated — he violated the breach of the peace statute because of the offensive content of his particular message. We accordingly applied more rigorous scrutiny and reversed his conviction. This suit falls into the same category.

Page 1345.   After section 2 of the Note, add the following:

2a. *Are signatures on a referendum petition "speech" within the meaning of the First Amendment?* In Doe v. Reed, 130 S. Ct. 2811 (2010), the Court considered the constitutionality of a Washington state public records statute, which authorizes the public disclosure of the names of individuals who sign referendum petitions. The plaintiffs argued that public disclosure would chill the willingness of individuals to sign such petitions. Although upholding the statute on its face, the Court rejected the argument that such signatures are not "speech" because "signing a petition is a legally operative legislative act and therefore 'does not involve any significant expressive element.'" The Court concluded that "[p]etition signing remains expressive even when it has legal effect in the electoral process." Although concurring in the result, Justice Scalia expressed "doubt whether signing a petition" that has legal effect "fits within 'the freedom of speech' at all." He explained: "When [a] voter signs a referendum [petition], he is acting as a legislator. [A] voter who signs a referendum petition [is] exercising legislative power because his signature, somewhat like a vote for or against a bill in the legislature, seeks to affect the legal force of the measure at issue. [There] is no precedent from this Court holding that legislating is protected by the First Amendment."

2b. *Are legislative votes "speech" within the meaning of the First Amendment?* In Nevada Comm'n on Ethics v. Carrigan, 131 S. Ct. _____ (2011), Carrigan, a state legislator, voted to approve a casino project that had used his long-time friend and campaign manager as a paid consultant. The commission held that, by so doing, Carrigan had violated a state ethics rule prohibiting public officials from voting on legislative matters with respect to which they have a conflict of interest. Carrigan claimed that this finding violated his rights under the First Amendment. The key issue was whether the casting of a vote by a state legislator is constitutionally protected speech. In a unanimous decision, the Court rejected Carrigan's claim.

Justice Scalia delivered the opinion of the Court: "Laws punishing libel and obscenity are not thought to violate 'the freedom of speech' [because] such laws existed in 1791 and have been in place ever since. The same is true of legislative recusal rules. [Such] rules have been commonplace for over 200 years. '[E]arly congressional enactments "provid[e] contemporaneous and weighty evidence of the Constitution's meaning,"' [and that] evidence is dispositive here. Within 15 years of the founding, both the House of Representatives and the Senate adopted recusal rules. [Moreover, today,] virtually every State has enacted some type of recusal law. . . . "But how can it be that restrictions upon legislators' voting are not restrictions upon legislators' protected speech? The answer is that a legislator's vote is the commitment of his apportioned share of the legislature's power to the passage or defeat of a particular proposal. The legislative power thus committed is not personal to the legislator but belongs to the people; the legislator has no personal right to it. [In] this respect, voting by a legislator is different from voting by a citizen. . . .

"There are, to be sure, instances where action conveys a symbolic meaning — such as the burning of a flag to convey disagreement with a country's policies. But the act of voting symbolizes nothing. It *discloses*, to be sure, that the legislator wishes (for whatever reason) that the proposition on the floor be adopted, just as a physical assault discloses that the attacker dislikes the victim. But neither the one nor the other is an act of communication. Moreover, the fact that a nonsymbolic act is the product of deeply held persona belief — even if the actor would like it to *convey* his deeply held personal belief — does not transform action into First Amendment speech. . . .

"Carrigan and Justice Alito [cite] *Doe v. Reed* as establishing 'the expressive character of voting.' But *Reed* did no such thing. That case held only that a citizen's signing of a petition—'"core political speech"'—was not deprived of its protected status simply because, under state law, a petition that garnered a sufficient number of signatures would suspend the state law to which it pertained, pending a referendum. It is one thing to say that an inherently expressive act remains so despite its having governmental effect, but it is altogether another thing to say that a governmental act becomes expressive simply because the governmental actor wishes it to be so." Justice Alito filed a concurring opinion rejecting the Court's distinction of *Doe v. Reed*, but agreeing with the result because "legislative recusal rules were not regarded during the founding era as *impermissible* restrictions on freedom of speech." Justice Kennedy also filed a concurring opinion.

Are you persuaded by the Court's distinction of *Doe v. Reed*? What do you think of the Court's "originalist" argument? Note that Justice Scalia was wrong about obscenity laws. In fact, there were no anti-obscenity laws in the United States until the nineteenth century. See Stone, Sex, Violence, and the First Amendment, 74 U. Chi. L. Rev. 1857, 1861-1863 (2007). What does this tell you about the dangers of "originalism" as a method of constitutional interpretation? Does Carrigan suggest that *New York Times v. Sullivan* was wrong and that a modern Sedition Act based on the Sedition Act of 1798 would be constitutional?

Page 1357. After section 2e of the Note, add the following:

3. *A comparative perspective.* The Canada Elections Act of 2000 set limits for third party spending in elections. Specifically, the Act provides that a third-party (that is, a group or individual who is not a candidate) "shall not incur election advertising expenses of a total amount of more than $150,000 during an election period in relation to a general election" and "not more than $3,000 [to] promote or oppose the election of one or more candidates in a given electoral district." The act defines "election advertising expenses" as including any paid message that names candidates, shows their likeness, or takes a position on an issue "with which they are particularly associated." Stephen Harper, the head of a conservative political group, brought suit claiming that the act violated the Canadian Charter of Rights and Freedoms, which guarantees to every person the fundamental "freedom of thought, belief, opinion and expression." The Charter provides that fundamental freedoms may be subjected "only to such reasonable limits [as] can be demonstrably justified in a free and democratic society." In

Harper v. Canada, 1 S.C.R. 827 (2004), excerpted in Hasen, Regulation of Campaign Finance, in V. Amar and M. Tushnet, Global Perspectives on Constitutional Law 198 (2009), the Supreme Court of Canada upheld these provisions of the act, therefore reaching a different result than the Supreme Court of the United States in *Buckley*.

Justice Bastarache delivered the opinion of the court: "Third party advertising is political expression. [As such, it] lies at the core of the expression guaranteed by the Charter and warrants a high degree of constitutional protection. [In] some circumstances, however, third party advertising will be less deserving of constitutional protection. Indeed, it is possible that third parties have access to significant financial resources can manipulate political discourse to their advantage through political advertising. [Advertising] expense limits may restrict free expression to ensure that participants are able to meaningfully participate in the electoral process. For candidates, political parties and third parties, meaningful participation means the ability to inform voters of their position. For voters, meaningful participation means the ability to hear and weigh many points of view. The difficulties of striking this balance are evident. ...

"The question, then, is what promotes an informed voter? For voters to be able to hear all points of view, the information disseminated by third parties, candidates, and political parties cannot be unlimited. In the absence of spending limits, it is possible for the affluent or a number of persons or groups pooling their resources and acting in concert to dominate the political discourse. [If] a few groups are able to flood the electoral discourse with their message, it is possible, indeed likely, that the voices of some will be drowned out. Where those having access to the most resources monopolize the election discourse, their opponents will be deprived of a reasonable opportunity to speak and be heard. This unequal dissemination of points of view undermines the voter's ability to be adequately informed of all views. In this way, equality in the political discourse is necessary for meaningfully participation in the electoral process and ultimately enhances the right to vote."

Page 1360. At the end of the Note, *Subsidy and Disclosure,* insert the following:

5. *Disclosure reaffirmed.* In subsequent decisions, the Court has reaffirmed *Buckley*'s conclusion that disclosure requirements in the context of campaign finance regulations are presumptively constitutional. See McConnell v. Federal Election Commission, 540 U.S. 93 (2003) (upholding disclosure requirements in the Bipartisan Campaign Reform Act of 2002); Citizens United v. Federal

Election Commission, 130 S. Ct. 876 (2010) (same). The Court in *Citizens United* also upheld the Act's disclaimer provision, which requires that televised electioneering communications must include a disclaimer that "X is responsible for the content of this advertising." The Court in *Citizens United* explained that disclaimer and disclosure requirements "may burden the ability to speak, but they 'impose no ceiling on campaign-related activities' and 'do not prevent anyone from speaking.'" Thus, although such requirements might be unconstitutional when, as in *Brown*, there is a "reasonable probability" that disclosure would subject contributors "to threats, harassment, or reprisals," they are generally constitutional because they "help citizens 'make informed choices in the political marketplace.'"

Dissenting from this facet of *Citizens United*, Justice Thomas argued that disclaimer and disclosure requirements were *per se* unconstitutional. Thomas insisted that "Congress may not abridge the "right to anonymous speech" based on the "simple interest in providing voters with additional relevant information." Pointing to alleged examples of harassment of supporters of California's Proposition 8, which banned same-sex marriage, Thomas suggested that the "success of such intimidation tactics has apparently spawned a cottage industry that uses forcibly disclosed donor information to *pre-empt* citizens' exercise of their First Amendment rights." Moreover, Thomas cited alleged threats of retaliation from elected officials against those who supported their opponents. Thomas concluded that he could not "endorse a view of the First Amendment that subjects citizens of this Nation to death threats, ruined careers, damaged or defaced property, or pre-emptive and threatening warning letters as the price for engaging in 'core political speech.'"

6. *Disclosure of referendum petition signatures.* The Court followed *Buckley* and *Brown* in *Doe v. Reed*, ___ U.S. ___ (2010), which involved the constitutionality of a Washington state public records statute, which authorizes the public disclosure of the names of individuals who sign referendum petitions. The plaintiffs argued that public disclosure would chill the willingness of individuals to sign such petitions. The Court held that the state's interest in "preserving the integrity of the electoral process by combating fraud, detecting invalid signatures, and fostering government transparency and accountability" is sufficient to justify the generally modest impact on those who sign such petitions. On the other hand, the Court made clear that if those who sign any *particular* petition can demonstrate "a reasonable probability that the compelled disclosure [of personal information] will subject them to threats, harassment, or reprisals from either Government officials or private parties," then disclosure might well violate the First Amendment.

Page 1360. **Move the Note beginning on page 1363,** *Contribution Limits, PACs, and Political Parties*, **to page 1360, after the Note,** *Subsidy and Disclosure.* **After the relocated Note, insert the following:**

McCONNELL v. FEDERAL ELECTION COMM'N, 540 U.S. 93 (2003). The Bipartisan Campaign Reform Act of 2002 (BCRA), which amended the Federal Election Campaign Act of 1971 (FECA), sought to address several important developments in the years since *Buckley,* including the increased importance of "soft money," the proliferation of "issue ads," and the disturbing findings of a Senate investigation into campaign practices related to the 1996 federal elections.

Prior to BCRA, FECA's contribution limitations extended only to so-called "hard money" contributions made for the purpose of influencing an election for federal office. Political parties and candidates were able to contribute "soft money" — money unregulated under FECA — to support activities intended to influence state or local elections, for get-out-the-vote (GOTV) drives and generic party advertising, and for legislative advocacy advertisements, even if they mentioned a federal candidate's name, as long as the ads did not expressly advocate the candidate's election or defeat. In BCRA, Congress sought to close these soft-money "loopholes" on the premise that they facilitated widespread circumvention of FECA's requirements.

Justices Stevens and O'Connor, joined by Justices Souter, Ginsburg, and Breyer, delivered the opinion of the Court: "The solicitation, transfer, and use of soft money [has] enabled parties and candidates to circumvent FECA's limitations on the source and amount of contributions in connection with federal elections.

"In 1998 the Senate Committee on Governmental Affairs issued a six-volume report summarizing the results of an extensive investigation into the campaign practices in the 1996 federal elections. The report gave particular attention to the effect of soft money on the American political system, including elected officials' practice of granting special access in return for political contributions. [The report concluded] that both parties promised and provided special access to candidates and senior Government officials in exchange for large soft-money contributions. ...

"[BCRA's] central provisions are designed to address Congress' concerns about the increasing use of soft money and issue advertising to influence federal elections. [Title I] is Congress' effort to plug the soft-money loophole. The cornerstone of Title I [is] § 323(a), which prohibits national party committees and their agents from soliciting, receiving, directing, or spending any soft money. In short, § 323(a) takes national parties out of the soft-money business.

"In *Buckley* and subsequent cases, [we] recognized that contribution limits, unlike limits on expenditures, 'entai[l] only a marginal restriction upon the contributor's ability to engage in free communication.' [The] less rigorous standard of review we have applied to contribution limits [shows] proper deference to Congress' ability to weigh competing constitutional interests in an area in which it enjoys particular expertise. [Like] the contribution limits we upheld in *Buckley*, § 323's restrictions have only a marginal impact on the ability of contributors, candidates, officeholders, and parties to engage in effective political speech. Complex as its provisions may be, § 323, in the main, does little more than regulate the ability of wealthy individuals, corporations, and unions to contribute large sums of money to influence federal elections, federal candidates, and federal officeholders. . . .

"The core of Title I [is] § 323(a), which provides that 'national committee[s] of a political party . . . may not solicit, receive, or direct to another person a contribution, donation, or transfer of funds or any other thing of value, or spend any funds, that are not subject to the limitations, prohibitions, and reporting requirements of this Act.' [Before the enactment of this provision], national parties were able to use vast amounts of soft money in their efforts to elect federal candidates. Consequently, as long as they directed the money to the political parties, donors could contribute large amounts of soft money for use in activities designed to influence federal elections. New § 323(a) is designed to put a stop to that practice.

"The Government defends § 323(a)'s ban on national parties' involvement with soft money as necessary to prevent the actual and apparent corruption of federal candidates and officeholders. Our cases have made clear that the prevention of corruption or its appearance constitutes a sufficiently important interest to justify political contribution limits. [The] idea that large contributions to a national party can corrupt or, at the very least, create the appearance of corruption of federal candidates and officeholders is neither novel nor implausible. . . .

"The question for present purposes is whether large *soft-money* contributions to national party committees have a corrupting influence or give rise to the appearance of corruption. Both common sense and the ample record in these cases confirm Congress' belief that they do. [The] evidence in the record shows that candidates and donors alike [have] exploited the soft-money loophole, the former to increase their prospects of election and the latter to create debt on the part of officeholders, with the national parties serving as willing intermediaries. . . .

"For their part, lobbyists, CEOs, and wealthy individuals alike all have candidly admitted donating substantial sums of soft money to national committees not on ideological grounds, but for the express purpose of securing influence over federal officials. [Particularly] telling is the fact that, in 1996 and 2000, more than half of the top 50 soft-money donors gave substantial sums to *both* major national parties, leaving room for no other conclusion but that these donors were seeking influence, or avoiding retaliation, rather than promoting any particular ideology. [We] reject the plaintiffs' First Amendment challenge [to] § 323(a).

"In constructing a coherent scheme of campaign finance regulation, Congress recognized that, given the close ties between federal candidates and state party committees, BCRA's restrictions on national committee activity would rapidly become ineffective if state and local committees remained available as a conduit for soft-money donations. Section 323(b) is designed to foreclose wholesale evasion of § 323(a)'s anticorruption measures by sharply curbing state committees' ability to use large soft-money contributions to influence federal elections.

"The core of § 323(b) is a straightforward contribution regulation: It prevents donors from contributing [soft-money] to state and local party committees to help finance 'Federal election activity.' The term 'Federal election activity' encompasses four distinct categories of electioneering: (1) voter registration activity during the 120 days preceding a regularly scheduled federal election; (2) voter identification, get-out-the-vote (GOTV), and generic campaign activity that is 'conducted in connection with an election in which a candidate for Federal office appears on the ballot'; (3) any 'public communication' that 'refers to a clearly identified candidate for Federal office' and 'promotes,' 'supports,' 'attacks,' or 'opposes' a candidate for that office; and (4) the services provided by a state committee employee who dedicates more than 25% of his or her time to 'activities in connection with a Federal election.' ...

"[In] addressing the problem of soft-money contributions to state committees, Congress both drew a conclusion and made a prediction. Its conclusion, based on the evidence before it, was that the corrupting influence of soft money does not insinuate itself into the political process solely through national party committees. Rather, state committees function as an alternate avenue for precisely the same corrupting forces. [Congress] also made a prediction. Having been taught the hard lesson of circumvention by the entire history of campaign finance regulation, Congress knew that soft-money donors would react to § 323(a) by scrambling to find another way to purchase influence. [We] 'must accord substantial deference to the predictive judgments of Congress.' [Preventing] corrupting activity from shifting wholesale to state committees and thereby eviscerating FECA clearly qualifies as an important governmental interest. [Because] voter registration, voter identification, GOTV, and generic campaign activity all confer substantial benefits on federal candidates, the funding of such activities creates a significant risk of actual and apparent corruption. Section 323(b) is a reasonable response to that risk."

The Court also upheld other sections of Title I, including § 323(d), which prohibits political parties from soliciting and donating funds to tax-exempt organizations that engage in electioneering activities; § 323(e), which restricts federal candidates and officeholders from receiving, spending, or soliciting soft money in connection with federal elections and limits their ability to do so in connection with state and local elections; and § 323(f), which prohibits state and local candidates from raising and spending soft money to fund advertisements and other public communications that promote or attack federal candidates.

Justice Scalia concurred in part and dissented in part: "We are governed by Congress, and this legislation prohibits the criticism of Members of Congress by those entities most capable of giving such criticism loud voice: national political parties. [To] be sure, the legislation is evenhanded: It similarly prohibits criticism of the candidates who oppose Members of Congress in their reelection bids. But as everyone knows, this is an area in which evenhandedness is not fairness. [If] incumbents and challengers are limited to the same quantity of electioneering, incumbents are favored. [Beyond] that, however, the present legislation *targets* for prohibition certain categories of campaign speech that are particularly harmful to incumbents. Is it accidental, do you think, that incumbents raise about three times as much 'hard money' — the sort of funding generally *not* restricted by this legislation — as do their challengers? Or that lobbyists [give] 92 percent of their money in 'hard' contributions? [Is] it mere happenstance [that] national-party funding, which is severely limited by the Act, is more likely to assist cash-strapped challengers than flush-with-hard-money incumbents."

Justice Kennedy, joined in part by Chief Justice Rehnquist and Justices Scalia and Thomas, filed an opinion concurring in part and dissenting in part: "Today's decision [replaces] respected First Amendment principles with new, amorphous, and unsound rules, rules which dismantle basic protections for speech. [Our] precedents teach, above all, that Government cannot be trusted to moderate its own rules for suppression of speech. The dangers posed by speech regulations have led the Court to insist upon principled constitutional lines and a rigorous standard of review. The majority now abandons these distinctions and limitations. ...

"In *Buckley,* the Court held that one, and only one, interest justified the significant burden on the right of association involved there: eliminating, or preventing, actual corruption or the appearance of corruption stemming from contributions to candidates. [The] Court [today] ignores these constitutional bounds and in effect interprets the anticorruption rationale to allow regulation not just of 'actual or apparent *quid pro quo* arrangements,' but of any conduct that wins goodwill from or influences a Member of Congress. [The] very aim of *Buckley*'s standard [was] to define undue influence by reference to the presence of *quid pro quo* involving the officeholder. The Court, in contrast, concludes that access, without more, proves influence is undue. [This] new definition of corruption sweeps away all protections for speech that lie in its path."

Justice Thomas, joined in part by Justice Scalia, concurred in part and dissented in part: "[At] root, the *Buckley* Court was concerned that bribery laws could not be effectively enforced [and] it approved the $1,000 contribution ceiling on this ground. [Section § 323(a)] is intended to prevent [circumvention of that] contribution ceiling, [and] the remaining provisions [of] § 323 are [intended to prevent] circumvention of § 323(a). [It] is not difficult to see where this leads. Every law has limits, and there will always be behavior [easily] characterized as 'circumventing' the law's prohibition. Hence, speech regulation will again expand to cover new forms of 'circumvention,' only to spur supposed circumvention of the new regulations, and so forth. Rather than permit this never-ending and self-justifying process, I would require that the Government explain why proposed speech restrictions are needed in light of actual Government interests, and, in particular, why the bribery laws are not sufficient."

Page 1360.

After McConnell, read *Davis v. Federal Election Commission* on pages 1373-1375 of the main volume and then read the following:

ARIZONA FREE ENTERPRISE CLUB'S FREEDOM CLUB PAC v. BENNETT, 131 S. Ct. 2806 (2011). The Arizona Citizens Clean Elections Act of 1998 created a voluntary public financing system to fund the primary and general election campaigns of candidates for state office. All eligible candidates may opt to receive public funding. Eligibility is contingent on the collection of a specified number of five-dollar contributions from Arizona voters and the acceptance of certain campaign restrictions and obligations. Publicly funded candidates must agree to limit their expenditure of personal funds to $500, participate in at least one public debate, adhere to an overall expenditure cap, and return all unspent public moneys to the State. In exchange for accepting these conditions, participating candidates are granted public funds to conduct their campaigns. When certain conditions are met, publicly funded candidates are granted additional "equalizing" or matching funds. Equalizing funds are made available to a publicly funded candidate when the amount of money a *privately* financed candidate receives in contributions (including expenditures of his own funds), combined with the expenditures of independent groups made in support of the privately financed candidate or in opposition to the publicly financed candidate, exceed the initial allotment of funds to the publicly financed candidate. Once matching funds are triggered, each additional dollar that a privately financed candidate spends or is spent on his behalf results in one dollar in additional state funding to his publicly financed opponent. Matching funds top out at two times the initial authorized grant of public funding to the publicly financed candidate.

Under Arizona law, a privately financed candidate may raise and spend unlimited funds.

The Court, in a five-to-four decision, held that this scheme violate the First Amendment. Chief Justice Roberts wrote the opinion of the Court: "Although the speech of the candidates and independent expenditure groups that brought this suit is not directly capped by Arizona's matching funds provision, those parties contend that their political speech is substantially burdened by the state law in the same way that speech was burdened by the law we recently found invalid in *Davis*. [The] logic of *Davis* largely controls our approach to this case. Much like the burden placed on speech in *Davis*, the matching funds provision "imposes an unprecedented penalty on any candidate who robustly exercises [his] First Amendment right[s].". . .

"The penalty imposed by Arizona's matching funds provision is [even] *more* constitutionally problematic [than the one we invalidated in *Davis*]. First, the penalty in *Davis* consisted of raising the contribution limits for one of the candidates. The candidate who benefited from the increased limits still had to go out and raise the funds. [Here] the benefit to the publicly financed candidate is the direct and automatic release of public money. That is a far heavier burden than in *Davis*. [Second,] unlike the law at issue in *Davis*, all of this is to some extent out of the privately financed candidate's hands. Even if that candidate opted to spend less than the initial public financing cap, any spending by independent expenditure groups to promote the privately financed candidate's election — regardless whether such support was welcome or helpful — could trigger matching funds. What is more, that state money would go directly to the publicly funded candidate to use as he saw fit. That disparity in control — giving money directly to a publicly financed candidate, in response to independent expenditures that cannot be coordinated with the privately funded candidate — is a substantial advantage for the publicly funded candidate. That candidate can allocate the money according to his own campaign strategy, which the privately financed candidate could not do with the independent group expenditures that triggered the matching funds. . . .

"Arizona, the Clean Elections Institute, and the United States offer several arguments attempting to explain away the existence or significance of any burden imposed by matching funds. None is persuasive. [Arizona] argues that the matching funds provision actually results in more speech by 'increas[ing] debate about issues of public concern' [and] 'promot[ing] the free and open debate that the First Amendment was intended to foster.' In the State's view, this promotion of First Amendment ideals offsets any burden the law might impose on some Arizona speakers. Not so. Any increase in speech resulting from the Arizona law is of one kind and one kind only — that of publicly financed candidates. The burden imposed on privately financed candidates and independent expenditure groups reduces their speech. . . . Thus, even if the matching funds provision did result in more speech by publicly financed candidates and more speech in general, it would do so at the expense of impermissibly burdening (and thus reducing) the speech of privately financed candidates and independent expenditure groups. This sort of "beggar thy neighbor" approach to free speech— "restrict[ing] the speech of some elements of our society in order to enhance the relative voice of others" — is "wholly foreign to the First Amendment.". . .

"The State and the Clean Elections Institute assert that the candidates and independent expenditure groups have failed to 'cite specific instances in which they decided not to raise or spend funds.' The record in this case does not support those assertions. That record contains examples of specific candidates curtailing fundraising efforts, and actively discouraging supportive independent expenditures, to avoid triggering matching funds. The record also includes examples of independent expenditure groups deciding not to speak in opposition to a candidate, or in support of a candidate, to avoid triggering matching funds. [In] addition, some candidates may be willing to bear the burden of spending above the cap. That a candidate is willing to do so does not make the law any less burdensome. If the State made privately funded candidates pay a $500 fine to run as such, the fact that candidates might choose to pay it does not make the fine any less burdensome. [In any event, as] in *Davis*, we do not need empirical evidence to determine that the law at issue is burdensome. [The] United States as *amicus* contends that '[p]roviding additional funds to petitioners' opponents does not make petitioners' own speech any less effective' and thus does not substantially burden speech. Of course it does. . . .

"Because the Arizona matching funds provision imposes a substantial burden on the speech of privately financed candidates and independent expenditure groups, 'that provision cannot stand unless it is 'justified by a compelling state interest.' There is a debate between the parties in this case as to what state interest is served by the matching funds provision. The privately financed candidates and independent expenditure groups contend that the provision works to 'level[] electoral opportunities' by equalizing candidate 'resources and influence.' The State [counters] that the provision 'furthers Arizona's interest in preventing corruption and the appearance of corruption.'

"There is ample support for the argument that the matching funds provision seeks to 'level the playing field in terms of candidate resources.' [We] have repeatedly rejected the argument that the government has a compelling state interest in 'leveling the playing field' that can justify undue burdens on political speech. [Citing *Citizens United* and *Buckley*]. 'Leveling the playing field' can sound like a good thing. But in a democracy, campaigning for office is not a game. It is a critically important form of speech. The First Amendment embodies our choice as a Nation that, when it comes to such speech, the guiding principle is freedom — the 'unfettered interchange of ideas' — not whatever the State may view as fair.

"[The] State [insists] that the [challenged] provision serves the compelling interest in combating corruption and the appearance of corruption. But even if the ultimate objective of the matching funds provision is to combat corruption — and not 'level the playing field' — burdens that the matching funds provision imposes on protected political speech are not justified. [We] have observed in the past that '[t]he interest in alleviating the corrupting influence of large contributions is served by ... contribution limitations." Arizona already has some of the most austere contribution limits in the United States. [Arizona] also has stringent fundraising disclosure requirements. In the face of such ascetic contribution limits, strict disclosure requirements, and the general availability of public funding, it is hard to imagine what marginal corruption deterrence could be generated by the matching funds provision. ...

"We do not today call into question the wisdom of public financing as a means of funding political candidacy. That is not our business. But determining whether laws governing campaign finance violate the First Amendment is very much our business. In carrying out that responsibility over the past 35 years, we have upheld some restrictions on speech and struck down others. We have said that governments 'may engage in public financing of election campaigns' and that doing so can further 'significant governmental interest[s],' such as the state interest in preventing corruption. [Quoting *Buckley*.] But the goal of creating a viable public financing scheme can only be pursued in a manner consistent with the First Amendment. The dissent criticizes the Court for standing in the way of what the people of Arizona want. But the whole point of the First Amendment is to protect speakers against unjustified government restrictions on speech, even when those restrictions reflect the will of the majority. When it comes to protected speech, the speaker is sovereign."

Justice Kagan, joined by Justices Ginsburg, Breyer and Sotomayor, dissented: "The First Amendment's core purpose is to foster a healthy, vibrant political system full of robust discussion and debate. Nothing in Arizona's anticorruption statute [violates] this constitutional protection. To the contrary, the Act promotes the values underlying both the First Amendment and our entire Constitution by enhancing the 'opportunity for free political discussion to the end that government may be responsive to the will of the people.'

"Campaign finance reform over the last century has focused on one key question: how to prevent massive pools of private money from corrupting our political system. If an officeholder owes his election to wealthy contributors, he may act for their benefit alone, rather than on behalf of all the people. [To] prevent both corruption and the appearance of corruption — and so protect our democratic system of governance — citizens have implemented reforms designed to curb the power of special interests. Among these measures, public financing of elections has emerged as a potentially potent mechanism to preserve elected officials' independence. By supplanting private cash in elections, public financing eliminates the source of political corruption. For this reason, [almost] one-third of the States have adopted some form of public financing, and so too has the Federal Government for presidential elections. . . .

"We declared the presidential public financing system constitutional in *Buckley*. [We] reiterated "that public financing as a means of eliminating the improper influence of large private contributions furthers a significant governmental interest." And finally, in rejecting a challenge based on the First Amendment, we held that the program did not 'restrict[] or censor speech, but rather . . . use[d] public money to facilitate and enlarge public discussion and participation in the electoral process.' [But] this model, which distributes a lump-sum grant at the beginning of an election cycle, has a significant weakness: It lacks a mechanism for setting the subsidy at a level that will give candidates sufficient incentive to participate, while also conserving public resources. [Candidates] will choose to sign up only if the subsidy provided enables them to run competitive races. If the grant is pegged too low, it puts the participating candidate at a disadvantage: Because he has agreed to spend no more than the amount of the subsidy, he will lack the means to respond if his privately funded opponent spends over that threshold. [But] if the subsidy is set too high, it may impose an unsustainable burden on the public fisc. [The] difficulty, then, is in finding the Goldilocks solution — not too large, not too small, but just right. . . .

"The hallmark of Arizona's program is its inventive approach to the challenge that bedevils all public financing schemes: fixing the amount of the subsidy. [Arizona's] matching funds arrangement responds to the shortcoming of the lump-sum model by adjusting the public subsidy in each race to reflect the expenditures of a privately financed candidate and the independent groups that support him. Arizona can therefore assure candidates that, if they accept public funds, they will have the resources to run a viable race against those who rely on private money. And at the same time, Arizona avoids wasting taxpayers' dollars. In this way, the Clean Elections Act creates an effective and sustainable public financing system. [The] majority contends that the matching funds provision "substantially burdens protected political speech" and does not "serv[e] a compelling state interest." But the Court is wrong on both counts.

"Arizona's statute does not impose a "restriction," or "substantia[l] burde[n]," on expression. The law has quite the opposite effect: It subsidizes and so produces *more* political speech. [Except] in a world gone topsy-turvy, additional campaign speech and electoral competition is not a First Amendment injury.

"At every turn, the majority tries to convey the impression that Arizona's matching fund statute is of a piece with laws prohibiting electoral speech. The majority [insists] that the statute 'restrict[s] the speech of some elements of our society' to enhance the speech of others. And it concludes by reminding us that the point of the First Amendment is to protect 'against unjustified government restrictions on speech.' There is just one problem. Arizona's matching funds provision does not restrict, but instead subsidizes, speech. The law 'impose[s] no ceiling on [speech] and do[es] not prevent anyone from speaking.' [What] the law does — all the law does — is fund more speech. And under the First Amendment, that makes all the difference. In case after case, we have distinguished between speech restrictions and speech subsidies. [Government] subsidies of speech, designed "to stimulate ... expression[,] ... [are] consistent with the First Amendment," so long as they do not discriminate on the basis of viewpoint. That is because subsidies, by definition and contra the majority, do not restrict any speech. [No] one can claim that Arizona's law discriminates against particular [ideas.] Republicans and Democrats, conservatives and liberals may [participate.] Arizona disburses funds based not on a candidate's (or supporter's) ideas, but on the candidate's decision to sign up for public funding. So under our precedent, Arizona's subsidy statute should easily survive First Amendment scrutiny.

"This suit, in fact, may merit less attention than any challenge to a speech subsidy ever seen in this Court. In the usual First Amendment subsidy case, a person complains that the government declined to finance his speech, while bankrolling someone [else's.] But the candidates bringing this challenge do not make that claim — because they were never denied a subsidy. Arizona, remember, offers to support any person running for state office. Petitioners here *refused* that assistance. So they are making a novel argument: that Arizona violated *their* First Amendment rights by disbursing funds to *other* speakers even though they could have received (but chose to spurn) the same financial assistance. Some people might call that *chutzpah*. [Petitioners] are able to convey their ideas without public financing — and they would prefer the field to themselves, so that they can speak free from response. To attain that goal, they ask this Court to prevent Arizona from funding electoral speech — even though that assistance is offered to every state candidate, on the same (entirely unobjectionable) basis. And this Court gladly obliges. ...

"According to the Court, the special problem here lies in Arizona's matching funds mechanism, which the majority claims imposes a "substantia[l] burde[n]" on a privately funded candidate's speech. [The] majority is wrong to see a substantial burden on expression. [Arizona] imposes nothing remotely resembling a coercive penalty on privately funded candidates. [The] only 'burden' in this case comes from the grant of a subsidy to another person, and the opportunity that subsidy allows for responsive speech. [I] will not quarrel with the majority's assertion that responsive speech by one candidate may make another candidate's speech less effective; that, after all, is the whole idea of the First

185

Amendment, and a *benefit* of having more responsive speech. [Citing *Abrams* (Holmes, J., dissenting).] And I will assume that the operation of this statute may on occasion deter a privately funded candidate from spending money, and conveying ideas by that means. [Still], does that effect count as a severe burden on expression? [The] answer is no.

"Our decisions about disclosure requirements show the Court is wrong. Starting in *Buckley* and continuing through [*Citizens United*], the Court has repeatedly declined to view these requirements as a substantial First Amendment burden, even though they discourage some campaign speech. "It is undoubtedly true," we stated in *Buckley*, that public disclosure obligations 'will deter some individuals' from engaging in expressive activity. Yet we had no difficulty upholding these requirements there. And much more recently [we] followed that precedent. 'Disclosure requirements may burden the ability to speak,' we reasoned, but they 'do not prevent anyone from speaking.' [Quoting *Citizens United*.]. So too here. Like a disclosure rule, the matching funds provision may occasionally deter, but 'impose[s] no ceiling' on electoral expression. . . .

"This case arose because Arizonans wanted their government to work on behalf of all the State's people. [They] wished [to] stop corrupt dealing — to ensure that their representatives serve the public, and not just the wealthy donors who helped put them in office. The legislation that Arizona's voters enacted [put] into effect a public financing system that attracted large numbers of candidates at a sustainable cost to the State's taxpayers. The system discriminated against no ideas and prevented no speech. [The] people of Arizona might have expected a decent respect for those objectives. Today, they do not get it."

Page 1363.   Insert the following at the end of the Note, Corporate Contributions and Expenditures:

4. *Electioneering Communications.* In *McConnell v. Federal Election Comm'n*, 540 U.S. 93 (2003), the Court, in a five-to-four decision, upheld § 203 of the Bipartisan Campaign Reform Act of 2002 (BCRA), which prohibited corporations and labor unions from funding "electioneering communications" from their general treasuries. BCRA defined an "electioneering communication" as any "broadcast, cable, or satellite communication" that refers to a clearly identified candidate for federal office, is made within 60 days before a general election or 30 days before a primary election, and is targeted to the relevant electorate.

Justices Stevens and O'Connor delivered the opinion of the Court. At the outset, the Court noted that Congress' "power to prohibit corporations and unions from using funds in their treasuries to finance advertisements expressly advocating the election or defeat of [particular] candidates in federal elections has been firmly embedded in our law." The ability of such organizations to create PACs, the Court observed, has "provided corporations and unions with a constitutionally sufficient opportunity to engage in [such] advocacy."

In the Court's view, all BCRA did was to extend this principle from advertisements that expressly advocate the election or defeat of named candidates ("Vote Against Smith") to advertisements that purport to address general issues but that expressly refer to named candidates, without literally calling for their election or defeat, in circumstances in which the underlying point of the advertisement is clear ("Tell Smith to stop raising your taxes.").

Those challenging the Act argued that *Buckley* "drew a constitutionally mandated line between express advocacy [of a named-candidate's election or defeat] and so-called issue advocacy, and that speakers possess an inviolable First Amendment right to engage in the latter category of speech." The Court rejected this contention, noting that the First Amendment does not erect such "a rigid barrier between express advocacy and so-called issue advocacy." Indeed, the Court reasoned, the express advocacy concept in this context would be "functionally meaningless, because speakers could "easily evade the line by eschewing the use of magic words." Although "electioneering communications," as defined by BCRA, "do not urge the viewer to vote for or against a candidate in so many words, they are no less clearly intended to influence the election." The Court rejected the argument that BCRA's regulation of "electioneering communications" was an unconstitutional limitation on the speech rights of corporations and unions to sponsor issue ads, because they remain free to "finance genuine issue ads [by] simply avoiding any specific reference to federal candidates, or in doubtful cases by paying for the ad from a segregated fund."

Justice Scalia dissented: "This is a sad day for the freedom of speech. Who could have imagined that the same Court which, within the past four years, has sternly disapproved of restrictions upon such inconsequential forms of expression as virtual child pornography, *Ashcroft* v. *Free Speech Coalition,* tobacco advertising, *Lorillard Tobacco,* [and] sexually explicit cable programming, *Playboy Entertainment,* would smile with favor upon a law that cuts to the heart of what the First Amendment is meant to protect: the right to criticize the government. [To] be sure, the legislation is evenhanded: It similarly prohibits criticism of the candidates who oppose Members of Congress in their reelection bids. But as everyone knows, this is an area in which evenhandedness is not fairness. [If] incumbents and challengers are limited to the same quantity of electioneering, incumbents are favored. [The] premise of the First Amendment is that the American people are neither sheep nor fools, and hence fully capable of considering both the substance of the speech presented to them and its proximate and ultimate source. If that premise is wrong, our democracy has a much greater problem to overcome than merely the influence of amassed wealth. Given the premises of democracy, there is no such thing as *too much* speech."

Justice Kennedy, joined in part by Chief Justice Rehnquist and Justices Scalia and Thomas, dissented: "Our precedents teach, above all, that Government cannot be trusted to moderate its own rules for suppression of speech. [The] majority permits a new and serious intrusion on speech when it upholds § 203, [which] prohibits corporations and labor unions from using money from their general treasury to fund electioneering communications. The majority compounds the error made in *Austin*, and silences political speech central to the civic discourse that sustains and informs our democratic processes. Unions and corporations, including nonprofit corporations, now face severe criminal penalties for broadcasting advocacy messages that 'refe[r] to a clearly identified candidate' in an election season. [The] Government is unwilling to characterize § 203 as a ban, citing the possibility of funding electioneering communications out of a separate segregated fund. This option, though, does not alter the categorical nature of the prohibition. '[T]he corporation *as a corporation* is prohibited from speaking. What the law allows — permitting the corporation 'to serve as the founder and treasurer of a different association of individuals that can endorse or oppose political candidates' — 'is not speech by the corporation.' [Moreover, our] cases recognize the practical difficulties [individuals and corporations] face when they are limited to communicating through PACs."

5. *Electioneering Communications Revisited.* Four years later, after Justice Alito had replace Justice O'Connor, who had voted with the majority in *McConnell*, the Court in a five-to-four decision in *Federal Election Commission v. Wisconsin Right to Life*, 551 U.S. 449 (2007), held § 203 unconstitutional *as applied* to Wisconsin Right to Life's televised political advertisements that criticized Wisconsin's senators for participating in a filibuster to block the confirmation of several of President Bush's judicial nominees. Because the ads expressly mentioned Senator Russ Feingold by name and called upon viewers to contact Feingold to urge him to oppose the filibuster, they clearly violated § 203.

In an opinion joined only by Justice Alito, Chief Justice Roberts argued that the Court in *McConnell* had upheld § 203 only insofar as it regulated political advertising that "was the 'functional equivalent' of express campaign speech." The question in this case, Roberts declared, was whether the WRTL ads were "the 'functional equivalent' of speech expressly advocating the election or defeat of a candidate for federal office," which could constitutionally be regulated under *McConnell*, or whether they were "genuine" issue ads, which, he maintained, could not be regulated consistent with the First Amendment:

"In drawing that line, the First Amendment requires us to err of the side of protecting political speech rather than suppressing it. We conclude that the speech at issue in this as-applied challenge is not the 'functional equivalent' of express campaign speech. We further conclude that the interests held to justify restricting corporate campaign speech or its functional equivalent do not justify restricting issue advocacy, and accordingly we hold that BCRA § 203 is unconstitutional as applied to the advertisements at issue. . . .

"Because BCRA § 203 burdens political speech, it is subject to strict scrutiny. Under strict scrutiny, the Government must prove that applying BCRA to WRTL's ads furthers a compelling interest and is narrowly tailored to achieve that interest. [This] Court has already held [in *McConnell*] that [§ 203] survives strict scrutiny to the extent it regulates express advocacy or its functional equivalent. [But] no precedent of this Court has yet [decided whether the government may constitutionally regulate ads that] are *not* express advocacy or its equivalent [nor has the Court decided on the definition of "functional equivalent." [The dissent contends] that *McConnell* already established the constitutional test for determining if an ad is the functional equivalent of express advocacy: whether the ad is intended to influence elections and has that effect. [We disagree.] *McConnell* did not adopt any test as the standard for future as-applied challenges. . . .

"[The] proper standard for an as-applied challenge to [§ 203] must be objective, focusing on the substance of the communication rather than amorphous considerations of intent and effect. [A] court should find that an ad is the functional equivalent of express advocacy only if the ad is susceptible of no reasonable interpretation other than as an appeal to vote for or against a specific candidate. Under this test, WRTL's [ads] are plainly not the functional equivalent of express advocacy. [§ 203] can be constitutionally applied to WRTL's ads only if it is narrowly tailored to further a compelling interest. This Court has never recognized a compelling interest in regulating ads, like WRTL's, that are neither express advocacy nor its functional equivalent. [This] Court has long recognized 'the governmental interest in preventing corruption and the appearance of corruption' in election campaigns [and] *McConnell* arguably applied this interest [to] ads that were the 'functional equivalent of express advocacy. But to justify regulation of WRTL's ads, this interest must be stretched yet another step. . . . Enough is enough. [We] hold that the interest recognized in *Austin* as justifying regulation of corporate campaign speech and extended in *McConnell* to the functional equivalent of such speech has no application to issue advocacy of the sort engaged in by WRTL."

Justice Scalia, joined by Justices Kennedy and Thomas, concurred in the result: "[It] was adventurous for *McConnell* to extend *Austin* beyond corporate speech constituting express advocacy. Today's cases make it apparent that the adventure is a flop. [Which] brings me to the question of *stare decisis*. [*Stare*

189

decisis carries] little weight when an erroneous 'governing decisio[n]' has created an 'unworkable' regime. [The] *McConnell* regime is unworkable because of the inability of any acceptable as-applied standard to validate the facial constitutionality of § 203. [Neither] do any of the other considerations relevant to *stare decisis* suggest adherence to *McConnell*. These cases do not involve property or contract rights, where reliance interests are involved. And *McConnell*'s § 203 holding has assuredly not become 'embedded' in our 'national culture.' [I] would overrule that part of the Court's decision in *McConnell* upholding § 203(a) of the BCRA."

Justice Souter, joined by Justices Stevens, Ginsburg, and Breyer, dissented: "[In] *McConnell*, we found [§ 203] to be 'easily understood and objective[e]' [and] we held that the [line] separating regulated election speech from general political discourse does not, on its face, violate the First Amendment. [We] found '[l]ittle difference ... between an ad that urged viewers to "vote against Jane Doe" and one that condemned Jane Doe's record on a particular issue before exhorting viewers to "call Jane Doe and tell her what you think"'. ...

"*McConnell*'s holding that § 203 is facially constitutional is overruled. [It] is hard to imagine the Chief Justice would ever find an ad to be 'susceptible of reasonable interpretation other than as an appeal to vote for or against a specific candidate' unless it contained words of express advocacy. The Chief Justice thus effectively reinstates the same toothless 'magic words' criterion [that] led Congress to enact BCRA in the first place. [The] price of *McConnell*'s demise [seems] to me a high one. The Court (and I think the country) loses when important precedent is overruled without good reason, and there is no justification for departing from our usual rule of *stare decisis* here."

6. *Impasse?* Consider BeVier, Full of Surprises — And More to Come: Randall v. Sorrell, The First Amendment, and Campaign Finance Regulation, 2006 Supreme Court Review 173, 195-196:

[D]ebate on these issues has reached an impasse. [The] chasm that separates the Justices from one another appears unbridgeable. After all that has been written on the issue already, one who thinks that basic freedoms are not at stake when campaign finance regulations are enacted is not likely to become persuaded that they are. On the other hand, one who embraces the intuition that legislative judgments tend to be hostages to incumbent self-interest is unlikely to think that legislators are trustworthy rule-makers when it comes to deciding how much their challengers may spend in future elections. [And] one who believes that the integrity of the very democratic process that the First Amendment protects is put at risk by excessive and unregulated spending on political campaigns and that the rights of the entire electorate cannot be secured without limiting the rights of some within it is likely to find the threat to political freedom too abstract and in any case too trivial in a state as active as ours to stand in the way of campaign finance reform efforts. There would seem to be little if anything that could be said and little if any evidence that could be marshaled, by either side, which would stand much of a chance of persuading those on the other to reconsider their positions.

CITIZENS UNITED v. FEDERAL ELECTION COMMISSION
130 S. Ct. 876 (2010)

JUSTICE KENNEDY delivered the opinion of the Court.

Federal law prohibits corporations and unions from using their general treasury funds to make independent expenditures for speech defined as an "electioneering communication" or for speech expressly advocating the election or defeat of a candidate. Limits on electioneering communications were upheld in [*McConnell*]. The holding of *McConnell* rested to a large extent on [*Austin*, which] had held that political speech may be banned based on the speaker's corporate identity.

In this case we are asked to reconsider *Austin* and, in effect, *McConnell*. [We] hold that *stare decisis* does not compel the continued acceptance of *Austin*. ...

I

Citizens United is a nonprofit corporation. [In] January 2008 Citizens United released a film entitled *Hillary: The Movie*. [It] is a 90-minute documentary about then-Senator Hillary Clinton, who was a candidate in the Democratic Party's 2008 Presidential primary elections. ...

Before the Bipartisan Campaign Reform Act of 2002 (BCRA), federal law prohibited — and still does prohibit — corporations and unions from using general treasury funds [to] make independent expenditures that expressly advocate the election or defeat of a candidate. 2 U.S.C. § 441b. [BCRA § 203 prohibited] any "electioneering communication" as well. [The Federal Elections Commission held that *Hillary* was an "electioneering communication" within the meaning of BCRA § 203.] ...

III

[T]he law before us is an outright ban [on speech], backed by criminal sanctions. Section 441b makes it a felony for all corporations — including nonprofit advocacy corporations — either to expressly advocate the election or defeat of candidates or to broadcast electioneering communications within 30 days of a primary election and 60 days of a general election. ... As a "restriction of the amount of money a person or group can spend on political communication during a campaign," that statute "necessarily reduces the quantity of expression of restricting the number of issues discussed, the depth of their exploration, and the size of the audience reached." [*Buckley*]. [If] § 441b applied to individuals, no one would believe it is merely a time, place, or manner restriction on speech. Its purpose and effect are to silence entities whose voices the Government deems to be suspect.

[P]olitical speech must prevail against laws that would suppress it. ... Laws that burden political speech are "subject to strict scrutiny," which requires the Government to prove that the restriction "furthers a compelling interest and is narrowly tailored to achieve that interest." [*WRTL*]. ...

Premised on mistrust of governmental power, the First Amendment stands against attempts to disfavor certain subjects or viewpoints. Prohibited, too, are restrictions distinguishing among different speakers, allowing speech by some but not others. [Citing *Bellotti*.] As instruments to censor, these categories are interrelated: Speech restrictions based on the identity of the speaker are all too often simply a means to control content. [By] taking the right to speak from some and giving it to others, the Government deprives the disadvantaged person or class of the right to use speech to strive to establish worth, standing, and respect for the speaker's voice. The Government may not by these means deprive the public of the right and privilege to determine for itself what speech and speakers are worthy of consideration. The First Amendment protects speech and speaker, and the ideas that flow from each. [We] find no basis for the proposition that, in the context of political speech, the Government may impose restrictions on certain disfavored speakers. ...

A

The Court has recognized that First Amendment protection extends to corporations. [Citing *Bellotti*; *Cox Broadcasting*; *New York Times v. United States*; *New York Times v. Sullivan*.] Under the rationale of these precedents, political speech does not lose First Amendment protection "simply because its source is a corporation." [*Bellotti*]. The Court [has] rejected the argument that political speech of corporations or other associations should be treated differently under the First Amendment simply because such associations are not "natural persons." [*Bellotti*.] ...

Austin "uph[eld] a direct restriction on the independent expenditure of funds for political speech for the first time in [this Court's] history." [To] bypass *Buckley* and *Bellotti*, the *Austin* Court identified a new governmental interest in limiting political speech: an antidistortion interest. *Austin* found a compelling governmental interest in preventing "the corrosive and distorting effects of immense aggregations of wealth that are accumulated with the help of the corporate form and that have little or no correlation to the public's support for the corporation's ideas."

B

This Court is thus confronted with conflicting lines of precedent: a pre-*Austin* lines that forbids restrictions on political speech based on the speaker's corporate identity and a post-*Austin* line that permits them. [In] its defense of the corporate-speech restrictions in § 441b, the Government notes the antidistortion rationale. ... [This] rationale cannot support § 441b. If the First Amendment has any force, it prohibits Congress from fining or jailing citizens, or associations of citizens, for simply engaging in political speech. If the antidistortion rationale were to be accepted, however, it would permit Government to ban political speech simply because the speaker is an association that has taken on the corporate form. [*Austin*] sought to defend the antidistortion rationale as a means to prevent corporations from obtaining "an unfair advantage in the political marketplace" by using "resources amassed in the economic marketplace." But *Buckley* rejected the premise that the Government has an interest "in equalizing the relative ability of individuals and groups to influence the outcome of elections."

[T]he *Austin* majority undertook to distinguish wealthy individuals from corporations on the ground that "[s]tate law grants corporations special advantages — such as limited liability, perpetual life, and favorable treatment of the accumulation and distribution of assets." This does not suffice, however, to allow laws prohibiting speech. "It is rudimentary that the State cannot exact as the price of those special advantages the forfeiture of First Amendment rights." [*Austin* (Scalia, J., dissenting)]. ...

The censorship we now confront is vast in its reach. The Government has "muffle[d] the voices that best represent the most significant segments of the economy." [*McConnell* (Scalia, J., dissenting)]. ... The purpose and effect of this law is to prevent corporations, including small and nonprofit corporations, from presenting both facts and opinions to the public. [The] speech that § 441b forbids [is] public, and all can judge its content and purpose. References to massive corporate treasuries should not mask the real operation of this law. Rhetoric ought not obscure reality. [When] Government seeks to use its full power, including the criminal law, to command where a person may get his or her information or what distrusted source he or she may not hear, it uses censorship to control thought. This is unlawful. The First Amendment confirms the freedom to think for ourselves. ...

What we have said also shows the invalidity of other arguments made by the Government. [The] Government falls back on the argument that corporate political speech can be banned in order to prevent corruption or its appearance. In *Buckley*, the Court found this interest "sufficiently important" to allow limits on contributions but did not extend that reasoning to expenditure limits. [Indeed], 26 States do not restrict independent expenditures by for-profit corporations. The Government does not claim that these expenditures have corrupted the political process in those States. [The] appearance of influence or access, furthermore, will not cause the electorate to lose faith in our democracy. [The] fact that a corporation, or any other speaker, is willing to spend money to try to persuade voters presupposes that the people have the ultimate influence over elected officials. . . .

When Congress finds that a problem exists, we must give that finding due deference; but Congress may not choose an unconstitutional remedy. If elected officials succumb to improper influences from independent expenditures; if they surrender their best judgment; and if they put expediency before principle, then surely there is cause for concern. [The] remedies enacted by law, however, must comply with the First Amendment; and, it is our law and our tradition that more speech, not less, is the governing rule. An outright ban on corporate political speech is not a permissible remedy. . . .

The Government contends further that corporate political expenditures can be limited because of its interest in protecting dissenting shareholders from being compelled to fund corporate political speech. This asserted interest, like *Austin*'s antidistortion rationale, would allow the Government to ban the political speech even of media corporations. [In any event], the remedy is not to restrict speech but to consider and explore other regulatory mechanisms. . . .

C

[F]or the reasons above, it must be concluded that *Austin* was not well reasoned. [Due] consideration leads to this conclusion: *Austin* should be and now is overruled. We return to the principle established in *Buckley* and *Bellotti* that the Government may not suppress political speech on the basis of the speaker's corporate identity. No sufficient governmental interest justifies limits on the political speech [of] corporations. [Given] our conclusion we are further required to overrule the part of *McConnell* that upheld BCRA § 203's extension of § 441b's restrictions on corporate independent expenditures.

The CHIEF JUSTICE, with whom JUSTICE ALITO joins, concurring.

The Government urges us in this case to uphold a direct prohibition on political speech. It asks us to embrace a theory of the First Amendment that, [if] accepted, would empower the Government to prohibit newspapers from running editorials or opinion pieces supporting or opposing candidates for office, so long as the newspapers were owned by corporations — as the major ones are. First Amendment rights could be confined to individuals, subverting the vibrant public discourse that is at the foundation of our democracy. The Court properly rejects that theory. ...

The text and purpose of the First Amendment point in the same direction: Congress may not prohibit political speech, even if the speaker is a corporation or union. What makes this case difficult is the need to confront our prior decision in *Austin.* ...

Fidelity to precedent—the policy of *stare decisis*—is vital to the proper exercise of the judicial function. "*Stare decisis* is the preferred course because it promotes the evenhanded, predictable, and consistent development of legal principles, fosters reliance on judicial decisions, and contributes to the actual and perceived integrity of the judicial process." For these reasons, we have long recognized that departures from precedent are inappropriate in the absence of a "special justification."

At the same time, *stare decisis* is neither an "inexorable command," [*Lawrence v. Texas*], nor "a mechanical formula of adherence to the latest decision," especially in constitutional cases. If it were, segregation would be legal, minimum wage laws would be unconstitutional, and the Government could wiretap ordinary criminal suspects without first obtaining warrants. ... *Stare decisis* is instead a "principle of policy." When considering whether to reexamine a prior erroneous holding, we must balance the importance of having constitutional questions *decided* against the importance of having them *decided right.* ...

In conducting this balancing, we must keep in mind that *stare decisis* is not an end in itself. It is instead "the means by which we ensure that the law will not merely change erratically, but will develop in a principled and intelligible fashion." Its greatest purpose is to serve a constitutional ideal—the rule of law. It follows that in the unusual circumstance when fidelity to any particular precedent does more to damage this constitutional ideal than to advance it, we must be more willing to depart from that precedent. ...

These considerations weigh against retaining our decision in *Austin.* First, [that] decision was an "aberration" insofar as it departed from the robust protections we had granted political speech in our earlier cases. *Austin* undermined the careful line that *Buckley* drew to distinguish limits on contributions to candidates from limits on independent expenditures on speech. *Buckley* rejected the asserted government interest in regulating independent expenditures, concluding that "restrict[ing] the speech of some elements of our society in order to enhance the relative voice of others is wholly foreign to the First Amendment." *Austin*, however, allowed the Government to prohibit these same expenditures out of concern for "the corrosive and distorting effects of immense aggregations of wealth" in the marketplace of ideas. *Austi*'s reasoning was—and remains—inconsistent with *Buckley*'s explicit repudiation of any government interest in "equalizing the relative ability of individuals and groups to influence the outcome of elections." *Austin* was also inconsistent with

195

Bellotti's clear rejection of the idea that "speech that otherwise would be within the protection of the First Amendment loses that protection simply because its source is a corporation." . . .

Second, the validity of *Austin*'s rationale [has] proved to be the consistent subject of dispute among Members of this Court ever since. [Citing *WRTL and McConnell*]. The simple fact that one of our decisions remains controversial is, of course, insufficient to justify overruling it. But it does undermine the precedent's ability to contribute to the stable and orderly development of the law. In such circumstances, it is entirely appropriate for the Court [to] address the matter with a greater willingness to consider new approaches capable of restoring our doctrine to sounder footing.

Third, the *Austin* decision is uniquely destabilizing because it threatens to subvert our Court's decisions even outside the particular context of corporate express advocacy. The First Amendment theory underlying *Austin*'s holding is extraordinarily broad. *Austin*'s logic would authorize government prohibition of political speech by a category of speakers in the name of equality. . . . If taken seriously, *Austin*'s logic would apply most directly to newspapers and other media corporations. They have a more profound impact on public discourse than most other speakers. These corporate entities are, for the time being, not subject to § 441(b)'s otherwise generally applicable prohibitions on corporate political speech. But this is simply a matter of legislative grace. The fact that the law currently grants a favored position to media corporations is no reason to overlook the danger inherent in accepting a theory that would allow government restrictions on their political speech. These readings of *Austin* do no more than carry that decision's reasoning to its logical endpoint. In doing so, they highlight the threat *Austin* poses to First Amendment rights generally. . . . Because *Austin* is so difficult to confine to its facts — and because its logic threatens to undermine our First Amendment jurisprudence and the nature of public discourse more broadly — the costs of giving it *stare decisis* effect are unusually high. . . .

Because continued adherence to *Austin* threatens to subvert the "principled and intelligible" development of our First Amendment jurisprudence, I support the Court's determination to overrule that decision.

JUSTICE SCALIA, with whom JUSTICE ALITO joins, and with whom JUSTICE THOMAS joins in part, concurring.

I join the opinion of the Court. I write separately to address JUSTICE STEVENS' discussion of *"Original Understandings."* This section of the dissent purports to show that today's decision is not supported by the original understanding of the First Amendment. The dissent attempts this demonstration, however, in splendid isolation from the text of the First Amendment. It never shows why "the freedom of speech" that was the right of Englishmen did not include the freedom to speak in association with other individuals, including association in the corporate form. To be sure, in 1791 (as now) corporations could pursue only the objectives set forth in their charters; but the dissent provides no evidence that their speech in the pursuit of those objectives could be censored.

Instead of taking this straightforward approach to determining the Amendment's meaning, the dissent embarks on a detailed exploration of the Framers' views about the "role of corporations in society." The Framers didn't like corporations, the dissent concludes, and therefore it follows (as night the day) that corporations had no rights of free speech. Of course the Framers' personal affection or disaffection for corporations is relevant only insofar as it can be thought to be reflected in the understood meaning of the text they enacted — not, as the dissent suggests, as a freestanding substitute for that text. ...

Despite the corporation-hating quotations the dissent has dredged up, it is far from clear that by the end of the 18th century corporations were despised. If so, how came there to be so many of them? [What] seems like a small number by today's standards surely does not indicate the relative importance of corporations when the Nation was considerably smaller. As I have previously noted, "[b]y the end of the eighteenth century the corporation was a familiar figure in American economic life."
[*McConnell*].

Even if we thought it proper to apply the dissent's approach of excluding from First Amendment coverage what the Founders disliked, and even if we agreed that the Founders disliked founding-era corporations; modern corporations might not qualify for exclusion. Most of the Founders' resentment towards corporations was directed at the state-granted monopoly privileges that individually chartered corporations enjoyed. Modern corporations do not have such privileges, and would probably have been favored by most of our enterprising Founders. ...

But to return to, and summarize, my principal point, which is the conformity of today's opinion with the original meaning of the First Amendment. The Amendment is written in terms of "speech," not speakers. Its text offers no foothold for excluding any category of speaker, from single individuals to partnerships of individuals, to unincorporated associations of individuals, to incorporated associations of individuals — and the dissent offers no evidence about the original meaning of the text to support any such exclusion. We are therefore simply left with the question whether the speech at issue in this case is "speech" covered by the First Amendment. No one says otherwise. A documentary film critical of a potential Presidential candidate is core political speech, and its nature as such does not change simply because it was funded by a corporation. [To] exclude or impede corporate speech is to muzzle the principal agents of the modern free economy. We should celebrate rather than condemn the addition of this speech to the public debate.

JUSTICE STEVENS, with whom JUSTICE GINSBURG, JUSTICE BREYER, and JUSTICE SOTOMAYOR join, concurring in part and dissenting in part.

The real issue in this case concerns how, not if, the appellant may finance its electioneering. Citizens United is a wealthy nonprofit corporation that runs a political action committee (PAC) with millions of dollars in assets. Under the Bipartisan Campaign Reform Act of 2002 (BCRA), it could have used those assets to televise and promote *Hillary: The Movie* wherever and whenever it wanted to. It also could have spent unrestricted sums to broadcast *Hillary* at any time other than the 30 days before the last primary election. Neither Citizens United's nor any other corporation's speech has been "banned." ...

The basic premise underlying the Court's ruling is its iteration, and constant reiteration, of the proposition that the First Amendment bars regulatory distinctions based on a speaker's identity, including its "identity" as a corporation. While that glittering generality has rhetorical appeal, it is not a correct statement of the law. [In] the context of election to public office, the distinction between corporate and human speakers is significant. Although they make enormous contributions to our society, corporations are not actually members of it. They cannot vote or run for office. [The] financial resources, legal structure, and instrumental orientation of corporations raise legitimate concerns about their role in the electoral process. Our lawmakers have a compelling constitutional basis, if not also a democratic duty, to take measures designed to guard against the potentially deleterious effects of corporate spending in local and national races.

The majority's approach to corporate electioneering marks a dramatic break from our past. Congress has placed special limitations on campaign spending by corporations ever since the passage of the Tillman Act in 1907. [The] Court today rejects a century of history when it treats the distinction between corporate and individual campaign spending as an invidious novelty born of *Austin*. Relying largely on individual dissenting opinions, the majority blazes through our precedents, overruling or disavowing a body of case law including *WRTL* [and] *McConnell*. ...

II

[I] am not an absolutist when it comes to *stare decisis,* [but] if this principle is to do any meaningful work in supporting the rule of law, it must at least demand a significant justification, beyond the preferences of five Justices, for overturning settled doctrine. [No] such justification exists in this case, and to the contrary there are powerful prudential reasons to keep faith with our precedents. The Court's central argument for why *stare decisis* ought to be trumped is that it does not like *Austin*. [I] am perfectly willing to concede that if one of our precedents were dead wrong in its reasoning or irreconcilable with the rest of our doctrine, there would be a compelling basis for revisiting it. But neither is true of *Austin*. [The] Court proclaims that *"Austin* is undermined by experience since its announcement." [But it] has no empirical evidence with which to substantiate [this claim.] Nor does the majority bother to specify in what sense *Austin* has been "undermined." ...

In the end, the Court's rejection of *Austin* and *McConnell* comes down to nothing more than its disagreement with their results. Virtually every one of its arguments was made and rejected in those cases, and the majority opinion is essentially an amalgamation of resuscitated dissents. The only relevant thing that has changed since *Austin* and *McConnell* is the composition of this Court. Today's ruling thus strikes at the vitals of *stare decisis*, "the means by which we ensure that the law will not merely change erratically, but will develop in a principled and intelligible fashion" that "permits society to presume that bedrock principles are founded in the law rather than in the proclivities of individuals."

III

The novelty of the Court's [approach] to *stare decisis* is matched by the novelty of its ruling on the merits. The ruling rests on several premises. First, the Court claims that *Austin* and *McConnell* have "banned" corporate speech. Second, it claims that the First Amendment precludes regulatory distinctions based on speaker identity, including the speaker's identity as a corporation. Third, it claims that *Austin* and *McConnell* were radical outliers in our First Amendment tradition. ... Each of these claims is wrong.

The So-Called "Ban". Pervading the Court's analysis is the ominous image of a "categorical ba[n]" on corporate speech. [This] characterization is highly misleading. ... For starters, both statutes provide exemptions for PACs, separate segregated funds established by a corporation for political purposes. [During] the most recent election cycle, corporate and union PACs raised nearly a billion dollars. [The] laws upheld in *Austin* and *McConnell* leave open many additional avenues for corporations' political speech. Consider the statutory provision we are ostensibly evaluating in this case, BCRA § 203. It has no application to genuine issue advertising [or] to Internet, telephone, and print advocacy. [Indeed, at] the time Citizens United brought this lawsuit, the only types of speech that could be regulated under § 203 were: (1) broadcast, cable, or satellite communications; (2) capable of reaching at least 50,000 persons in the relevant electorate; (3) made within 30 days of a primary or 60 days of a general federal election; (4) by a labor union or [a] nonmedia corporation; (5) paid for with general treasury funds; and (6) "susceptible of no reasonable interpretation other than as an appeal to vote for or against a specific candidate." The category of communications meeting all of these criteria is not trivial, but the notion that corporate political speech has been "suppress[ed] ... altogether" [is] nonsense. [In] many ways, then, § 203 functions as a [a] time, place, and manner restriction. It applies in a viewpoint-neutral fashion to a narrow subset of advocacy messages about clearly identified candidates for federal office, made during discrete time periods through discrete channels....

So let us be clear: Neither *Austin* nor *McConnell* held or implied that corporations may be silenced; the FEC is not a "censor"; and in the years since these cases were decided, corporations have continued to play a major role in the national dialogue. Laws such as § 203 [burden] political speech, and that is always a serious matter, demanding careful scrutiny. But the majority's incessant talk of a "ban" aims at a straw man.

Identity-Based Distinctions. The second pillar of the Court's opinion is its assertion that "the Government cannot restrict political speech based on the speaker's ... identity." The case on which it relies for this proposition is *Bellotti,* [but] the holding in that case was far narrower than the Court implies. [In] a variety of contexts, we have held that speech can be regulated differentially on account of the speaker's identity, when identity is understood in categorical or institutional terms. The Government routinely places special restrictions on the speech rights of students, prisoners, members of the Armed Forces, foreigners, and its own employees. [In] contrast to the blanket rule that the majority espouses, our cases recognize that the Government's interests may be more or less compelling with respect to different classes of speakers. [It] is fair to say that our First Amendment doctrine has "frowned on" certain identity-based distinctions, particularly those that may reflect invidious discrimination or preferential treatment of a politically powerful group. But it is simply incorrect to suggest that we have prohibited all legislative distinctions based on identity....

The election context is distinctive in many ways, and the Court, of course, is right that the First Amendment closely guards political speech. But in this context, too, the authority of legislatures to enact viewpoint-neutral regulations based on content and identity is well settled. We have, for example, allowed state-run broadcasters to exclude independent candidates from televised debates. [Citing *Forbes*]. ... The same logic applies to this case with additional force because it is the identity of corporations, rather than individuals, that the Legislature has taken into account. [Not] only has the distinctive potential of corporations to corrupt the electoral process long been recognized, but [campaign] finance distinctions based on corporate identity tend to be less worrisome [because] the "speakers" are not natural persons, much less members of our political [community]. ...

In short, the Court dramatically overstates its critique of identity-based distinctions, without ever explaining why corporate identity demands the same treatment as individual identity. Only the most wooden approach to the First Amendment could justify the unprecedented line it seeks to draw.

Our First Amendment Tradition. A third fulcrum of the Court's opinion is the idea that *Austin* and *McConnell* are radical outliers [in] our First Amendment tradition. The Court has it exactly backwards. It is today's holding that is the radical departure from what had been settled First Amendment law. To see why, it is useful to take a long view.

1. *Original Understandings.* [T]here is not a scintilla of evidence to support the notion that anyone believed [the First Amendment] would preclude regulatory distinctions based on the corporate form. To the extent that the Framers' views are discernible and relevant to the disposition of this case, they would appear to cut strongly against the majority's position.

[T]he Framers [held] very different views [than the majority does today] about the nature of the First Amendment right and the role of corporations in society. Those few corporations that existed at the founding were authorized by grant of a special legislative charter. [Corporations] were created, supervised, and conceptualized as quasi-public entities, "designed to serve a social function for the state." It was "assumed that [they] were legally privileged organizations that had to be closely scrutinized by the legislature because their purposes had to be made consistent with public welfare." [The] Framers thus took it as a given that corporations could be comprehensively regulated in the service of the public welfare. Unlike our colleagues, [the Framers] had little trouble distinguishing corporations from human beings, and when they constitutionalized the right to free speech in the First Amendment, it was the free speech of individual Americans that they had in mind. While individuals might join together to exercise their speech rights, business corporations, at least, were plainly not seen as facilitating such associational or expressive ends. Even "the notion that business corporations could invoke the First Amendment would probably have been quite a novelty," given that "at the time, the legitimacy of every corporate activity was thought to rest entirely in a concession of the sovereign." ...

As a matter of original expectations, then, it seems absurd to think that the First Amendment prohibits legislatures from taking into account the corporate identity of a sponsor of electoral advocacy. [This] case sheds a revelatory light on the assumption of some that an impartial judge's application of an originalist methodology is likely to yield more determinate answers [than] his or her views about sound policy.

JUSTICE SCALIA criticizes the foregoing discussion for failing to adduce statements from the founding era showing that corporations were understood to be excluded from the First Amendment's free speech guarantee. Of course, JUSTICE SCALIA adduces no statements to suggest the contrary proposition. ... Nothing in his account dislodges my basic point that members of the founding generation held a cautious view of corporate power and a narrow view of

corporate rights (not that they "despised" corporations), and that they conceptualized speech in individualistic terms. If no prominent Framer bothered to
articulate that corporate speech would have lesser status than individual speech,
that may well be because the contrary proposition — if not also the very notion
of "corporate speech" — was inconceivable. . . .

2. *Legislative and Judicial Interpretation.* A century of more recent history
puts to rest any notion that today's ruling is faithful to our First Amendment
tradition. At the federal level, the express distinction between corporate and
individual political spending on elections stretches back to 1907, when Congress passed the Tillman Act, banning all corporate contributions to candidates.
[By] the time Congress passed FECA in 1971, the bar on corporate contributions and expenditures had become such an accepted part of federal campaign
finance regulation that [in *Buckley*] no one even bothered to argue that the bar
as such was unconstitutional. [Thus], it was unremarkable, that [in a 1982
decision] then-Justice Rehnquist wrote for a unanimous Court that [the] governmental interest in preventing both actual corruption and the appearance of
corruption of elected representatives has long been recognized" [and that]
"there is no reason why it may not . . . be accomplished by treating . . . corporations . . . differently from individuals." [Several] years later, in *Austin*, we [held
that] corporations [could] be barred from using general treasury funds to make
independent expenditures in support of, or in opposition to, candidates. In the 20
years since *Austin*, we have reaffirmed its holding and rationale a number of
times, most importantly in *McConnell*, where we upheld the provision challenged here. . . .

3. *Buckley and Bellotti.* Against [the] extensive background of congressional
regulation of corporate campaign spending, and our repeated affirmation of this
regulation as constitutionally sound, the majority dismisses *Austin* as "a significant departure from ancient First Amendment principles." How does the
majority attempt to justify this claim? Selected passages from two cases,
Buckley and *Bellotti*, do all of the work. [The] case on which the majority
places [its primary emphasis] is *Bellotti*, claiming it "could not have been
clearer" that *Bellotti*'s holding forbade distinctions between corporate and
individual [expenditures]. The Court's reliance is odd. The only thing about
Bellotti that could not be clearer is that it declined to adopt the majority's
position. *Bellotti* ruled, in an explicit limitation on the scope of its holding, that
"our consideration of a corporation's right to speak on issues of general public
interest implies no comparable right in the quite different context of participation in a political campaign for election to public office." *Bellotti*, in other
words, did not touch the question presented in *Austin* and *McConnell*, and the
opinion squarely disavowed the proposition for which the majority cites it.

The majority attempts to explain away the distinction *Bellotti* drew — between general corporate speech and campaign speech intended to promote or

prevent the election of specific candidates for office — as inconsistent with the rest of the opinion and with *Buckley*. Yet the basis for this distinction is perfectly coherent: The anticorruption interests that animate regulations of corporate participation in candidate elections, the "importance" of which "has never been doubted," do not apply equally to regulations of corporate participation in referenda. A referendum cannot owe a political debt to a corporation, seek to curry favor with a corporation, or fear the corporation's retaliation. ...

Austin and *McConnell*, then, sit perfectly well with *Bellotti*. Indeed, all six Members of the *Austin* majority had been on the Court at the time of *Bellotti*, and none so much as hinted in *Austin* that they saw any tension between the decisions. The difference between the cases is not that *Austin* and *McConnell* rejected First Amendment protection for corporations whereas *Bellotti* accepted it. The difference is that [the] State has a greater interest in regulating independent corporate expenditures on candidate elections than on referenda, because in a functioning democracy the public must have faith that its representatives owe their positions to the people, not to the corporations with the deepest pockets. ...

IV

Having explained [why] *Austin* and *McConnell* [sit] perfectly well with "First Amendment principles," I come at last to the interests that are at stake. ...

The Anticorruption Interest. [O]n numerous occasions we have recognized Congress' legitimate interest in preventing the money that is spent on elections from exerting an "undue influence on an officeholder's judgment" and from creating "the appearance of such influence," beyond the sphere of *quid pro quo* relationships. [Our] "undue influence" cases [have recognized that when] private interests are seen to exert outsized control over officeholders solely on account of the money spent on (or withheld from) their campaigns, the result can depart so thoroughly "from what is pure or correct" in the conduct of Government that it amounts to a "subversion ... of the electoral process." [This] understanding of corruption has deep roots in the Nation's history. ...

Rather than show any deference to a coordinate branch of Government, the majority [rejects] the anticorruption rationale without serious analysis. Today's opinion provides no clear rationale for being so dismissive of Congress, but the prior individual opinions on which it relies have offered one: the incentives of the legislators who passed BCRA. Section 203, our colleagues have suggested, may be little more than "an incumbency protection plan," a disreputable attempt at legislative self-dealing rather than an earnest effort to facilitate

First Amendment values and safeguard the legitimacy of our political system. This possibility, the Court apparently believes, licenses it to run roughshod over Congress' handiwork.

In my view, we should instead start by acknowledging that "Congress surely has both wisdom and experience in these matters that is far superior to ours." [This] is not to say that deference would be appropriate if there were a solid basis for believing that a legislative action was motivated by the desire to protect incumbents or that it will degrade the competitiveness of the electoral process. [But] it is the height of recklessness to dismiss Congress' years of bipartisan deliberation and its reasoned judgment on this basis, without first confirming that the statute in question was intended to be, or will function as, a restraint on electoral competition. . . .

We have no record evidence from which to conclude that BCRA § 203, or any of the dozens of state laws that the Court today calls into question, reflects or fosters such invidious discrimination. Our colleagues have opined that "'*any* restriction upon a type of campaign speech that is equally available to challengers and incumbents tends to favor incumbents.'" [*McConnell* (opinion of SCALIA, J.)]. This kind of airy speculation could easily be turned on its head. The electioneering prohibited by § 203 might well tend to *favor* incumbents, because incumbents have pre-existing relationships with corporations and unions, and groups that wish to procure legislative benefits may tend to support the candidate who, as a sitting officeholder, is already in a position to dispense benefits and is statistically likely to retain office. If a corporation's goal is to induce officeholders to do its bidding, the corporation would do well to cultivate stable, long-term relationships of dependency. [We] do not have a solid theoretical basis for condemning § 203 as a front for incumbent self-protection, and it seems equally if not more plausible that restrictions on corporate electioneering will be self-denying.

Austin and Corporate Expenditures. Just as the majority gives short shrift to the general societal interests at stake in campaign finance regulation, it also overlooks the distinctive considerations raised by the regulation of *corporate* expenditures. The majority fails to appreciate that *Austin*'s antidistortion rationale is itself an anticorruption rationale, tied to the special concerns raised by corporations. Understood properly, "antidistortion" is simply a variant on the classic governmental interest in protecting against improper influences on officeholders that debilitate the democratic process. It is manifestly not just an "equalizing" ideal in disguise. . . .

1. *Antidistortion.* The fact that corporations are different from human beings might seem to need no elaboration, except that the majority opinion almost completely elides it. *Austin* set forth some of the basic differences. Unlike natural persons, corporations have "limited liability" for their owners and managers, "perpetual life," separation of ownership and control, "and favorable

treatment of the accumulation and distribution of assets...that enhance their ability to attract capital and to deploy their resources in ways that maximize the return on their shareholders' investments." "[T]he resources in the treasury of a business corporation [are] not an indication of popular support for the corporation's political ideas." "They reflect instead the economically motivated decisions of investors and customers. The availability of these resources may make a corporation a formidable political presence, even though the power of the corporation may be no reflection of the power of its ideas." [Corporations] help structure and facilitate the activities of human beings, to be sure, and their "personhood" often serves as a useful legal fiction. But they are not themselves members of "We the People" by whom and for whom our Constitution was established.

These basic points help explain why corporate electioneering is not only more likely to impair compelling governmental interests, but also why restrictions on that electioneering are less likely to encroach upon First Amendment freedoms. One fundamental concern of the First Amendment is to "protec[t] the individual's interest in self-expression." [A] regulation such as BCRA § 203 may affect the way in which individuals disseminate certain messages through the corporate form, but it does not prevent anyone from speaking in his or her own voice. [Take] away the ability to use general treasury funds for some of those ads, and no one's autonomy, dignity, or political equality has been impinged upon in the least.

[R]ecognizing the weakness of a speaker-based critique of *Austin*, the Court places primary emphasis not on the corporation's right to electioneer, but rather on the listener's interest in hearing what every possible speaker may have to say. [There] are many flaws in this argument. [*Austin*] recognized that there are substantial reasons why a legislature might conclude that unregulated general treasury expenditures will give corporations "unfai[r] influence" in the electoral process and distort public debate in ways that undermine rather than advance the interests of listeners. [In] addition to [the] drowning out of non-corporate voices, [corporate] "domination" of electioneering can generate the impression that corporations dominate our democracy. [Citizens] may lose faith in their capacity, as citizens, to influence public policy. [The] predictable result is cynicism and disenchantment. . . .

The Court's facile depiction of corporate electioneering assumes away all of these complexities. Our colleagues ridicule the idea of regulating expenditures based on "nothing more" than a fear that corporations have a special "ability to persuade," as if corporations were our society's ablest debaters and viewpoint-neutral laws such as § 203 were created to suppress their best arguments. [Our] colleagues simply ignore the fundamental concerns of the *Austin* Court and the legislatures that have passed laws like § 203: to safeguard the integrity, competitiveness, and democratic responsiveness of the electoral process. All of the majority's theoretical arguments turn on a proposition with undeniable surface appeal but little grounding in evidence or experience, "that there is no such thing as too much speech." If individuals in our society had infinite free time to listen to and contemplate every last bit of speech uttered by anyone, anywhere; and if broadcast advertisements had no special ability to influence elections apart from the merits of their arguments (to the extent they make any); and if legislators always operated with nothing less than perfect virtue; then I suppose the majority's premise would be sound. In the real world, we have seen, corporate domination of the airwaves prior to an election may decrease the average listener's exposure to relevant viewpoints, and it may diminish citizens' willingness and capacity to participate in the democratic process....

2. *Shareholder Protection.* There is yet another way in which laws such as § 203 can serve First Amendment values. Interwoven with *Austin*'s concern to protect the integrity of the electoral process is a concern to protect the rights of shareholders from a kind of coerced [speech]. When corporations use general treasury funds to praise or attack a particular candidate for office, it is the shareholders [who] are effectively footing the bill. Those shareholders who disagree with the corporation's electoral message may find their financial investments being used to undermine their political convictions. The PAC mechanism, by contrast, helps assure that those who pay for an electioneering communication actually support its content and that managers do not use general treasuries to advance personal agendas. [*Austin*'s] acceptance of restrictions on general treasury spending "simply allows people who have invested in the business corporation for purely economic reasons" — the vast majority of investors, one assumes — "to avoid being taken advantage of, without sacrificing their economic objectives."

The concern to protect dissenting shareholders and union members has a long history in campaign finance reform. [Indeed], we have unanimously recognized the governmental interest in "protect[ing] the individuals who have paid money into a corporation or union for purposes other than the support of candidates from having that money used to support political candidates to whom they may be opposed." [See pages 1397-98 of the main volume.]

V

[O]ur colleagues have arrived at the conclusion that *Austin* must be overruled [only] after mischaracterizing both the reach and rationale of [the relevant] authorities, and after bypassing or ignoring rules of judicial restraint used to cabin the Court's lawmaking power. [While] American democracy is imperfect, few outside the majority of this Court would have thought its flaws included a dearth of corporate money in politics....

Note: Reflections on Citizens United

Consider the following views:

a. Sullivan, Two Concepts of Freedom of Speech, 124 Harv. L. Rev. 123 (2010):

Does *Citizens United* mark a reversal in the political valence of free speech? Have liberals grown weary of First Amendment values they once celebrated? Have conservatives flip-flopped and now become free speech devotees? [Both] sides in *Citizens United* are committed to free speech, but to two very different visions of free speech. Where the two visions align, lopsided victories for free speech claims are still possible. [Citing the 2009 dog-fighting case, *United States v. Stevens*.] But where the two visions diverge, divisions like that in *Citizens United* become sharp.

In the first vision, [free] speech rights serve an overarching interest in political equality. Free speech as equality embraces first an antidiscrimination principle: in upholding the speech rights of anarchists, syndicalists, communists, civil rights marchers, Maoist flag burners, and other marginal, dissident, or unorthodox speakers, the Court protects members of ideological minorities who are likely to be the target of the majority's animus or selective indifference. A vision of free speech as serving an interest in political equality also endorses a kind of affirmative action for marginal speech in the form of access to government subsidies without speech-restrictive strings attached. By invalidating conditions on speakers' use of public land, facilities, and funds, a long line of speech cases in the free-speech-as-equality tradition ensures public subvention of speech expressing "the poorly financed causes of little people." On the equality-based view of free speech, it follows that the well-financed causes of big people (or big corporations) do not merit special judicial protection from political regulation. And because, in this view, the value of equality is prior to the value of speech, politically disadvantaged speech prevails over regulation but regulation promoting political equality prevails over speech.

The second vision of free speech, by contrast, sees free speech as serving the interest of political liberty. On this view, [the] First Amendment is a negative check on government tyranny, and treats with skepticism all government efforts at speech suppression that might skew the private ordering of ideas. And on this view, members of the public are trusted to make their own individual evaluations of speech, and government is forbidden to intervene for paternalistic or redistributive reasons. Government intervention might be warranted to correct certain allocative inefficiencies in the way that speech transactions take place, but otherwise, ideas are best left to a freely competitive ideological market.

[T]he outcome of *Citizens United* is best explained as representing a triumph of the libertarian over the egalitarian vision of free speech.

b. Bebchuk & Jackson, Corporate Political Speech: Who Decides?, 124 Harv. L. Rev. 83 (2010):

[L]lawmakers might be concerned with minority shareholders' First Amendment interest in not being forced to be associated with political speech that they do not support. [The] Supreme Court has long recognized that the First Amendment's protection of "[f]reedom of association . . . plainly presupposes a freedom not to associate." [The] Court has generally addressed this principle in the context of legislation that imposes require- ments on associations that compromise the association's message — for example, a law requiring that the association admit certain members. But the Court has also acknowledged individuals' constitutional interest in avoiding association with political messages with which they disagree — holding, for example, that unions violate the First Amendment rights of their members when union leaders spend union funds for political speech that the individual members oppose. . . . In such cases, the Court has held, laws requiring individuals to be union members may be remedied by pro- viding those individuals with the right to opt out of spending in support of political speech with which they disagree. . . . [On the right not to associate, see the main text at pages 1429-1442.]

[The] *Citizens United* Court [seemed] to accept the legitimacy of the government's interest in protecting dissenting shareholders, but reasoned that "the remedy is not to restrict speech but [to] explore other regulatory mechanisms." [Mechanisms] that are properly tailored to the purpose of protecting minority shareholders may well be constitutionally permissible. [Suppose] that lawmakers adopt a rule under which companies are not permitted to spend on political speech unless a budget for that purpose is approved in the company's preceding annual meeting [and that the rule required approval by at least 60 percent of shareholders.] Is such a [rule] constitutionally permissible?

Pages 1365-1376.   **Skip the material (most of which has been relocated) beginning with *McConnell* on page 1365 up to the Note, "Additional Regulation of the Electoral Process," on page 1376.**

Page 1382. **At the end of the section 2 of the Note, add the following:**

Borough of Duryea, Pennsylvania v. Guarnieri, 131 S. Ct. 2438 (2011) (litigation by public employees against the government is governing by public concern standard).

Page 1385. **At the end of section 2 of the Note, add the following:**

In Borough of Duryea, Pennsylvania v. Guarnieri, 131 S. Ct. 2438 (2011), the Court held that "the Petition Clause protects the right of individuals to appeal to courts [for] the resolution of legal disputes. In a dissenting opinion, Justice Scalia concluded that "the proposition that a lawsuit is a constitutionally protected 'Petition'" is "quite doubtful." Scalia reasoned that "[t]here is abundant historical evidence that 'Petitions' were directed to the executive and legislative branches of government, not to the courts." Nonetheless, recognizing that some "scholars have made detailed historical arguments to the contrary," and because the parties had not litigated the issue, he agreed to "leave its resolution to another day." If litigation is not "Petition," can it still be "Speech"?

Page 1393. **After subsection c of the Note, add the following:**

3. *Prohibition v. subsidy.* Suppose *Dale* involved not a state law prohibiting discrimination, but a state law denying tax-exempt status to any organization that discriminates on the basis of sexual orientation or a public high school's policy that denies any student group the right to use school facilities if it discriminates on that basis. As applied to the Boy Scouts, would such restrictions be constitutional? See *Christian Legal Society v. Martinez*, which is in this Supplement as an insert for page 1305.

F.   Freedom of the Press

Page 1406.   At the end of section 2 of the Note, add the following:

For data on the number of subpoenas served on the press in recent years, see Jones, Avalanche or Undue Alarm? An Empirical Study of Subpoenas Received by the New Media, 93 Minn. L. Rev. 585 (2008).

Page 1426.   After section 2c of the Note, add the following:

cc. In FCC v. Fox Television Stations, 129 S. Ct. 1800 (2009), discussed *supra* in the Supplement to page 1274, Justice Thomas called *Red Lion* into question in a separate concurring opinion:

Red Lion [was] unconvincing when [it was] issued, and the passage of time has only increased doubt regarding [its] continued validity. [*Red Lion*] relied heavily on the scarcity of available broadcast frequencies. [Its] deep intrusion into the First Amendment rights of broadcasters [is] problematic on two levels. First, instead of looking to first principles to evaluate the constitutional question, the Court relied on a set of transitory facts [to] determine the applicable First Amendment standard. But the original meaning of the Constitution cannot turn on modern necessity. [Highlighting] the doctrinal incoherence of *Red Lion*, [the] Court has declined to apply the lesser standard of First Amendment scrutiny imposed on broadcast speech to federal regulation of telephone dial-in services [citing *Sable Communications*], cable television programming [citing *Turner Broadcasting*], and the Internet [citing Reno v. American Civil Liberties Union]. The justifications relied on by the Court in *Red Lion* [neither] distinguish broadcast from cable, nor explain the relaxed application of the principles of the First Amendment to broadcast. ...

Second, even if this Court's disfavored treatment of broadcasters under the First Amendment could have been justified at the time of *Red Lion*, dramatic technological advances have eviscerated the factual assumptions underlying [that decision]. Broadcast spectrum is significantly less scarce than it was 40 years ago. [And] the trend should continue. [Moreover], traditional broadcast television and radio are no longer the 'uniquely pervasive' media forms they once were. For most consumers, traditional broadcast media programming is now bundled with cable or satellite services.

210

Broadcast and other video programming is also widely available over the Internet. [The] extant facts that drove this Court to subject broadcasters to unique disfavor under the First Amendment simply do not exist today.

Page 1440.   After section 3 of the Note, add the following:

3a. *Preserving First Amendment value.* Consider Adelman & Deitrich, Extremist Speech and the Internet: The Continuing Importance of Brandenburg, 4 Harv. L. & Pol. Rev. 361 (2010).

[T]he diversity of human thought found on the web includes not just the inspired and the banal, but also the depraved. Due to its speed, global reach, and promise of anonymity, the internet has undoubtedly become a valuable means of communication for those of ill will. Perhaps not surprisingly, the use of the interest by people interested in promoting terrorism, racism, and the like has made many anxious. [But] it is [easy] to exaggerate the harm that can come from a new means of communication. [It] is critical that we not succumb to the temptation to weaken our protections of speech based on our concerns about terrorists and hatemongers and their use of the internet. [It] is particularly important that the internet be free from censorship because [the] internet empowers individual citizens and equalizes opportunities for communication. [Because] the internet expands both the number of people who are able to participate in the democratic conversation and the number of opinions available for consideration, an uncensored internet promotes democracy. . . .

Proponents of an internet-specific standard argue that extremist advocacy on the internet is more dangerous than elsewhere because it may reach a larger audience. But all previous advances in communications technology [allowed] speakers to reach larger audiences. [Justice] Brandeis's famous comment that "the fitting remedy for evil counsels is good ones" remains sound advice.

Page 1440.   After section 4 of the Note, add the following:

5. *Freedom of the press in a global society.* Consider L. Bollinger, Uninhibited, Robust, and Wide-Open: A Free Press for a New Century 105-106, 116-117 (2010):

[We] are facing the emergence of a global society, with the technological capacity to provide a free and independent press to a world in desperate need of such an institution, but there is also a myriad of laws, policies, practices, and conditions that inhibit and impede that from happening. Without a central, overriding system of constitutional protections, there is a risk of a collapse to the bottom, where jurisdictions that have the least degree of freedom will undermine the freedom of those that value it the most. . . .

This situation poses a significant challenge to the United States and the world. For a society uniquely committed to unconstrained public debate and for which knowledge of the entire world is increasingly vital, we must now see how we can achieve this goal — to make it a shared principle as well as a working reality — in a world that is not in full agreement with the American conception of a free press. [To help achieve this, the Supreme Court must] begin the process of making the shift from the constitutional paradigm of a national public forum to a global one.

Page 1441.   At the end of the Note, add the following:

Finally, consider D. Strauss, The Living Constitution 52-53 (2010):

[The] First Amendment — that is, the principles protecting free speech — has been a tremendous success story in American constitutional law. But where did these successful principles come from? They did not come from the text of the Constitution. The First Amendment was part of the Constitution for a century and a half before the central principles of the American regime of free speech [became established in the law. Nor did those principles come from the original understandings. [To] the extent that we can determine the views of [the Framers], they did not think they were establishing a system of freedom of expression resembling what we have today.

The central principles of the American system of freedom of expression, in other words, are not the product of a moment of inspired constitutional genius 200-plus years ago. We owe those principles, instead, to the living, common law Constitution. The central features of First Amendment law were hammered out in fits and starts, in a series of judicial decisions and extrajudicial developments, over the course of the twentieth century. The story of the emergence of the American constitutional law of free speech is a story of evolution and precedent, trial and error — a demonstration of how the living Constitution works.

8

THE CONSTITUTION AND RELIGION

A. Introduction: Historical and Analytic Overview

Page 1450.   At the end of section 4 of the Note, add the following:

For a discussion of the anti-corruption approach to the non-establishment principle, see Koppelman, Corruption of Religion and the Establishment Clause, 50 Wm. & Mary L. Rev. 1831, 1896-1898 (2009), describing the anti-corruption approach's claims:

> Religious behavior, without sincerity, is devoid of religious value. [Establishment] exaggerates the importance of doctrinal divisions. [The] state is an unreliable source of religious authority. [Religious] teachings are likely to be altered, in a pernicious way, if the teachers are agents of the state. [Establishment] tends to produce underserved contempt toward religion. [The] legitimate authority of the state does not extend to religious questions.

With respect to the claim about altering religious teachings, why should religious leaders be precluded from considering or reconsidering their faith commitments in light of government policies? Should the fact that the anti-corruption argument is founded on a contestable theological view rule it out as a general approach to the religion clauses? Do other general approaches have analogous religious foundations?

Page 1454.   At the end of section 4 of the Note, add the following:

What does it mean, really, for a court [to] take a "hands-off approach to religious doctrine"? [It] is certainly *not* the case that government officials and courts may not render decisions that touch upon, affect, motivate, or even regulate religious believers and religiously motivated individuals. ["Religion'] and law are (almost) everywhere, and so there is no avoiding contact between them. [It] also seems misguided to see the rule simply as the specification of a general "neutrality" requirement. [It] is [a] rule that state actors should not render [decisions] involving the resolution of religious questions.

Garnett, A Hands-Off Approach to Religious Doctrine, 84 Notre Dame L. Rev. 837, 850-851, 853, 854 (2009). Garnett develops his argument in connection with church-property disputes. Is it relevant to other religion-clause questions?

B.   The Establishment Clause

Page 1481.   At the end of the second paragraph of section 5 of the Note, add the following:

See also Corbin, Ceremonial Deism and the Reasonable Religious Outsider, 57 UCLA L. Rev. 1545 (2010), which draws on the law under Title VII of the 1964 Civil Rights Act for the argument that the perspective to adopt for determining whether a ceremonial practice constitutes an establishment of religion is that of the reasonable religious outsider.

Page 1482.   Before the final paragraph of section 6 of the Note, add the following:

For a discussion of the early history of the congressional chaplaincy, see Lund, The Congressional Chaplaincies, 17 Wm. & Mary Bill of Rts. J. 1171 (2009), which describes antebellum controversies over the selection of Catholic and Unitarian chaplains.

Page 1482.   At the end of section 6 of the Note, add the following:

Lund, Legislative Prayer and the Secret Costs of Religious Endorsements, 94 Minn. L. Rev. 972 (2010), reviews post-*Marsh* litigation on legislative prayer at city councils and other settings. Consider his summary and suggestion: "[Courts] have [required] that legislative prayers be thoroughly nondenominational or 'nonsectarian' [and] have [prohibited] picking and choosing prayergivers based on their religious affiliations. [What] these restrictions give to religious freedom with one hand, they take [with] the other. Insisting that prayer be nondenominational [protects] listeners from denominationally exclusive speech. But it [requires] discrimination against speakers who insist on praying in denominational terms. [The] only way to really protect religious liberty [is] by not having legislative prayer at all." Lund suggests that "[o]stensibly benign religious endorsements can grow to have real meaning and real power, and they can be a real force for religious division in our society. Religious endorsements that initially seem innocuous can grow into something quite pernicious." Id. at 977, 1050. Consider whether the same might be said of banning legislative prayer.

Page 1483.   After section 6 of the Note, add the following:

6a. *A cross as a war memorial?* Salazar v. Buono, 130 S. Ct. 1803 (2010), considered but did not definitively resolve an Establishment Clause challenge to the 2004 transfer to private ownership of federal land on which a Latin cross had been erected in 1934. The cross was located in a remote area of the Mojave National Preserve, accessible via a blacktop road. Justice Kennedy, in an opinion joined by Chief Justice Roberts and Justice Alito, wrote, "Although certainly a religious symbol, the cross was not emplaced [to] promote a Christian message. [Time] also has played a role. The cross had stood [for] nearly seven decades before the [transfer]. By then, the cross and the cause it commemorated had become entwined in the public consciousness. Members of the public gathered regularly [to] pay their respects. [Congress] ultimately designated the cross as a national memorial. [It] is reasonable to interpret the congressional designation as giving recognition to the historical meaning that the cross had attained. ... The goal of avoiding governmental endorsement does not require eradication of all religious symbols in the public realm. [The] Constitution does not oblige government to avoid any public acknowledgement of religion's role in society. Rather, it leaves room to accommodate divergent values within a constitutionally permissible framework. ... [A] Latin cross is not merely a reaffirmation of Christian beliefs. It is a symbol often used to honor and respect those whose heroic acts, noble contributions, and patient striving help secure an honored place in history for this Nation and its people. Here, one Latin cross in the desert evokes far more than religion. It evokes thousands of small crosses in foreign fields marking the graves of Americans who fell in battles [whose] tragedies are compounded if the fallen are forgotten."

Concurring, Justice Alito observed that "Congress' consistent goal [has] been to commemorate our Nation's war dead and to avoid the disturbing symbolism that would have been created by the destruction of the monument." Justices Scalia and Thomas concurred in the judgment, finding that the challenger lacked standing.

Justice Stevens, joined by Justices Ginsburg and Sotomayor, dissented. " [After] the transfer it would continue to appear to any reasonable observer that the Government has endorsed the cross, [particularly because] the Government has designated the cross as a national memorial. ... After the transfer, a well-informed observer would know that the cross was no longer on public land, but would additionally be aware [that the] cross was once on public land, [Congress] transferred it to a specific purchaser in order to preserve its [display], and the Government maintained a reversionary interest in the land. ... Even though Congress recognized this cross for its military associations, the solitary cross conveys an inescapable sectarian message. [Making] a plain, unadorned Latin cross a war memorial does not make the cross secular. It makes the war memorial sectarian." In a footnote, Justice Stevens observed, "The cross is not a universal symbol of sacrifice. It is a symbol of one particular sacrifice, and that sacrifice carries deeply significant meaning for those who adhere to the Christian faith." Justice Breyer also dissented.

Page 1488.   At the end of section 3 of the Note, add the following:

See also Pleasant Grove City, Utah v. Summum, 129 S. Ct. 1129 (2009), discussed *supra* in the Supplement to page 1317.

Page 1507.   After section 9 of the Note, add the following:

10. *Facially-neutral statutes that incidentally burden religion.* To what extent may government officials take religion into account in seeking to deter crime?

May police officials direct special attention to religious institutions whose doctrine — as interpreted by the officials — suggests that church members are more likely to commit crime than members of other religious institutions? Huq, The Signaling Function of Religious Speech in Domestic Counterterrorism, 89 Tex. L. Rev. 833 (2011), argues that such actions pose threats to the "epistemic authority" of religious institutions in defining their doctrine (by deterring the development of definitions that public officials might misinterpret as signaling a greater propensity to commit crime), but that current doctrine does not afford robust protection to epistemic authority. Should it?

D. Permissible Accommodation

Page 1537.   At the end of the first paragraph, add the following:

For a related view, see Gellman & Looper-Friedman, Thou Shalt Use the Equal Protection Clause for Religion Cases (Not Just the Establishment Clause), 10 U. Pa. J. Const'l L. 666 (2008).

9
STATE ACTION, BASELINES, AND THE PROBLEM OF PRIVATE POWER

B. Pure Inaction and the Theory of Governmental Neutrality

Page 1556.   At the bottom of the page, add the following:

Consider the following defense of the state action doctrine:

[The] state action principle does not rest on the presence or absence of public power because its justification does not depend on the claim that private rights that are governmentally enforced somehow do not rest on state power. Rather, the distinction the principle draws rests on the thesis that private individuals are principals, entitled to act to pursue their own interests, whereas government decisionmakers are agents, whose function is to further the interests of citizens. Thus the presence or absence of a decisive choice by a private person, which the state action principle uses to categorize actions as private or governmental, is normatively central and justifies the application of constitutional rules to one choice and not the other.

BeVier & Harrison, The State Action Principle and Its Critics, 96 Va. L. Rev. 1767, 1785 (2010).

Notice that Flagg Brothers and Brooks are both private individuals or entities who are principals and not merely agents. How, then, does the state action doctrine help in deciding whether it is constitutionally permissible for the government to intervene on one side or the other of their private dispute?

Page 1565.   Before section 4 of the Note, add the following:

Alternatively, consider the extent to which substantive constitutional law questions are really state action questions in disguise. For example, are establishment clause issues really questions about state responsibility for religious conduct? *See* McConnell, State Action and the Supreme Court's Emerging Consensus on the Line between Establishment and Private Religious Expression, 28 Pepp. L. Rev. 681 (2001). For an argument that "when the sectarian nature of constitutionally questioned activity is determined, the state action doctrine furnishes courts with a clearer and more coherent legal framework for evaluating Establishment Clause cases than does automatic application of the [test enunciated in Lemon v. Kurtzman, 4903 U.S. 602 (1971)]," see Developments in the Law-State Action and the Public/Private Distinction, 123 Harv. L. Rev. 1248, 1279 (2010). For a discussion of the *Lemon* test, see page 1460 of the main volume.